Know Accounting Graphically

Value added tax international edition

Mike Darlow

The Melaleuca Press

First published May 2017.

The typefaces used within this book are Minion Pro for the body text, Gill Sans MT in figures and for figure captions, Rockwell for the column and row heads of pro formas, and *Lucida Handwriting Italic* for text which imitates that entered by hand. The Minion Pro text is set 11/15, the Gill Sans MT is set 11/14.

The computer software used to lay out and illustrate this book was: Adobe InDesign CS5.5®, Adobe Illustrator CS5.5®, and Adobe Photoshop CS5.5®.

National Library of Australia Cataloguing-in-Publication entry

Author:	Darlow, Mike, 1943–
Title:	Know Accounting Graphically: Value Added Tax International Edition / Mike Darlow
ISBN:	978-0-9589609-7-7
Notes:	Includes index.
Subjects:	Accounting—International—Graphic Methods
	Bookkeeping—International—Graphic Methods
	Taxation—International—Graphic Methods

Published by: The Melaleuca Press, 21 Wilsons Lane, Exeter, NSW 2579, Australia.
Website: www.knowaccountinggraphically.com
Contact email address: mike@knowaccountinggraphically.com

CONTENTS

PREFACE

I found the notes supplied for a correspondence course I was taking in bookkeeping difficult to understand. Chatting to others who had taken accounting-related courses revealed that my difficulties weren't unusual. There had to be a better way to explain accounting than with text alone.

I was fortunate to come across Anthony Rice's book *Accounts Demystified*. It shows that an entity's financial state can be represented by a wonderfully elegant two-tower (or bar) structure as shown below. This struc-

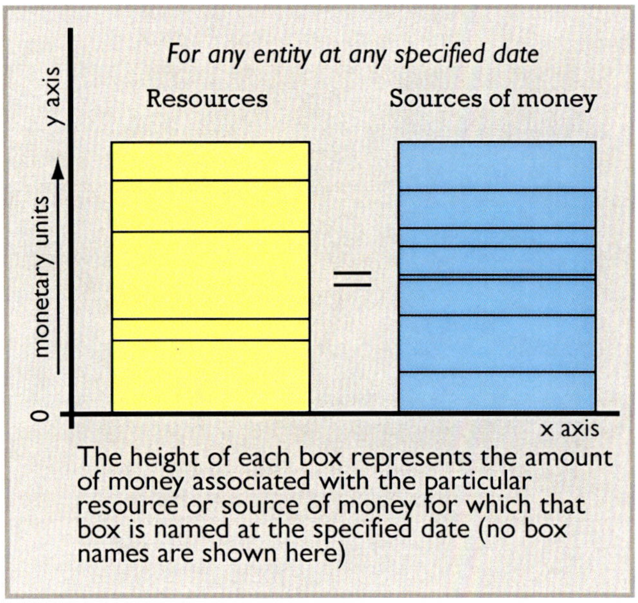

ture's left-hand bar records the monetary value of the resources an entity controls. The right-hand bar records the sources of the money which enable the entity to control those resources. Each bar consists of a stack of boxes on a horizontal x axis. The two bar heights continually vary during an entity's active life, but must always be equal. Rice exploits this two-bar structure to represent a business entity's activities by a series of what he calls *balance sheet charts*.

I saw that dollar amounts could also be represented by boxes below the x axis, and thus invented what I call *balance charts*. This name is appropriate because, as will be explained, the net heights of a balance chart's two bars of boxes should always be equal, that is balance.

I initially developed balance charts to explain bookkeeping and accounting to myself. However I soon realised that the charts, complemented by appropriate text, could portray and communicate accounting ideas, situations, problems and solutions far more easily than text alone. And the understanding thus achieved would enable purely textual accounting explanations and information to be more readily absorbed. The mystery is why something as powerful, versatile and simple as the balance chart wasn't invented decades ago.

I therefore resolved to write a book which would explain the basics of accounting with balance charts. I envisaged three types of reader:

1. those who wish to know the basics of accounting sufficiently to complement their efforts in fields such as business and investing
2. those who want to become accounting professionals
3. those who already know accounting, and wish to better communicate accounting information or teach accounting.

Particularly for the second type of reader for whom *Know Accounting Graphically* would be an introductory text, I have ensured that the book is both short and inexpensive.

Will balance charts catch on? One accounting lecturer told me, "I don't care how good your charts are, I'm not going to change the way I teach". It will be interesting to see whether this reaction prevails.

ACKNOWLEDGMENTS

I am solely responsible for the content of this book. However Mr Ian Hodgson of Hodgson & Associates Pty Ltd, Mr Matt Ingall of Allan Hall Business Advisors Pty Ltd, and Mrs Abigail Santos of Harvey Norman Holdings Limited have provided valuable assistance.

I thank my wife, Aliki, for her great patience and encouragement.

Chapter 1

INTRODUCTION

Over the past five centuries accounting has been continuously developed to enable particular types of entity to:

i. be run more efficiently, and

ii. comply with their legal and other obligations.

Such entities may be profit-seeking; these include individuals, sole traders (unincorporated business entities run by one person), partnerships, companies, and superannuation funds. Alternatively such entities may be not-for-profit; these include charities, clubs, associations, and government bodies.

To achieve the objectives i and ii above, four accounting processes have been developed:

1. **identifying** separating the entity's activities into events consisting of transactions. (An *event* is a 'discrete happening'. A *transaction* is 'an event or part of an event which produces a financial change in an entity'.)
2. **measuring** recording the transactions in accounts
3. **preparing the financial statements** summarising the information in the accounts to show the state of the entity as at the ends of regular intervals and the changes in the entity during those intervals
4. **communicating** facilitating appropriate access for the entity's staff to the entity's accounts and financial statements. Also reporting, with appropriate analysis and interpretation, financial information tailored to the needs of particular entity managers, and to external parties including potential lenders, investors, taxing authorities, government regulators, and stock exchanges.

An entity keeps accounts and prepares and communicates financial statements and reports to enable and assist decision making. Therefore decision makers who have an appropriate level of accounting understanding are likely to make better decisions than those who haven't.

Different countries levy different taxes. This international edition of *Know Accounting Graphically* assumes that income tax and value added tax are levied, but not retail sales tax. A second international edition of this book is available which assumes that income tax and retail sales tax are levied, but not value added tax.

The rules and practices which govern how entities should financially record and report in the country which is relevant to you, the reader, may differ in detail from those explained in this book. These differences shouldn't significantly affect the ability of this book to convey by using balance charts a holistic understanding of accounting. This understanding will then form a sound base from which you can seek further accounting knowledge.

I've had to choose a monetary unit for this book. I chose dollars because every reader will have heard of them. If you live in a country which doesn't use dollars, you can choose to substitute an appropriate multiple of a different currency.

Different nations may use different terms for the same accounting-related meaning. Even within a nation the use of accounting synonyms and terms with overlapping or ill-defined meanings can be rife. I've therefore had to select terms for this book for which a reader may have to determine his or her national equivalents.

The first edition of this book was written for an Australian readership. This international edition's real examples are therefore drawn from Australia.

This book first explains the basics of the first three accounting processes introduced above; it then explains financial analysis, valuing businesses, and budgeting. These explanations are ordered so that understanding builds serially. Readers who seek to understand accounting should therefore first read from start to finish omitting content which appears irrelevant or too advanced. Those who instead wish to focus on the potential of balance charts in financial communication and education should first study the introduction to balance charts in the Appendix. They should then skim through the book where they'll find several additional varieties of balance chart introduced and explained.

The next chapter introduces the foundation of double-entry accounting: the balance sheet equation.

Chapter 2

THE BALANCE SHEET EQUATION

This chapter explains the balance sheet equation, the arithmetical basis of accounting; it also introduces the terms *account balance* and *account*.

2.1 THE BALANCE SHEET EQUATION

An equation is a statement that:

Something = Something else

For example:

$$\$21 - \$9 = \$12$$

An equation whose amounts are also measured in dollars can be used to connect the three amounts which define the financial position (situation) of an entity:

$$\begin{bmatrix}\text{The amount}\\ \text{that the entity}\\ \text{owns and is}\\ \text{owed (controls)}\end{bmatrix} - \begin{bmatrix}\text{The amount}\\ \text{that the}\\ \text{entity owes}\end{bmatrix} = \begin{bmatrix}\text{The amount}\\ \text{that the}\\ \text{entity is}\\ \text{worth}\end{bmatrix}$$

Equation 2.a

Figure 2.1 represents equation 2.a graphically.

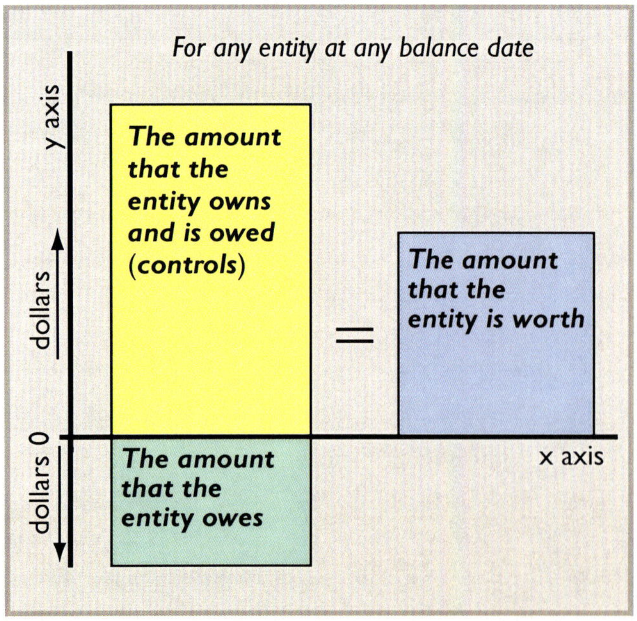

Figure 2.1 A form of bar chart called a *balance chart*. Balance charts are the main graphical tool used to explain accounting in this book. They consist of boxes arranged in vertical two bars located above and/or below an x axis. The two bars lie to the right of a vertical y axis which is usually drawn to a suitable monetary scale. If because of the need to restrain the height of a balance chart, a chart's box heights and depths aren't all drawn to the same monetary scale, the y axis is labelled *nts* meaning 'not to scale'. The x axis is drawn horizontally at y = $0. The x axis doesn't have a horizontal scale, and therefore the width of a box has no significance.

The name printed in bold italic type at the top of each box is an account name.

In literature an account is a story. In accounting an *account* is the 'story (chronological record) of amounts called *postings* becoming associated with and disassociated from the centre of interest (subject) for which the account is named'. The 'total of the postings to an account from when that account was first started (opened) to a specified date (called the *balance date)*' is the *balance* of that account. And when, as in this chapter, each box represents the balance of an account, the amount of the balance is represented by the height or depth of the box which is drawn to the monetary scale of the y axis. Because an account balance can change several times during the course of a day, account balances are measured as at midnight on a balance date.

The terms on the left-hand side of the equals sign in equation 2.a are represented by the yellow- and green-filled boxes in this chart's left-hand bar. The green-filled box is located below the x axis because it's balance is subtracted.

The blue-filled box is located in the right-hand bar because it represents the term in equation 2.a to the right of the equals sign. When, as is usual, an entity's worth is positive, the blue-filled box is located above the x axis. A negative worth would be represented by a blue-filled box below the x axis.

For active entities, account balances vary in amount through time. However those variations aren't independent because they're governed by the imperative of equation 2.a.

If in figure 2.1 the amount represented by the green-filled box [The amount that the entity owes] is added above the x axis to both bars, the two green-filled boxes in the left-hand bar cancel each other to produce figure 2.2.

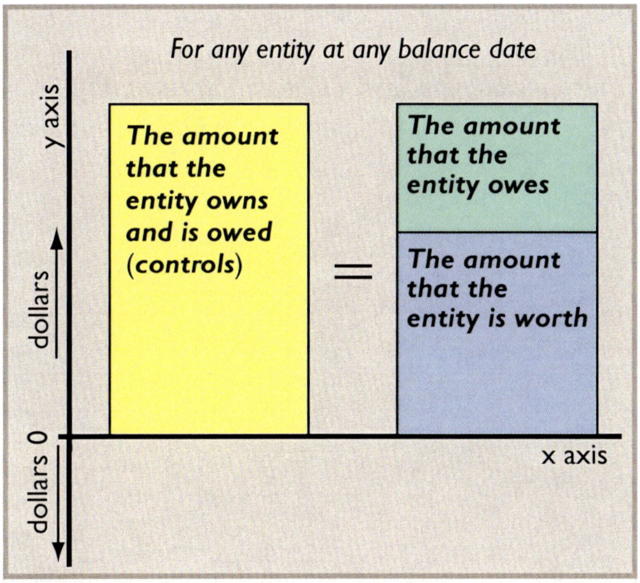

Figure 2.2 A balance chart which has a different format to that of figure 2.1. Both figures equally represent the entity's financial position.

The account balances represented by the heights of the three boxes change continually through time for an active entity. However the height of the yellow box must always equal that of the green box plus the blue box.

The equation which figure 2.2 represents is:

$$\left[\text{The amount that an entity owns and is owed (controls)}\right] = \left[\text{The amount that the entity owes}\right] + \left[\text{The amount that the entity is worth}\right]$$

Equation 2.b

The account names used in equations 2.a and 2.b and in figures 2.1 and 2.2 and are long and therefore inconvenient. Figure 2.3 introduces the one-word terms accounting uses instead. Substituting *assets*, *liabilities* and *equity* for their phrase equivalents in equation 2.b gives:

$$\text{Assets} = \text{Liabilities} + \text{Equity}$$

Equation 2.c

Equation 2.c is called the *accounting equation* or the *balance sheet equation*. It can be restated more clearly: for any entity at any balance date,

$$\left[\text{The total of the entity's assets}\right] = \left[\text{The total of the entity's liabilities}\right] + \left[\text{The total of the entity's equity}\right]$$

Equation 2.d

Because this simple monetary equation is the arithmetical basis of accounting, it's essential that you fully understand and agree with it before continuing.

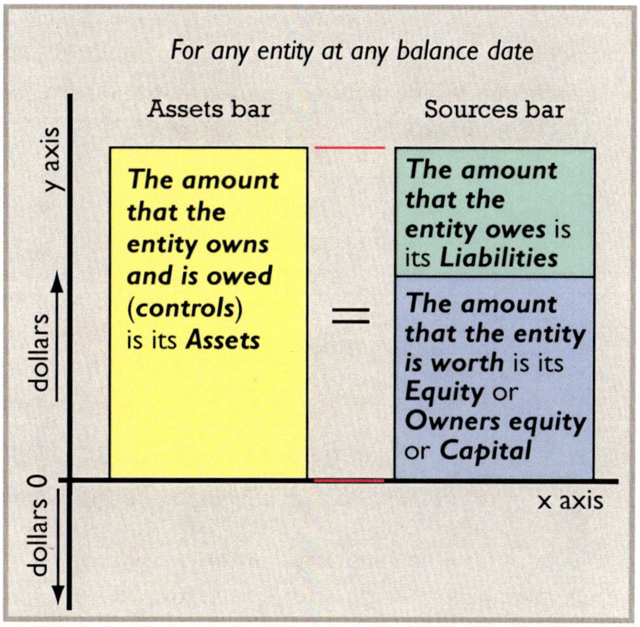

Figure 2.3 A balance chart which represents balance-sheet equations 2.c and 2.d, and summarises the subject entity's financial position at the specified balance date. The preferred one-word accounting terms used in the boxes above are defined below:

- ***Assets*** are what an entity owns and is owed, that is controls. More formally an *asset* is a 'resource whose cost or value can be measured reliably which is controlled by the entity as a result of past events and from which future economic benefits are expected to flow to the entity'. (An *economic benefit* is an 'amount of money which will be saved or generated as the result of an action'.) **>**

- ***Liabilities*** are what an entity owes. A *liability* is a 'present obligation of the entity arising from past events, the settlement of which is expected to result in an outflow of resources and thus a reduction in economic benefits'.

- ***Equity***, also called ***owners equity*** or ***capital***, is what the entity is worth, that is the 'residual interest in the assets of the entity after deducting all its liabilities'. This is the amount the owners would receive if on the balance date all the entity's assets could be sold or otherwise realised for their recorded amounts in the accounts, and the entity paid its debts in full. This difference is theoretically claimable from the entity by the entity's owners. It's called *equity* because in England disputes about ownership were decided in the Court of Chancery (figure 2.4), supposedly according to the principle of fairness or equity.

  In government entities *equity* is usually called *accumulated surplus*. In other not-for-profit entities *equity* it's usually called *accumulated funds*.

  Not-for-profit doesn't mean that the entity doesn't make a profit, but that any excess accumulated funds will instead of being distributed to the entity's owners, managers or staff be used to further the entity's objectives. These objectives are usually socially desirable.

A proviso which applies to every liability and equity, not just to every asset, is that its amount must be reliably measurable. (*Measurable* includes, as will be explained later, reliably estimable.)

In balance charts the left-hand bar is called the *assets bar* because it records the carrying amounts of the entity's assets. (A *carrying amount*, also called a *book value*, is the 'net amount at which an asset or liability is recorded in an entity's accounts'.) As explained in later chapters, carrying amounts can change through time.

To gain control of the assets recorded in a balance chart's assets bar, the entity may have borrowed (with the entity liable to repay the borrowings to their lenders who therefore have a claim on the entity). The entity will also have used (which includes not yet spent) all the monies which its owners could claim according to the amounts recorded in the equity accounts. Hence the right-hand bar can be called the *claims bar*.

The right-hand bar can also be called the *sources bar* because it records the sources of the amounts of the monies which enable the entity to control the assets recorded in the assets bar at the balance date. *Sources bar* will be preferred to *claims bar* in this book.

Balance sheet equations 2.c and 2.d both have an equals sign; so therefore does this balance chart. However in later charts the magenta balance-signifying lines connecting the top and bottom internal corners of the two bars will appear alone. Besides omitting the equals sign, most later balance charts will also omit x and y axis and assets- and sources-bar labels.

Figure 2.4 The Court of Chancery sitting in Lincoln's Inn Hall in London in 1808.

Illustration courtesy of Wikimedia Commons.

Chapter 3

THE CHART OF ACCOUNTS

Derived from figure 2.3 on page 3, figure 3.1 contains only three account balances. It therefore doesn't provide any detailed financial information about the subject entity's financial position. For example, the balance of the assets account doesn't reveal the carrying amounts of particular asset centres of interest controlled by the entity such as land, buildings or vehicles. To provide the detail required to manage the entity and enable it to meet its reporting obligations, the balances of figure 3.1's three accounts are each separated into many centre-of-interest account balances as this chapter explains. The resulting three-branch structure of accounts is called a *chart of accounts*.

A chart of accounts which shows an entity's financial position even in detail won't shed much light on that entity's performance. Performance and changes in performance (which of course produce changes in financial position) are best measured by dividing the life of an entity into periods of constant and appropriate length. Indeed accounting-related legislation requires that. Therefore before explaining the chart of accounts, this chapter will explain the periods used in accounting.

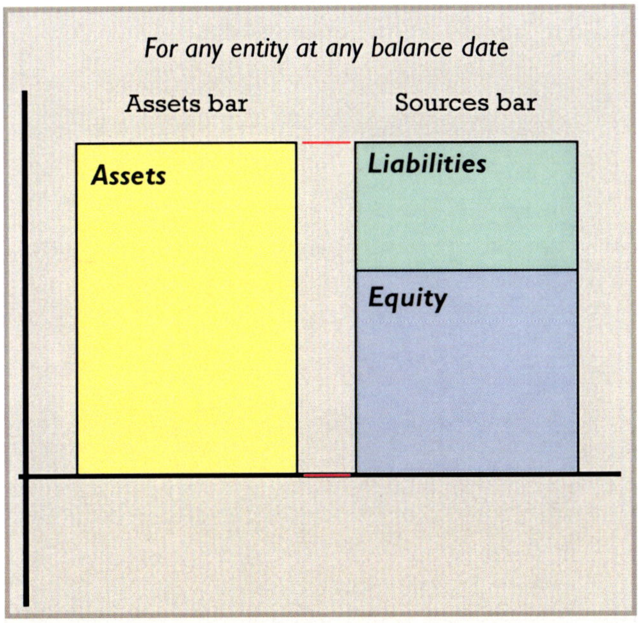

Figure 3.1 A balance chart representing the balance sheet equation, Assets = Liabilities + Equity.

3.1 PERIODS

In accounting, an entity's life is divided into periods of two types:

- **those not specified by legislation** These are used mainly by those working within entities to enable changes in an entity's financial position and performance to be better recorded, assessed and compared
- **those specified by legislation** Legislated periods are of two types: reporting periods which are periods as at the end of which affected entities must report to regulators and other non-taxing authorities, and those periods prescribed by taxing authorities.

Reporting periods

Some types of entity are required by law to financially report to a government regulator or similar as at the ends of prescribed periods this book calls *reporting periods*. The most common duration of reporting period is 12 months. All the reporting entities in this book use 12-months-long reporting periods which can also be called *annual reporting periods*. Some entities are also required to or choose to report more frequently than annually using interim reports. Whether all a nation's reporting entities have to use coincident reporting periods will be specified in the relevant legislation.

The scope and depth of the financial reporting required to be made as at the end of a reporting period are usually determined by the entity's public accountability and size. The reporting will require an entity to provide financial statements.

The use by entities of reporting periods which are of equal length, and especially when the reporting periods used by different entities coincide, greatly aids:

- comparisons by an entity's managers of that entity's performances and changes in financial position through time
- comparisons between entities by entity managers, regulators, taxing authorities, investors, analysts

and others. The value of such comparisons depends on the breadth and depth of the financial and other information accessible.

Income tax periods

Most nations levy income tax. The amounts of income tax an entity has to pay are typically based upon that entity's income-taxable income during successive 12-months periods which this book will call *income tax years*. The tax legislation (tax law) of many nations stipulates an income tax year; for example, income tax years start at:

- midnight on 30 June for Australia
- midnight on 31 March for India.

However each of the USA's income-tax payers is allowed to choose when that taxpayer's income year starts.

An entity's accounting workload is less if its annual reporting period coincides with its income tax year.

3.2 WHY MULTIPLE ACCOUNTS?

As explained at the start of this chapter, entities need to keep more than three accounts to enable them to prepare reports, financial statements, and tax returns. (A *tax return* is a 'statement made to a taxing authority which supports the entity's determination of the amount of tax payable to or claimable from the taxing authority'.) A sole trader might keep tens of accounts, a major bank millions. Each of these accounts is not isolated, but has to be located and linked to one or more other accounts within a multi-level chart of accounts. A chart of accounts thus provides an elegant and mathematically correct means to aggregate the balances of the accounts which receive the postings which record the entity's transactions (the *ledger accounts*) in order to satisfy different informational needs. Creating a chart of accounts from scratch uses mainly the reverse of aggregation, namely separation. Starting from the three account balances in figure 3.1, the five steps required are:

1. separate the assets account balance into current and non-current assets account balances
2. separate the liabilities account balance into current and non-current liabilities account balances
3. separate the equity account balance into capital invested, reserves, and retained profits account balances
4. create the temporary accounts whose balances are closed as at the end of each reporting period into the balance of the retained profits account.
5. separate as required any of the account balances or accounts created in steps 1 to 4 above to create more account balances or accounts.

Each of the account balances (which may be zero) created in the steps above should be the balance of a named account. Each account should have a different account name which clearly identifies that account's centre of interest.

3.3 SEPARATING THE ASSETS, LIABILITIES AND EQUITY ACCOUNT BALANCES

This section explains the first three separations listed above.

3.3.1 Separating the assets account balance

As explained in chapter 2, an *asset* is a 'resource controlled by the entity as a result of past events'. A resource which isn't owned by an entity but is controlled by the entity can therefore be an asset. (An example of such a resource is a finance lease which substantially transfers all the risks and rewards of ownership to the lessee.)

An asset may be:

- used alone or in combination with other assets to produce goods or services to be sold by the entity
- exchanged for other assets
- used to settle a liability, or
- distributed to the entity's owners.

Most assets have a physical (tangible) form. (Shares in companies are regarded as tangible.) Intangible assets include patents, copyrights and other legal rights from which future economic benefits are expected to flow and whose cost or value can be measured reliably.

The concept of periods was introduced earlier in this chapter. Accounting applies this concept to separate the assets account balance in figure 3.1 into a current assets account balance and a non-current assets account balance as shown in figure 3.2. For assets, an alternative term to *non-current* is *fixed* (in ownership, not location).

In accounting a current asset is:

- cash, or is a cash equivalent which can be readily converted into cash
- one that the entity holds primarily for trading irrespective of how long the asset might take to sell or swap, or
- is one that the entity expects to realise, sell or consume within the later of 12 months after the end of the current reporting period or the end of the current operating cycle.

Thus accounting defines *current* in terms of an entity's reporting period, and an entity's operating cycle in those countries where the operating cycle concept is recognised. A retailer's or manufacturer's *operating cycle* is the 'average duration between the business purchasing stock (which can include raw materials and components) and, after any processing, receiving the cash or cash equivalent from selling that stock'. For mining businesses the operating cycle starts when the ore or mineral is dug out, and for annual crops it begins from when the crop is first planted. (Many entities don't have a clearly definable operating cycle. Most of those entities that do, have one which is no more than 12-months long and is therefore irrelevant to the definition of *current*.)

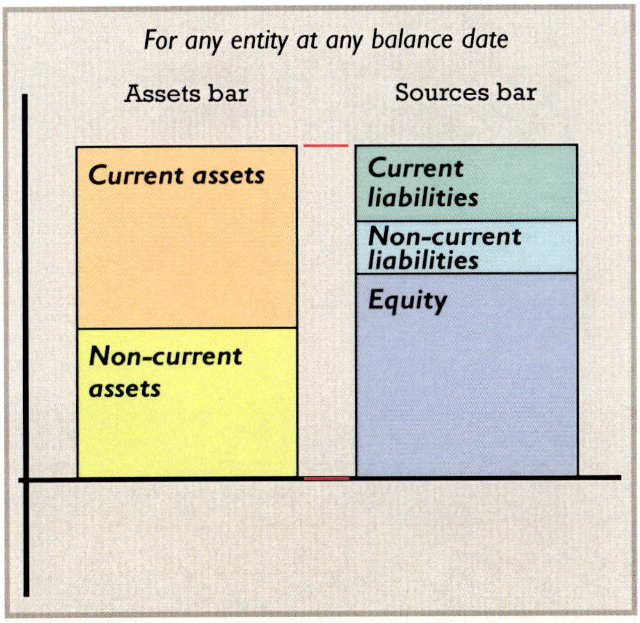

Figure 3.2 A balance chart with current and non-current assets and liabilities accounts.

The balance of an entity's figure 3.2 current assets account is then the total of the carrying amounts of all the entity's current assets at the balance date. Introduced on page 4, an asset's *carrying amount* is simply the 'net amount at which that asset is recorded in the accounts at the specified balance date'.

The second account balance separated from the figure 3.1 assets account balance is that of the entity's *non-current assets*. Its balance is the total of the carrying amounts of all the entity's non-current assets at the balance date. A *non-current asset* is 'any asset which isn't a current asset'.

3.3.2 Separating the liabilities account balance

The liabilities account balance in figure 3.1 can, similarly to that figure's assets account balance, be separated into a current liabilities account balance and a non-current liabilities account balance as shown in figure 3.2. Defined on page 4, a *liability* is a 'present obligation of an entity resulting from past events, the settlement of which is expected to result in an outflow of economic benefits'. However where an entity has raised an order for a supply, but that supply has not come under the control of the entity, a liability is not generally recognised. A *current liability* is therefore a current obligation (but not a future commitment) which:

- has been incurred primarily for the purpose of trading, or
- is due to be settled within the later of 12 months after the end of the current reporting period or, if operating cycles are recognised in the nation's accounting legislation, the end of the current operating cycle.

And any liability which isn't a current liability is a non-current liability.

3.3.3 Separating the equity account balance

The next separation is that of the equity account balance in figures 3.1 and 3.2 into the balances of the following three accounts shown in the sources bar of figure 3.3:

1. **Capital invested** records the amounts invested by an entity's owner or owners in the entity as at the balance date. These amounts aren't loans which the entity must repay. If the entity is a company (a separate legal entity), the capital invested belongs to the company and is under the control of the company's directors. Sole-trader businesses and partnerships aren't separate legal entities distinct from their owners, but are separate accounting entities. Their amounts of capital invested are controlled respectively by the sole trader, and by the partners subject to the terms of the partnership agreement.

   A sometimes-used synonym for *capital invested* is *contributed equity*, but because *contribution* usually means 'gift', this synonym is best avoided.

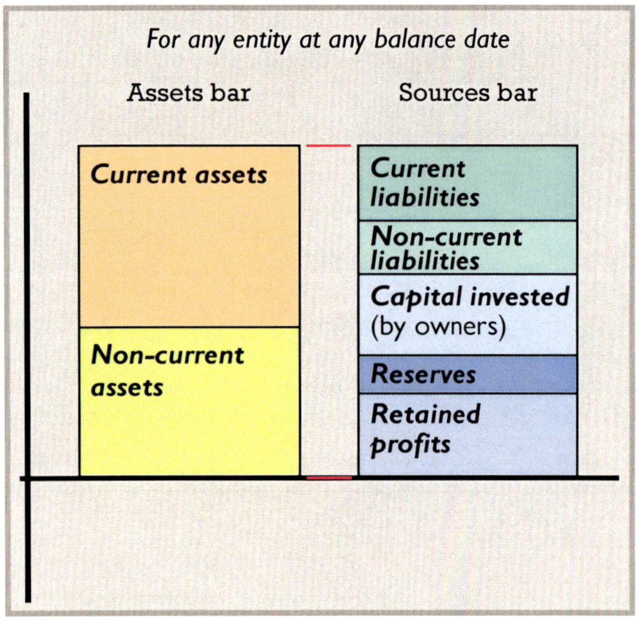

Figure 3.3 A balance chart with current and non-current assets and liabilities account balances, and the three accounts whose balances total the balance of the equity account.

For an active entity the amounts of the seven account balances will vary through time. Thus the actual and relative box heights can vary, but the two net bar heights must always be equal.

2. **Reserves** are amounts of equity currently reserved from being spent by the entity or from being distributed to the entity's owners. A reserves account may be:

   - created by the entity to signal that the amount of the reserve should be corralled for a specified future purpose. Such reserves can created by transferring amounts from retained profits. Unless equal amounts of cash are corralled in, say, separate bank accounts, such reserves act as reminders.

   - used to record amounts of profit which are unrealised and uncertain, and therefore shouldn't be spent or distributed. Such profits result from increases in the carrying amounts of particular assets whose carrying amounts are likely to unpredictably vary through time. When such an asset is later realised (say by being sold), the amount realised is likely to be different from, and may even be below, that asset's earlier recorded carrying amounts. Therefore in the as-at-the-ends-of-reporting-periods financial statements unrealised profits are reported in the statement of other comprehensive income, not in the profit or loss statement.

3. **Retained (undistributed) profits** is the total of the profits earned from when the entity started to operate to the balance date, less the total of any income tax paid and not yet paid but owing (payable) by the entity, less any amounts transferred to reserves, less all amounts that have been distributed to the entity's owners and that the entity has declared that it will distribute to the entity's owners.

The next step explained is the fourth in the list on page 6.

3.4 CREATING THE TEMPORARY ACCOUNTS

The fourth of the five steps listed on page 6 is creating the temporary accounts. As explained below this step is not a direct separation.

Reporting periods were introduced on pages 5 and 6. The profit earned by an entity during a reporting period is calculated using the formula:

$$\begin{bmatrix}\text{Profit or}\\ \text{loss for the}\\ \text{reporting}\\ \text{period}\end{bmatrix} = \begin{bmatrix}\text{Income}\\ \text{earned during}\\ \text{the reporting}\\ \text{period}\end{bmatrix} - \begin{bmatrix}\text{Expenses}\\ \text{incurred during}\\ \text{the reporting}\\ \text{period}\end{bmatrix}$$

Equation 3.a

There are two ways to determine the amounts of income earned and expenses incurred during a reporting period:

1. if the balances of the income and expenses accounts as at the end of the reporting period result from the continual recording of transactions throughout the life of the entity, subtract the income and expenses account balances at the beginning of the reporting period from those at the end of that period, or
2. at the beginning of each reporting period have the balances of the profit-related accounts set at (closed to) zero. The end-of-reporting-period balances of these accounts then record the income earned and expenses incurred during that reporting period.

Manual bookkeeping uses and accounting software simulates the second way. (Accounts whose balances are closed to zero as at the end of each reporting period by being transferred to another account are called *temporary* or *nominal* accounts. The closing process is explained in detail on pages 67 and 72.)

Rather than record all amounts of income in one income account and all expenses in one expenses account as equation 3.a implies, accounting first separates these two accounts into two income accounts and three expenses accounts as below:

$$\begin{bmatrix}\text{Profit or}\\ \text{loss for}\\ \text{the}\\ \text{reporting}\\ \text{period}\end{bmatrix} = \begin{bmatrix}\text{Revenue +}\\ \text{Other-income}\\ \text{earned during}\\ \text{the reporting}\\ \text{period}\end{bmatrix} - \begin{bmatrix}\text{Cost of sales +}\\ \text{Revenue expenses}\\ \text{+ Other-expenses}\\ \text{incurred during the}\\ \text{reporting period}\end{bmatrix}$$

Equation 3.b

In equation 3.b's middle term:

- **Revenue** is the 'amounts of income earned in the course of the entity's usual activities during a reporting period'.
- **Other-income** is 'income earned during a reporting period which the entity decides to classify not as revenue'. For example, a manufacturer might classify the relatively small income it receives from investments in other companies as other-income. (The hyphen in *other-income* signals that the term is a compound noun.)

An *expense* is the 'consumption or loss of future economic benefits during the current or future reporting periods resulting from a transaction during the current reporting period'. (Events and transactions will be further explained, particularly in chapters 6 and 7.) In equation 3.b's right-hand square brackets an entity's expenses are separated into three types:

1. **Cost of sales (COS)** records the cost to the entity of goods and/or services sold during the reporting period excluding administration and other general overhead costs. An expense is only a cost of sales if it would not have been incurred had no sales of the related goods and/or services been made during the reporting period.

   The amount of cost of sales recorded when a sale is made during the reporting period should include:

   a. the cost including freight-in of the finished goods purchased for resale sold. (*Freight-in* is the transport and other delivery costs of moving goods from a seller to a buyer that are paid by the buyer.)
   b. the purchase costs including freight-in of materials and components used in goods manufactured by the entity sold
   c. the direct labour, direct expenses, and manufacturing overheads for any goods manufactured by the entity sold
   d. the direct labour and other direct costs related to any service performed by the entity included in the sale.

When an entity's sales consist only of goods, the expenses account in which the costs of those sales is recorded is sometimes called *cost of goods sold* (*COGS*) instead of *cost of sales*.

2. **Revenue expenses** are those expenses incurred during a reporting period to earn revenue. They exclude expenses recorded as cost of sales which although incurred to earn revenue are required to be recorded separately. Revenue expenses can be separated into direct and indirect. Direct revenue expenses directly relate to the revenue earned during the reporting period. Indirect revenue expenses (also called *overhead expenses*) are incurred in the course of an entity's usual activities, but don't directly relate to any part of the revenue earned during the reporting period.

3. **Other-expenses** are those incurred during the reporting period to earn other-income.

The balances of these five accounts (and of any accounts directly separated from them in step 5 of the page 6 list) are closed to zero as at the end of each reporting period. Therefore the balance of each these accounts at any balance date equals only the amount of income earned or expenses incurred from the start of the reporting period containing the balance date to the balance date. These temporary account balances are therefore not directly separable from the equity or retained profits account balances, each of which records the total of the postings to that account from when the entity was started. (Accounts which aren't temporary accounts are called *permanent* or *real* accounts.)

How the balances of the temporary and other accounts are used to calculate the profit retained from a reporting period varies according to whether the entity is or isn't legally separate from its owner or owners. If the accounting entity isn't legally separate and isn't therefore an income-tax payer, the calculation is illustrated in figure 3.4. The calculation for an income-tax-paying entity such as a company is shown in figure 3.5.

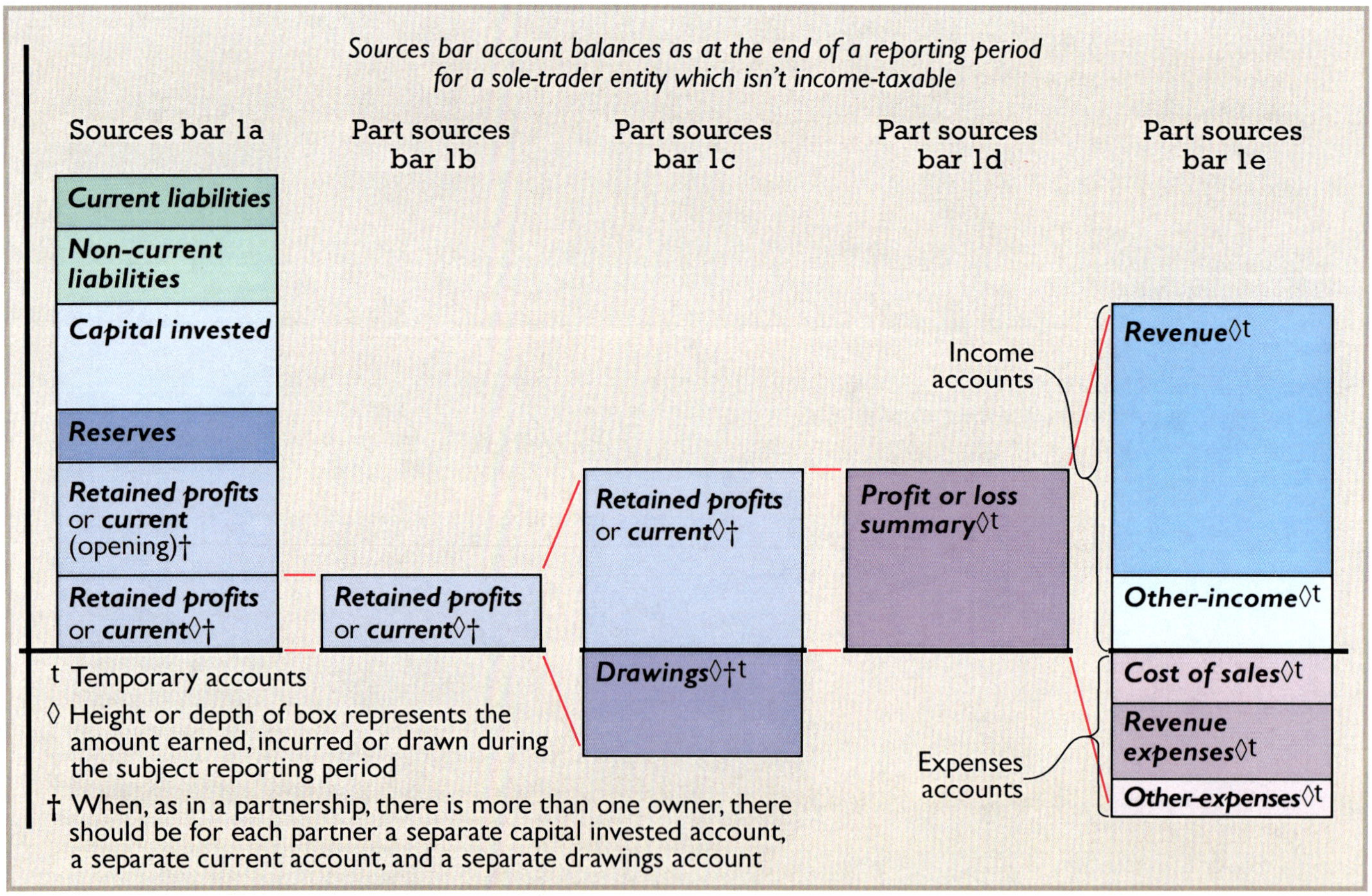

Figure 3.4 How the profit retained from a reporting period is calculated for an entity, here a sole trader (proprietorship), which isn't legally separate from its owner, and isn't therefore itself an income- >

tax payer. The owner, however, is an income-tax payer. (A partnership is an entity which isn't legally separate from its multiple owners called *partners*).

Sources bar 1a. This bar consists of the balances of the same five accounts as the sources bar in figure 3.3. *Current* is a synonym used in some partnerships' accounts for *retained profits*.

Here the balance of the retained profits account is separated into the balance as at the end of the previous reporting period (which equals the balance at the start of the subject reporting period), and the amount of profit retained from the whole of the subject reporting period.

The remaining explanation proceeds from right to left starting from part sources bar 1e.

Part sources bar 1e The boxes represent the income earned and the expenses incurred between the start and the end of the subject reporting period recorded according to the relevant accounting standards. These standards are introduced on page 23.

Part sources bar 1d In manual bookkeeping, the balances of the income and expenses accounts are as at the end of the subject reporting period closed (transferred) into and become the balance of a temporary processing account called the *profit or loss summary account*. Closing and how to transfer amounts between accounts are explained on pages 67 and 72. (In computerised bookkeeping the software simulates the same closing process.)

Part sources bar 1c The accounting profit for the reporting period recorded as the balance of the profit or loss summary account has as at the end of the reporting period been closed into the retained profits account.

Owners of entities which aren't financially separate from their owners can withdraw cash or equivalents as they wish for their own purposes (subject to any partnership agreement and hopefully prudence). These withdrawals are called *drawings*. All the amounts of the drawings by all the owners during the reporting period are here recorded in a separate equity, drawings account. To balance the total of these drawings there would be an equal total reduction in the entity's assets which isn't shown. >

Part sources bar 1b The total of the owners' drawings during the reporting period has been closed into the entity's retained profits account. The height of this bar's box therefore represents the profit earned by the entity during the reporting period less the owners' total drawings during that period. The resulting amount is the entity's retained profit for that reporting period.

Sources bar 1a The balance of the retained profits account as at the end of the reporting period is represented by the combined height of the bar's bottom two boxes. This balance then records the total profits or accumulated losses earned by the entity, less the total of the amounts of owners drawings withdrawn from those profits. Both totals are from when the entity was started to the end of the subject reporting period.

The process used to determine or estimate an entity's retained profits at any specified balance date is similar to that shown in this figure. Many entities only perform that determination accurately as at the end of reporting periods.

Because they're closed as at the end of reporting periods, the drawings account and the profit or loss summary account are, like the profit-related accounts, temporary accounts. The balances of temporary accounts don't appear in balance sheets.

The profits of entities which aren't themselves levied for income tax don't escape being taxed. Each income tax year's taxable income earned by such an entity flows-through to its owners, that is is notionally distributed to and thereby added to the taxable incomes from other sources of each of the entity's owners. Each owner then pays income tax on his or

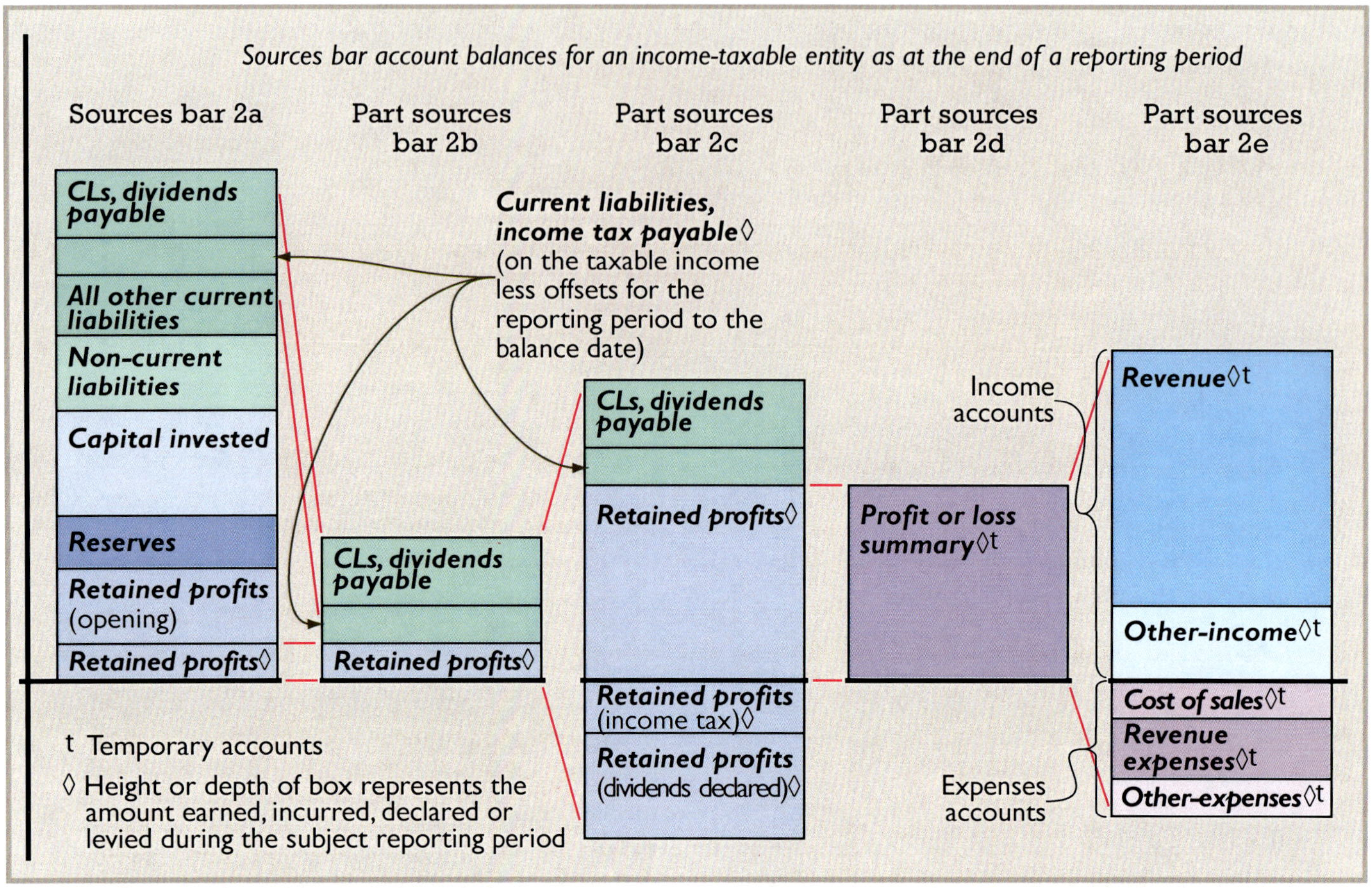

Figure 3.5 How the profit retained from a reporting period is calculated for an company entity which is legally separate from its owners and is therefore itself an income-tax payer.

Sources bar 2a The combination of this bar's bottom two boxes represents the balance of the retained profits account as at the end of the subject reporting period. The upper retained profits box represents the balance of the retained profits as at end of the previous reporting period. The bottom box represents the amount of profit retained from the whole of the subject reporting period.

The total of the entity's current liabilities has been separated into three account balances.

The remaining explanation proceeds from right to left starting from part sources bar 2e.

Part sources bar 2e Shows the amounts of income earned and expenses incurred during the reporting period according to the relevant accounting standards.

Part sources bar 2d In manual bookkeeping, the balances of the income and expenses accounts are as at the end of each reporting period closed into and become the balance of a temporary processing account called the *profit or loss summary account*. (In computerised bookkeeping the software simulates the same process.)

Part sources bar 2c The profit for the reporting period recorded as the balance of the profit or loss summary account in part sources bar 2d has been closed (transferred) into the retained profits account.

A company entity is income-taxable. The income tax which the entity should pay resulting from its activities during the whole of the reporting period is not based upon the profit amount recorded as the balance of the profit and loss summary account. Instead the income tax is levied on the entity's *taxable income*. Taxable income is a measure of taxable profit determined according to the tax law. (Tax law is introduced on page 27). As explained in chapter 10, the income tax payable on an income tax year's taxable income can be reduced by tax offsets (see page 75), and the taxable income itself may have been reduced by carried-forward tax losses (see page 75).

The income tax payable as at the end of the reporting period is represented by the height of the lower green box. To conform to the balance sheet equation imperative, the same amount is >

> simultaneously subtracted from retained profits, and is represented by the box immediately below the x axis.

Owners of a company typically receive rewards for their investments in that company by means of distributions of cash, other assets or the company's own shares. These distributions, which are usually of cash, are called *dividends.* A dividend may be limited by law to an amount which will not adversely affect the company's solvency (its ability to pay bills as they fall due).

Dividends are paid by a company on a payment date, typically several weeks after the dividend's details have been declared by the company's directors on a declaration date. When a dividend is declared the company incurs a legal liability as specified in the declaration. The total of the dividends declared by the entity company's directors during the reporting period is then represented by the depth of the bottom box in part sources bar 2c. Thus, unlike drawings which are usually recorded in a temporary account, dividend declarations are instead usually recorded as debits to the retained profits account (which is permanent). The height of the upper green box represents the amount of dividends declared but unpaid as at the end of the reporting period (here the height of the upper green box is less than the depth of the bottom grey box).

Part sources bar 2b The amount of income tax payable on the company's taxable income earned during the reporting period less any offsets reduces the balance of the retained profits account. Each amount of dividend declared during the reporting period also reduces that balance. The height of this bar's retained profits box therefore represents the profit retained in the company from the subject reporting period.

The three amounts represented by this bar's three boxes are already included in the account balances in part sources bar 2a as shown by the magenta lines.

Sources bar 2a All full and part account balances in this bar are of permanent accounts which aren't closed at the end of each reporting period.

The process used to determine or estimate a company entity's retained profits at any specified > balance date within a reporting period is similar to that shown in this figure. Many companies only perform that determination accurately as at the end of reporting periods.

3.5 CREATING A CHART OF ACCOUNTS

So far in this chapter about fifteen accounts have been created from the three accounts shown in figure 3.1. The last of the five steps listed on page 6 consists of as required separating the balances of those about fifteen accounts to create additional account balances, and then successively separating any of the account balances thereby created to create more. Thus all the different accounts which an entity needs to record and report its activities can be created. Figure 3.6 shows a typical example of the resulting three-branch linked arrangement of accounts called a *chart of accounts.*

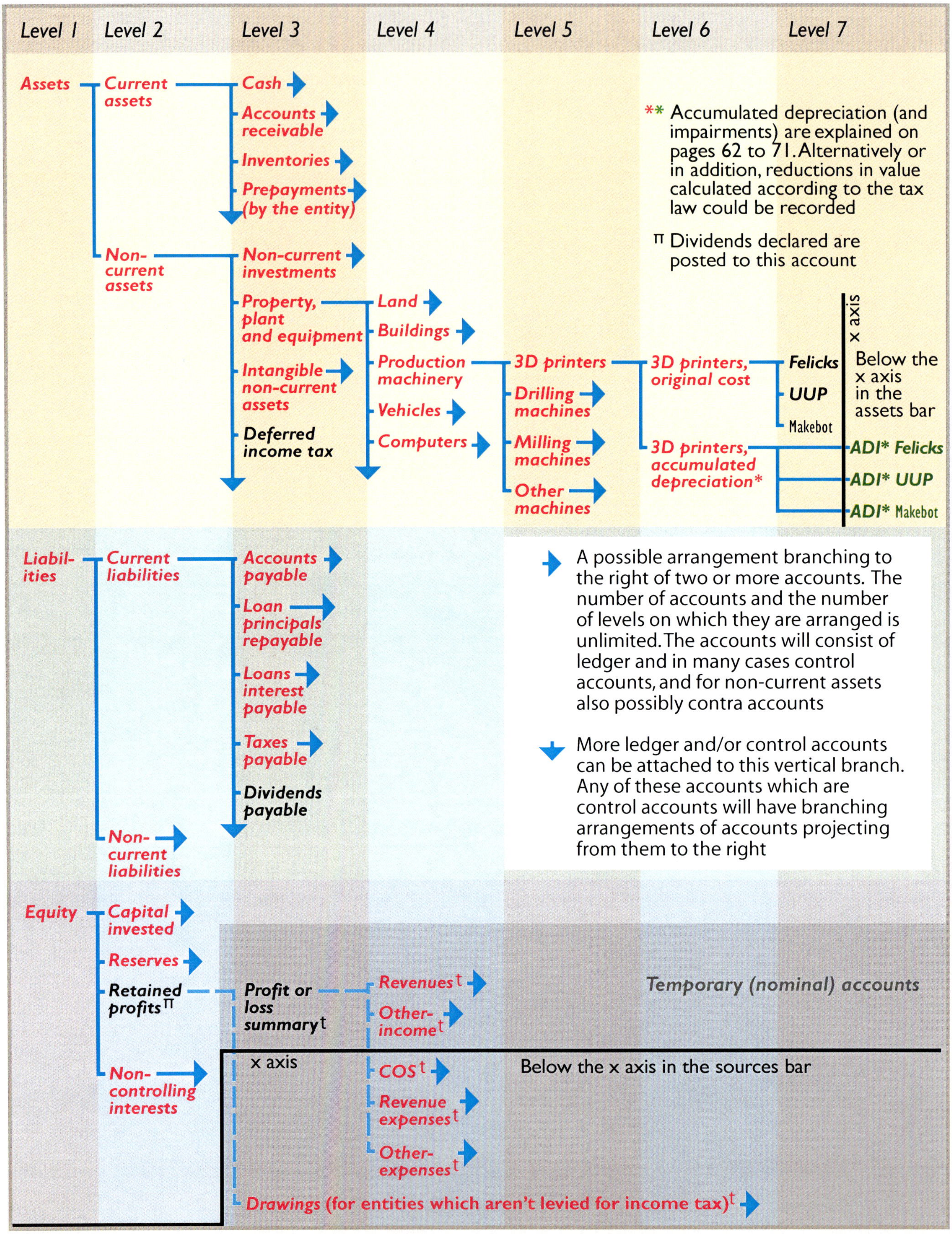

Figure 3.6 An example graphical chart of accounts, here for a company. This chart shows the accounts, their locations and the links between them created by successive account balance separations. Only the branch >

> projecting from the right of the level 5 3D printers control account is shown in full. The company controls three 3D printers made by Felicks, UUP and Makebot respectively, and keeps a ledger account and a contra account (both defined below) for each 3D printer.

The three accounts of the balance sheet equation 2.c on page 3 occupy level 1. A chart of accounts therefore consists of three separate branches of accounts which are connected by the balance sheet equation, but don't converge into one branch. Here the assets branch has a yellow-tinted background, the liabilities branch has a green-tinted background, and the equity branch has a blue-tinted background. The number, names, types and locations of the accounts and the links between them should be tailored to suit each entity.

Types of account

Charts of accounts always include ledger and control accounts, and usually contra accounts. These three account types are explained below:

1. **Ledger accounts** They are located only at the right-hand ends of branches. Here their names are printed in black bold-italic letters. Ledger accounts are sometimes called *posting accounts* because they and contra (ledger) accounts are the only accounts which should receive transaction postings. Such postings may result from the closing of other ledger accounts. Only the balances of ledger accounts are totalled in trial balances (pages 52, 72, and 79 and 80).
2. **Contra accounts** Their names are here printed in green bold-italic letters. A contra account is a special type of ledger account associated with the non-current asset's ledger account to which the asset's original cost is posted. This above-the-x-axis account is then called a *companion account*. By posting a reduction to the carrying amount of a non-current asset to that asset's contra account, not to the companion account, the non-current asset's original cost is more readily accessed. A companion asset's carrying amount at a specified date is then that asset's companion account balance less the balances of that asset's one or more contra accounts at that date. (As explained in chapter 9, amounts of depreciation and >

   > impairment losses related to a non-current asset can be recorded in separate contra accounts.)
3. **Control (totals) accounts** Their names are here printed in magenta bold-italic letters.

   Control accounts are summary accounts, should not receive postings, and their balances aren't used in trial balances. The balance of a control account is the total of the balances of all the control and ledger accounts which directly feed into it (here from the right). The number of control and ledger accounts which directly and indirectly feed into a control account, and the number of levels on which they're located is unlimited. The accounts whose balances feed into a control account should be chosen so that the resulting control account balance is useful.

When an account's type isn't stated, it's usually clear from the context.

Although the type of account is indicated by colour in this chart, the box outlines and the type within the boxes in this book's balance charts will be in black or in a few cases grey.

More information about accounts

In manual bookkeeping, postings must only be made to ledger and contra ledger accounts, not to control accounts. This ensures that the imperative of the balance sheet equation is satisfied because the balances of its three level 1 control accounts (assets, liabilities and equity) then consist respectively only of the balances of all the assets, liabilities and equity ledger accounts.

The balances of the ledger and control accounts which feed directly into a control account are usually located on the same branch as that control account. However they don't have to be; for example, the balance of the control account for one definition of working capital equals the balance of the current assets control account less the balance of the current liabilities control account.

Each account within the grey rectangle at the bottom of this chart (and whose account name is followed here by a ^{t}) is a temporary account. The linking lines to them are paler and dashed because the balances of the temporary accounts aren't directly separated from the balance of the retained profits account. >

> The level 2, equity, non-controlling interests account is kept only by entities which control, but don't wholly own, external companies. Non-controlling interests are explained in chapter 11.
>
> The *category* of an account is the name of the family of related ledger and/or control accounts to which that account belongs.

3.5.1 Deciding a chart's accounts

A chart of accounts tailored to an entity's particular needs can be created from scratch. Most entities however create their charts of accounts by amending an existing chart of accounts. Accounting software usually provides specimen charts of accounts for different types of entity which can be readily tailored to suit a particular entity's activities.

A chart of accounts should:

- be designed to ensure that the entity's managers have the information they need in the appropriate form for decision making
- exclude accounts called *miscellaneous* or similar because they're likely to be used to hold transaction postings which are difficult to classify or which someone doesn't wish to explain
- ensure that amounts will be appropriately classified so that the resulting accounting records and the financial statements, reports and tax returns prepared from those records comply with the relevant accounting standards and the tax law (these are introduced on pages 23 and 27 respectively).

In preparing its financial statements an entity may be required to analyse its expenses by nature or by function, and should design its chart of accounts accordingly. If analysing by nature, the layout of the income and expenses entries in the profit or loss statement should resemble that below:

Revenue		$$$$
Other-income		$$$$
Expenses related to revenue described by nature and listed alphabetically; e.g. COS, falls in asset carrying amounts, stationery, wages, etc.	($$$$)	
Other-expenses (not directly related to revenue)	($$$$)	
Total expenses		($$$$)
Profit before income tax		$$$$

If analysing expenses by function, the layout of the profit or loss statement should resemble that below:

Revenue	$$$$
Cost of sales expenses	($$$$)
Gross profit	$$$$
Other-income	$$$$
Distribution expenses	($$$$)
Administration expenses	($$$$)
Other-expenses	($$$$)
Profit before income tax	$$$$

To clarify the two methods of analysis, consider an entity's wages and salaries expenses:

- If analysing expenses by nature, wages and salaries would be recorded according to whether employees were employed in clerical, trade-related or managerial roles.
- If analysing by function, wages and salaries expenses would instead be separated and recorded under some or all of the expenses accounts headed *cost of sales*, *distribution*, *administration*, and *other-expenses*.

3.5.2 Classes

Some accounting software allows amounts to be posted to accounts and in parallel to classes. For example, each of the two factories a manufacturer operates could be defined as a separate class in the accounts. Then when a bookkeeper posts transactions, amounts could be associated with the appropriate factory by specifying that factory's class. This would save having to have separate accounts for, say, the same types of income and expenses for each factory. Similarly, classes can refer to particular departments, branches, projects or similar. Having classes also facilitates the decentralised employment of bookkeepers; for example, if a manufacturer installed the appropriate accounting software, bookkeepers at each of its factories could record in the same accounts by including the factory's class in their postings.

3.5.3 Numbering charts of accounts

Recording transactions would be unnecessarily slow if bookkeepers had to search for the relevant ledger accounts in charts of accounts drawn as branching arrangements similar to that in figure 3.6. Instead the account names and locations and the links between them are horizontally compressed and then stored, whether on paper or in a computer file, as a vertical list.

The account names in longer vertical lists may be numbered. One possible account numbering arrangement is shown below.

1-0000 to 1-9999 Assets
  1-0001 to 1-4999 Current assets
  1-5000 to 1-9999 Non-current assets
2-0000 to 2-9999 Liabilities
  2-0001 to 2-4999 Current liabilities
  2-5000 to 2-9999 Non-current liabilities
3-0000 to 3-9999 Equity
  3-0001 to 3-1999 Capital invested
  3-2000 to 3-2999 Reserves
  3-3000 to 3-3999 Retained profits
4-0000 to 4-9999 Revenue
5-0000 to 5-9999 Other-income
6-0000 to 6-9999 Cost of sales
7-0000 to 7-9999 Revenue expenses
8 0000 to 8-9999 Other-expenses

There isn't one recognised numbering system for charts of accounts. Therefore different brands of accounting software may use different account numberings.

When allocating numbers to a chart of accounts, allow ample uncommitted account numbers. As the entity's recording and reporting needs change, additional accounts can then be added without having to disturb the numbering of the existing accounts

A chart of accounts can be widely useful. With training, an entity's non-accounting staff can refer to the chart of accounts when raising source documents, and thus post the related transactions or clarify the accounts which should receive postings. (A *source document* is an 'original paper or electronic record of a transaction'.) Common types of source document include invoices, credit notes, and receipts. (An *invoice* is an 'itemised request for payment raised by a seller', a *credit note* is a 'negative invoice', and a *receipt* is a 'record of the seller receiving payment for the related sale and the buyer receiving the related supply'.) Also, an entity's staff will find it useful to be able to consult the financial information in the accounts on an appropriate view-only basis.

3.6 AMENDING A CHART OF ACCOUNTS

As an entity and its financial recording and reporting needs change through time, its chart of accounts should be amended to reflect those changes:

- Accounts can be added; for example, as an entity gains new credit customers it needs to add a accounts-receivable (debtors) ledger account for each (this category of accounts is explained on page 25). When a new ledger account is added, its initial balance must be zero, and it must also be linked 'up' (to the left in figure 3.6) to a control account. If the added account is a control account it must be linked both 'up' and 'down' (both to the left and to the right in figure 3.6).

- Over time some accounts will cease to receive any more postings. Bookkeeping is then slower than it could be because an unnecessarily large number of accounts need to be sorted through to make a posting. If using accounting software, posting efficiency can be restored by making accounts which will no longer receive postings inactive, that is hidden but preserved. Were such accounts deleted (equivalent to tearing out their pages from an entity's manual ledgers), the information they contained would be lost. Preservation of the information in the accounts which are inactive leaves what's called an *audit trail*. Correcting wrong postings by reversing, not deleting, them also preserves the audit trail. If the audit trail were broken by the deletion of transactional data, comprehensive checking of the accounts would be rendered more difficult if not impossible.

Chapter 4

THE ACCOUNTING CYCLE

Chapters 2 and 3 explained that an entity's activities are financially recorded in accounts located and linked in that entity's chart of accounts. Recording an entity's activities in its accounts is part of the *accounting cycle.* This chapter introduces that cycle, and five inventions which made its current version possible.

4.1 THE ACCOUNTING CYCLE

The accounting cycle is shown in figure 4.1, and is the 'process by which an entity records its activities financially in accounts, and from the resulting account balances prepares its financial statements'. These statements should according to IAS (International Accounting Standard) 1 *Presentation of Financial Statements* be intended 'to provide information about the financial position, financial performance and cash flows of an entity that is useful to a wide range of users in making economic decisions'. The statements should also 'show the results of the entity's management's stewardship of the resources entrusted to it'. The best-known examples of financial statements are those found in the annual reports of public companies (companies whose shares are quoted on stock exchanges). These reports are readily viewable on those companies' websites.

The accounting cycle's three processes were introduced on page 1. The first two processes are explained in chapters 5 to 7, and the third process in chapters 8 to 11. Communicating, a necessary and important process also mentioned on page 1 which isn't part of the accounting cycle, is introduced within figure 4.1's right-hand blue rectangle.

4.2 RELATED INVENTIONS

This section introduces five human inventions which have been essential to the development of the modern accounting cycle.

4.2.1 Complete writing

Complete writing (also called *full writing*) is intended for communication, and consists of artificial graphic marks which relate to articulate speech which are made on a durable or electronic surface. The first complete writing was achieved by about 2500 BC by the Sumerians who lived in part of what is now called Iraq. Their script, shown in figure 4.2, was cuneiform (from the Latin *cuneus* meaning 'wedge' and *forma* meaning 'shape'). However the modern alphabetic script used in this book evolved from the demotic (meaning 'of the people') script in use in Egypt by 700 BC.

Figure 4.2 Egyptian demotic script on baked clay from Luxor, 2nd to 1st centuries BC.

Illustration courtesy of Wikimedia Commons and the Oriental Institute Museum, University of Chicago.

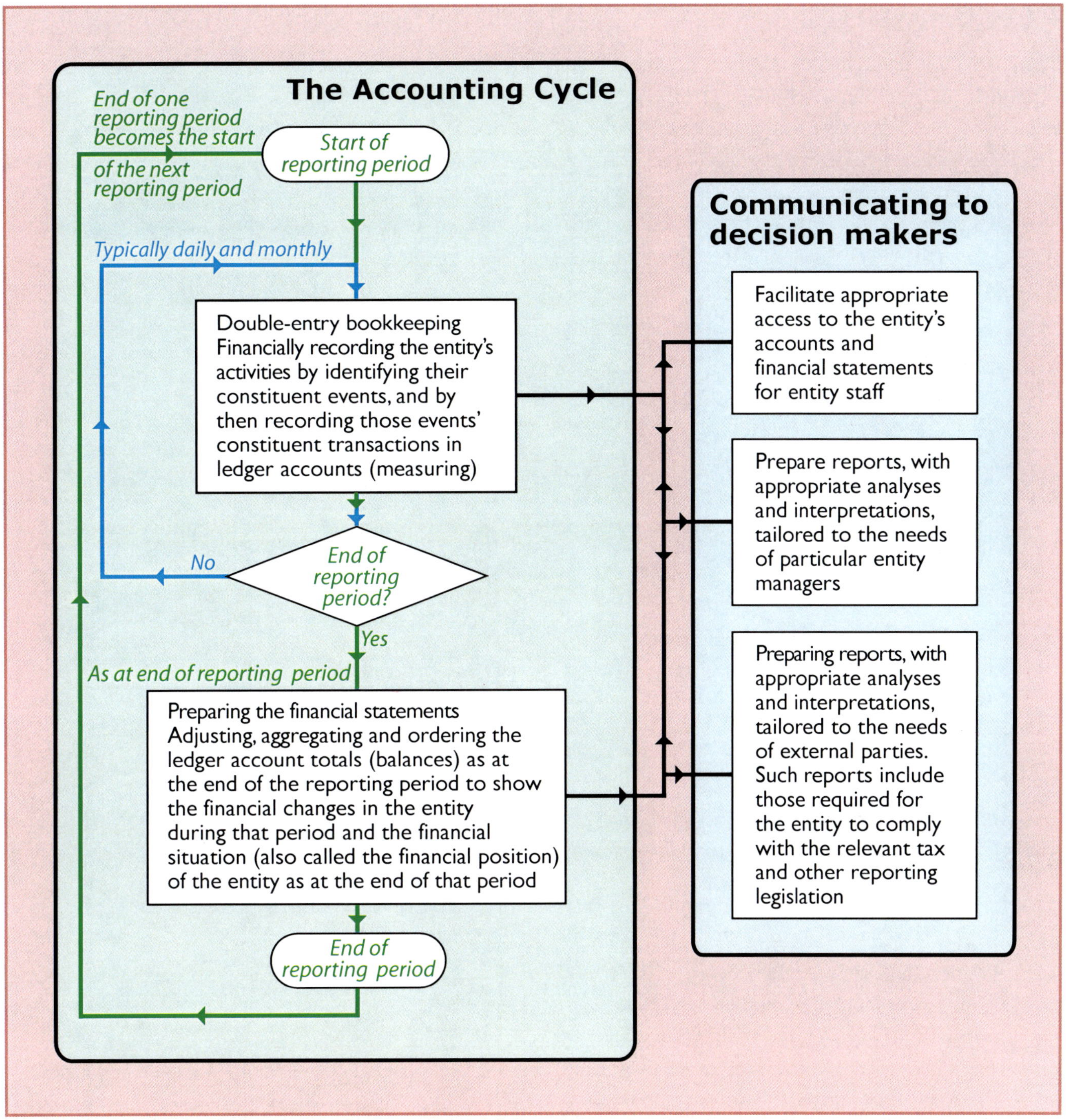

Figure 4.1 The accounting cycle consists of two cycles. The inner blue cycle consists of:

- identifying the entity's events, and then recording the entity events' constituent transactions. (These operations are ideally performed daily.)
- performing other bookkeeping operations.

Among the most important of these other bookkeeping operations is bank reconciliation. This consists of explaining why the balance of the entity's own ledger account for each bank account differs from the balance at the same date shown in the bank's bank statement for that same bank account. Many entities perform bank reconciliations monthly.

The account balances as at the end of a reporting period are used to prepare the entity's financial statements. These show the financial changes in the entity during, and its financial position as at the end of, the reporting period.

Entity managers who understand the accounting cycle will find it immensely useful to be able to access the accounts.

4.2.2 Money

Money enables the values of different goods and services to be measured and compared. Primitive money such as cowrie shells and cocoa beans enabled trading when time and/or distance was involved in an exchange. The first coins were introduced in Lydia (in what is now Turkey) in about 630 BC. The first international currency was the Greek drachma. Silver drachma coins (figure 4.3) were introduced in about 640 BC.

Figure 4.3 A Greek tetradrachm coin after 449 BC.

Illustration courtesy Wikimedia Commons and the Classical Numismatic Group.

4.2.3 Hindu-Arabic numerals

If you can imagine performing multiplication and division with Roman numerals, you'll realise the huge advantage of using Hindu-Arabic numerals (those used in this book) for computation. Hindu-Arabic numerals were first introduced into Europe in the 980s by Gerbert of Aurillac. They were reintroduced in 1202 by Leonardo of Pisa in his manuscript-form book *Liber abacci* ('Book of Calculation'). (Since 1838 Leonard of Pisa has also been known by the nickname Fibonacci.) However because of opposition from the guilds, the Church and others, it was not until about 1500 that Hindu-Arabic numerals were fully accepted in Europe.

No originals of the 1202 or 1228 editions of *Liber abacci* are extant. Fourteen, mostly incomplete, later copies of the 1228 edition are held in Italian libraries.

4.2.4 Double entry

How and when double entry was invented is unknown. One possibility is that in about 1300 AD an Italian merchant's bookkeeper conceived of what is now called double-entry bookkeeping, the processes of identifying transactions and then recording them so that the resulting account balances conform to the balance sheet equation.

The first printed description of double-entry bookkeeping was a treatise included in a book first self-published in Venice in 1494 called *Summa de Arithmetica* (figures 4.4 and 4.5). Pacioli's treatise was widely translated, and popularised the adoption of double-entry in other countries. The term *double entry* is recorded as

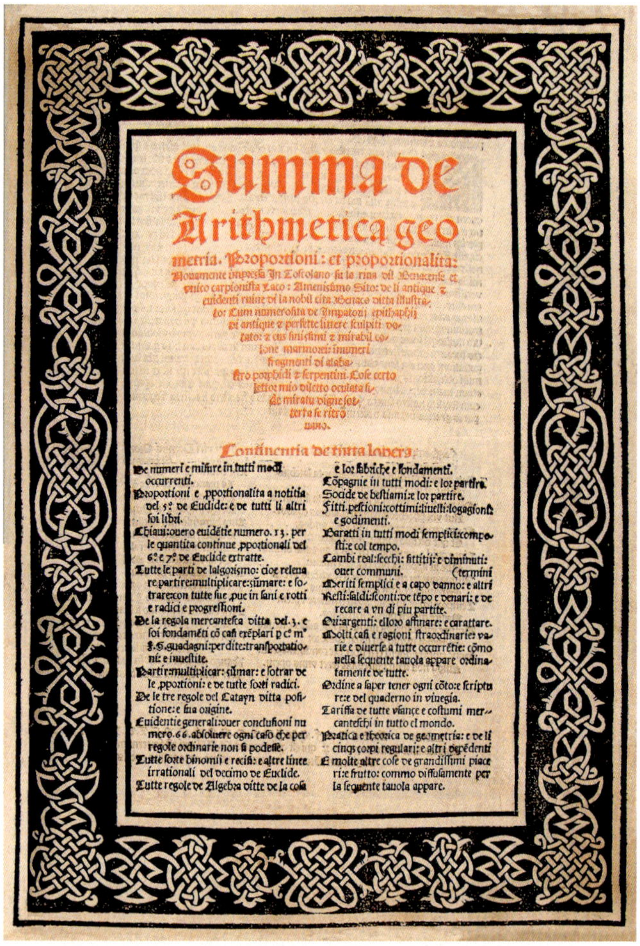

Figure 4.4 The title page of Pacioli's 1523 second edition of *Summa de Arithmetica*. This page is far more impressive than the title page of the 1494 first edition.

Illustration courtesy of Edinburgh University Library.

first being used in English in 1721—until then the process was known in English as the *Italian method.* (The 2011 book *Double Entry* by Jane Gleeson-White is an excellent first source for those wishing to learn more about the history of accounting.)

Figure 4.5 Luca Pacioli, the author of the first printed explanation of double-entry bookkeeping. This portrait was painted in 1495 by Jacopo de' Barbari. (The identity of the young man on the right is uncertain, but he may be Albrecht Dürer.)

Pacioli's 615-page book *Summa de Arithmetica, Geometria, Proportioni, et Proportionalita* (Sum of Knowledge of Arithmetic, Geometry, and Proportions) contains a 27-page treatise called "Particularis de Computis et Scripturis" which explains the practice of double-entry bookkeeping. A copy of the book (with the red cover) is pictured *bottom right* beneath the model of the dodecahedron.

Pacioli's left hand rests on a copy of Euclid's geometry text *Elements*. The pointer in Pacioli's right hand points to a fifteen-sided figure drawn in chalk using a method described in *Elements*. The glass model shown *top left* is of a twenty-six-faced rhomicuboctahedron half-filled with water.

Illustration reproduced by permission of the Museo de Gallerie Nazionale di Capodimonte, Naples.

4.2.5 The joint-stock company

A joint-stock company is one whose stock (ordinary shares representing the capital invested in the company or corporation) is owned jointly. A joint-stock company can have many owners who are commonly called *shareholders* or *stockholders* or *investors*. Most of a joint-stock company's owners will not be involved in the day-to-day running of the company. To try to ensure that owners of such companies are both adequately informed and protected from fraud committed by those running these companies, government regulators and stock exchanges require that joint-stock companies keep proper accounts and adequately, honestly and regularly inform owners of their companies' activities via financial and other statements.

The best-known, early, joint-stock company was the United Dutch Chartered East India Company chartered in 1602 (see figure 4.6).

The first legislation allowing a joint-stock company to be formed without legislation specific to that company was the British Joint Stock Companies Act 1844. The Joint Stock Companies Act 1856 provided for limited liability. The liability of an owner of a company with limited liability for that company's debts is limited, typically to the amount the owner has paid for and owes on the shares the owner owns.

Figure 4.6 Possibly the first company logo, that of the United Dutch Chartered East India Company (Vereenigde Nederlandsche Geoctroyeerde Oostindische Compagnie or VOC for short).

Illustration courtesy of Wikimedia Commons.

Chapter 5
PRINCIPLES, CONCEPTS, STANDARDS AND LAWS

National laws prescribe how different types of entity have to record and report their activities. These laws are intended to ensure that an entity's reporting:

i. is readily comparable with similar reporting from other entities

ii. is reliable

iii. results in the entity paying the correct amounts of the different taxes levied.

For reasons i and ii financial records and reporting which aren't prescribed by laws are also usually prepared to conform to those laws.

The laws which govern financial and tax recording and reporting are largely based upon certain principles and concepts. The resulting body of principles, concepts and laws which relate to a nation's accounting typically comprises:

1. the balance sheet equation
2. the concept of periods
3. the chart of accounts
4. the GAAP (Generally Accepted Accounting Principles)
5. any publications which form a bridge between the GAAP and the accounting standards which apply within the nation
6. the current accounting standards used within the nation and any interpretations of and amendments to those standards
7. the cash accounting and accrual accounting methods including revenue recognition and matching
8. debit and credit
9. what this book calls the *tax law* which comprises the current national tax legislation, rulings and determinations.

Those involved in processing transactional data through the accounting cycle and communicating financial information derived from that data should understood these nine principles, concepts and laws. An appreciation of them will also enable those who should use the resulting information to do so more effectively.

Items 1 to 3 in above list have already been explained in earlier chapters. This chapter will explain the remaining items numbered 4 to 9.

5.1 GAAP

The term *GAAP* refers to the accounting principles which should be followed by bookkeepers and accountants in measuring, recording and reporting transactions. Appreciate the GAAP and you'll understand the detail of accounting much more readily. Six principles are introduced below:

1. **Distinct accounting entity** An entity for which accounts are kept and financial statements are prepared must be financially isolated and distinct.
2. **Cost principle** Only transactional data that can be expressed in terms of money should be included in accounting records. These records should use the actual costs paid for goods and services, and the prices at which goods and services are sold.
3. **Amounts relevant** While actual (historical) amounts are reliable, they may not be relevant. For example, if rural land bought decades ago by an entity were now on the edge of a city and zoned residential, the land's original cost would be a small fraction of its current value. To reliably assess that land-owning entity's current financial position, that land would have to be valued at some current value, not at its original cost. (The most used measure of an asset's current value is *fair value* which is the 'amount for which the asset could be exchanged between a knowledgeable willing buyer and a knowledgeable willing seller in an arm's length transaction'.)
4. **The revenue recognition and matching principles** An entity's profit or loss for a period is the

income earned during the period less the expenses incurred during the period. To determine those two constituent amounts it's necessary to understand the principles of revenue recognition and matching.

Revenue recognition would be better called income recognition, and is the process of recording each amount of an entity's income in the entity's accounts during the appropriate reporting period. Usually an income is recognised when the entity passes control of an asset to another entity and the amount of money involved can be reliably measured and has been or will probably be received. However income can have been earned without control passing; for example, if a manufacturing entity has at the end of a reporting period partially completed a contract for a customer but not invoiced for the work done. Assuming that the manufacturer is reasonably certain of receiving payment, for the manufacturer's total income for that reporting period to be reliable, the cost of the work done on the partially completed contract plus an appropriate proportion of the anticipated profit should be included.

Determining the expenses for a reporting period may also not be straightforward. In matching, costs incurred in earning a particular income are recorded as being incurred in the reporting period in which that income was earned. For example, if an entity sells goods purchased in an earlier reporting period, the expense of the resulting fall in stocks is matched to the reporting period in which the sale was made. However the matching principle can't always be applied. For example, the fall in value of a production machine during a reporting period is an expense which isn't usually related to incomes earned through using that machine.

5. **Conservatism or prudence principle** To counter any desire to report optimistically, profits should not be anticipated but losses should be.

6. **Going concern principle** Unless an entity is about to close or fail, its financial statements should be prepared on the basis that the entity is what's called a *going concern*, that is it will continue to operate and is financially healthy. If it becomes known that an entity is likely to close or fail, its assets should then be revalued on that basis.

5.2 BRIDGE PUBLICATIONS

Some nations have publications which explain and clarify the principles on which that nation's accounting standards are based. These publications thus bridge between the GAAP and the nation's accounting standards.

5.3 NATIONAL ACCOUNTING STANDARDS

A nation's accounting standards define how affected entities should measure, and record their activities, and prepare their financial statements.

The number of entities which operate in multiple nations continues to increase. Therefore the accounting standards boards of those nations which have such a board are seeking to harmonise their national accounting standards with those of other nations. To do this, national accounting standards boards when revising their existing accounting standards and producing new ones usually try to ensure that those standards meet the requirements of the International Financial Reporting Standards (IFRSs) or the earlier International Accounting Standards (IASs) which are still current. These IFRSs and IASs are currently used by or form the basis of the accounting standards used by more than a hundred countries.

5.4 CASH AND ACCRUAL ACCOUNTING

An entity can measure its profit for a period in one of two ways:

1. the cash receipts of income received during the period less the cash expenditures on expenses during the period

2. the income earned during the period less the expenses incurred during the period.

The more an entity trades on credit and the longer the durations for which it controls its assets, the more the profits measured in the two ways diverge. Each of the two ways of measuring profit results from a different method of recording transactions. These two methods are respectively *cash accounting* and *accrual accounting*.

5.4.1 Cash accounting

In cash accounting only cash transactions (those involving a receipt or payment of cash) are recorded. Thus the purchase or acquisition of an asset, even if bought on credit, is recorded as taking place when the entity makes the related cash payment. Similarly sales, even if on credit, are recorded as taking place only when the seller receives the related cash from the buyer. Cash accounting therefore has four particular disadvantages:

1. Income and expenses resulting from changes in the values of assets due to non-cash transactions such as depreciations and revaluations (explained in chapter 9) aren't recorded.
2. Other transactions which don't involve a receipt or a payment of cash aren't recorded. For example, credit events consist of two or more related transactions. One will be a non-cash *core transaction* such as the purchase of a current asset, the acquisition of a non-current asset, or a sale. The other transaction or transactions will be one or more related payments or receipts of cash—these usually happen after the core transaction. Because in cash accounting the core transactions of credit events (the incurrences or acceptances of debts) aren't recorded, managing cash payments and receipts is more difficult under cash accounting than under accrual accounting.
3. When an event doesn't wholly occur within a reporting period, the profits for the reporting periods through which the event spans will be distorted under cash accounting. For example, if the cash for a credit sale made in one annual reporting period were received in the following reporting period, under cash accounting the reported profit for the earlier period would be lower, and that for the following period would be higher than under accrual accounting. (As will be explained shortly, accrual accounting represents the activities and financial positions of most entities more realistically than does cash accounting.)

Therefore cash accounting is only appropriate for members of some professions, and for small businesses which buy and sell for cash and not on credit, and whose assets are of little value and retained for very short durations.

How much freedom entities have to choose between the two accounting methods will depend upon the relevant national laws.

5.4.2 Accrual accounting

Accrual accounting attempts to represent an entity's activities through recording all that entity's transactions, not only those which involve cash, as happening when they do happen. Thus entities using accrual accounting:

1. post an event's core transfer-of-control transactions in addition to the related receipt or payment of cash transactions
2. post transactions for which there aren't any related payments or receipts of cash. These include internal transfers and changes to the carrying amounts of asset units
3. recognise income as it's earned (is reasonably certain and can be reliably measured), not when the related payments are received. This practice of revenue recognition was introduced on the preceding page.
4. recognise expenses as they're incurred.

These four practices conform to the accounting principle of prudence, and are the bases of accrual accounting. Accrual accounting is typically summarised by the statement, 'items of income are recognised as they are earned; and expenses are recognised as they are incurred, and both are recorded in the accounting records and reported in the financial statements of the reporting periods to which they relate'. This statement is shown graphically as equation 5.a.

Accounting profit before tax for a period	=	Total revenue and other-income earned during the period	—	Total expenses and other-expenses incurred during the period

Equation 5.a

Outside accounting an *accrual* is a 'natural accumulation or outgrowth'. According to Bangs & Hanselman, *Accounting for Engineers*, 1941, accrual accounting was so named because it was an accounting method which arose 'naturally' from the desire to keep financial records which more accurately represented the activities of entities. Consequently because accrual accounting requires bookkeepers to post all an entity's transactions, in accrual accounting:

- the carrying amounts of the entity's assets are tracked in the accounts
- ledger accounts are kept for those who owe the entity cash or cash equivalents, and for those to whom the entity owes cash or cash equivalents. It's therefore much easier to monitor amounts owing and owed
- processing is simpler because bookkeepers can post core transactions immediately they receive the relevant source documents, and don't have to wait until the related cash is received or paid

Overall therefore accrual accounting is the sensible choice even for the smallest entities.

5.5 DEBIT AND CREDIT

Accounting professionals don't usually use *positive, negative, add, subtract* and related terms when describing account balances or postings. Instead they use *debit* and *credit*, not out of contrariness, but because those two terms offer definite advantages. *Debit* and *credit* do however have the reputation of being difficult to understand. This reputation stems not from any inherent difficulties in the terms' meanings, but because they're so often poorly explained. In this section they're explained graphically.

Figure 5.1 represents an entity's financial position, and includes account balances both above and below the x axis in both bars. Above the x axis the chart includes the control account balances *debtors* and *creditors (*also called *accounts receivable* or *accounts payable*, although 'by the entity' needs to be added for these two account names to be understood).

When entity A is owed a debt by another entity B, entity A calls entity B a *debtor*. This term is derived from Old French. An alternative term was *debitor* from Latin. The positive balances of the debtors' ledger accounts kept by an entity for the debts of each of its debitors therefore came to be called *debit balances* or *debits*. The positive balances of all the above-the-x-axis assets bar accounts then also came to be called *debit balances*. And any posting which increased the balance of an above-the-x-axis assets account bar came to be called a *debit*.

If entity B allows entity A to borrow from it or buy from it on credit, entity A calls entity B a creditor because entity B has credence (faith) that entity A will repay the borrowing. The positive balances of the creditors' ledger accounts kept by an entity to record the entity's borrowings from other entities therefore came to be called *credit balances* or *credits*. The positive balances of all the above-the-x-axis sources bar accounts then also came to be called *credit balances*. And any posting which increased the positive balance of one of those accounts came to be called a *credit*.

Increasing the balance of a sources bar account below the x axis in a balance chart affects the balance between the two bars' net heights in the same way that increasing the balance of an assets bar account located above the x axis. Therefore the balances of sources bar accounts located below the x axis and postings which increased those balances came to be called *debits*. Similarly the balances of assets bar accounts located below the x axis and postings which increased those balances came to be called *credits*. Figure 5.1 therefore defines *debit* and *credit* graphically.

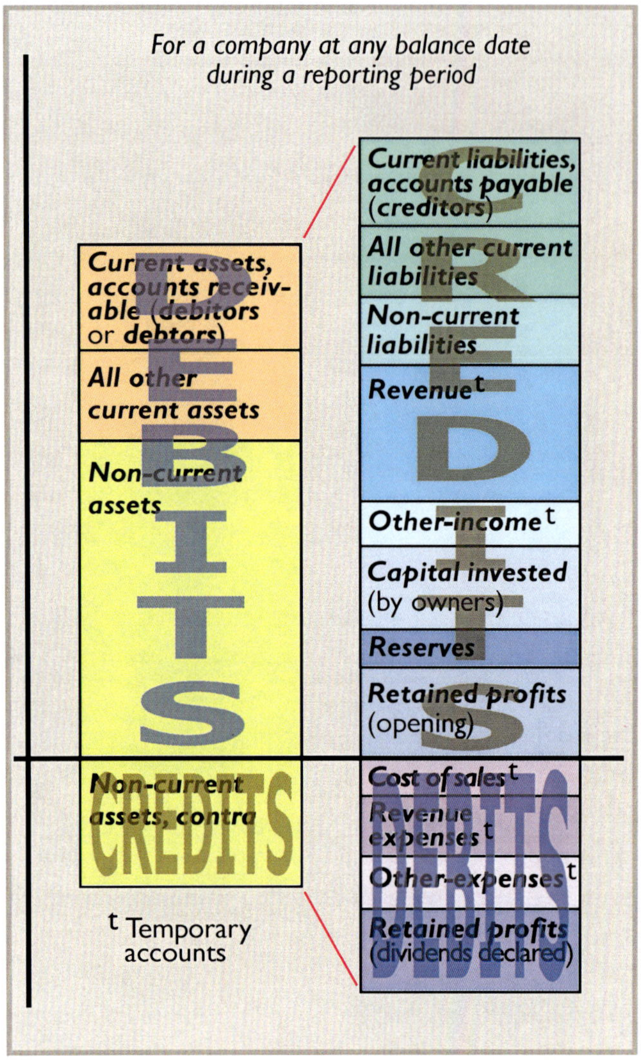

Figure 5.1 A balance chart representing a company entity's financial position or balance sheet. The locations of the boxes assumes that all the account balances are positive. The amounts of the account balances represented will vary according to the entity and the balance date, but must always conform to the balance sheet equation imperative.

The easiest way to decide the sign (that is whether a debit or a credit) of an account balance or of a posting to an account is to visualise the location of its representing box in a balance chart:

- when the account balance is positive or the posting would positively increase the balance of the account, its representing box would be located as in the above chart. The overlay over that box then shows the sign of the balance or posting
- when the account balance is negative or the posting would decrease the balance of the account, the location of the representing box would lie in > > the same bar but on the opposite side of the x axis from the location were the balance or posting positive. Thus the sign of a negative balance or negative posting is opposite to that of a positive balance of or a positive posting to that account.
- Amounts owing to creditors which aren't trade suppliers, such as a taxing authority or a credit card company aren't recorded in accounts-payable accounts, but in ledger accounts separated from the all other current liabilities control account represented by the second box down in the sources bar.

Debit and *credit* in recording transactions

Figure 3.6's caption explains that when a balance chart represents an entity's financial position, the monetary total of its assets bar must consist of only the balances of all the assets ledger accounts. Also the monetary total of its sources bar must consist of only the balances of all the liabilities and equity ledger accounts. If a posting to a ledger account or the balance of a ledger account were included twice in such a balance chart, the balance sheet equation imperative would be violated. Therefore at any balance date for any balance chart which represents a balance sheet:

$$\begin{bmatrix}\text{Total of}\\ \text{assets bar}\\ \text{ledger}\\ \text{account}\\ \text{debit}\\ \text{balances}\end{bmatrix} - \begin{bmatrix}\text{Total of}\\ \text{assets bar}\\ \text{ledger}\\ \text{account}\\ \text{credit}\\ \text{balances}\end{bmatrix} = \begin{bmatrix}\text{Total of}\\ \text{sources bar}\\ \text{ledger}\\ \text{account}\\ \text{credit}\\ \text{balances}\end{bmatrix} - \begin{bmatrix}\text{Total of}\\ \text{sources bar}\\ \text{ledger}\\ \text{account}\\ \text{debit}\\ \text{balances}\end{bmatrix}$$

Equation 5.b

If the terms within its second and fourth square brackets are added to both sides of equation 5.b, that equation becomes:

$$\begin{bmatrix}\text{Total of all}\\ \text{ledger account}\\ \text{debit balances}\end{bmatrix} = \begin{bmatrix}\text{Total of all}\\ \text{ledger account}\\ \text{credit balances}\end{bmatrix}$$

Equation 5.c

Equation 5.c is used in manual accounting to perform arithmetical checks called *trial balances*. These checks are explained on pages 52, 71 and 72, and 79 and 80.

A ledger account debit balance results when the total of all the debit postings to that account exceeds the total of all the credit postings to that account. Similarly, a ledger account credit balance results when the total of all the credit postings to that account exceeds the total of all the debit postings to that account. Therefore for any entity at any balance date, equation 5.c can be restated as:

$$\begin{bmatrix}\text{Total of all the debit}\\ \text{postings from when}\\ \text{the entity was started}\\ \text{to the balance date}\end{bmatrix} = \begin{bmatrix}\text{Total of all the credit}\\ \text{postings from when}\\ \text{the entity was started}\\ \text{to the balance date}\end{bmatrix}$$

Equation 5.d

All an entity's postings must conform to equation 5.d immediately before and immediately after a transaction is recorded. Therefore for every transaction:

$$\begin{bmatrix}\text{Total of all the}\\ \text{debit postings}\\ \text{which record}\\ \text{the transaction}\end{bmatrix} = \begin{bmatrix}\text{Total of all the}\\ \text{credit postings}\\ \text{which record}\\ \text{the transaction}\end{bmatrix}$$

Equation 5.e

Equation 5.e therefore provides a simple check of whether a transaction's postings are arithmetically correct. Also because equation 5.e applies to any one transaction, it must also apply to any series of transactions.

Instead of referring to postings as being *debited* or *credited* amounts, why not use the common words *added* and *subtracted*? The reason is that for a single transaction the sum of the additive postings doesn't always equal the sum of the subtractive postings, and therefore the useful checks provided by equations 5.c and 5.e would be lost.

The economic benefit criterion

An alternative criterion for deciding whether a posting is a debit or a credit is economic benefit. For example, when recording the transaction of a sale of some inventory (stock) for cash, the addition to the entity's cash is an economic benefit and therefore a debit; and the reduction in the entity's inventory is a loss of economic benefit, and therefore a credit.

Debit and credit in balance charts

As you'll see, boxes in a balance chart can represent control account balances, ledger account balances, and/or the postings for one or more transactions. As long as the balance chart's box heights and depths are accurately drawn to the y axis's monetary scale, and if any necessary boxes representing the balances of balancing-accounts are included (explained on page 34), for any balance chart at any balance date:

$$\begin{bmatrix}\text{Net height of}\\ \text{the assets bar}\end{bmatrix} = \begin{bmatrix}\text{Net height of}\\ \text{the sources bar}\end{bmatrix}$$

Equation 5.f

This equation is the *net-bar-heights imperative*. In it the *net height of a bar* is its 'total height above the x axis minus its total depth below the x axis'.

5.6 TAX LAW

This book calls the laws which govern the levying of the taxes within a country by the various levels of government the *tax law*. Any tax-related amounts in an entity's accounts, financial statements and reports which are required to comply with the country's accounting standards must be calculated according to the country's tax law.

5.7 CAUTION

In the remainder of this book the terms 'accounting standards' and 'tax law' should be understood as referring to those of the country in which the reader resides or in which the reader is interested. A nation's accounting standards typically occupy several hundred pages, and its tax law thousands of pages. Readers who wish to be sure in an accounting situation should therefore consult the appropriate accounting standards and tax law and/or an accounting professional.

Chapter 6

REPRESENTING AND RECORDING (MEASURING) AN EVENT

Figure 4.1 on page 19 shows a condensed version of the accounting cycle. To explain that cycle's identifying and measuring operations, this chapter:

- describes how an entity's bookkeepers analyse an entity's activities into financial events, and the financial events into transactions
- introduces an example fictional entity and describes an example event consisting of two transactions
- represents that example event using balance charts
- uses those balance charts to show how financial events are represented in balance charts
- explains how accounts and balance charts are balanced
- shows how the example event would be recorded manually (with pen and ink) and with bookkeeping software.

6.1 ANALYSING ACTIVITIES INTO TRANSACTIONS

An entity's activities form a continuing series of events. Events are of two sorts: those which don't affect the entity's financial position such as interviewing a prospective employee, and those which do such as making a sale. This second sort of event is called a *financial event* or usually just an *event* because events which aren't financial aren't recorded in an entity's accounts.

A financial event consists of one or more related transactions. For example, if an entity buys something for cash, that is an event consisting of a single cash transaction. (A *cash transaction* is one which 'involves a receipt or payment of cash by the entity'.) If an entity buys something on credit, that event typically consists of two transactions: a transaction in which the entity gains control over the something and simultaneously incurs a liability, and a later related transaction in which the entity pays the agreed cash to the something's seller thereby discharging the liability.

The first operation in the accounting cycle is termed *identifying*. It consists of continually analysing the entity's activities into events, and then analysing those events which are financial into their one or more constituent transactions. (A *transaction* is defined on page 1 as an 'event or part of an event which produces a financial change in an entity'.)

Bookkeepers usually work in offices remote from where the events which they identify and measure occur. How do bookkeepers know that a transaction which should be recorded has occurred? Usually by receiving the one or more related source documents. Source documents can be raised by the account-keeping entity itself; these include invoices, credit notes, and receipts. Source documents can also be raised by and received from other entities such as suppliers and banks. Such source documents include bank statements, receipts, bills, and credit notes (negative bills). (A *bill* is what a 'buyer calls a seller's invoice to distinguish it from the invoices raised by the buyer itself'.)

If the one or more source documents for a transaction can't be located or none has been prepared, an equivalent record may be created by the entity's bookkeeper after, where necessary, consulting with others.

As a bookkeeper identifies a financial event transaction, it should be correctly recorded. To illustrate this, the next section will explain an example credit acquisition event, and introduce the company entity making that acquisition. (To *buy* a non-current asset is to *acquire* it, to *buy* a current asset is to *purchase* it.)

6.2 THE EXAMPLE EVENT

The example event is the credit acquisition of a 3D printing machine by the imaginary entity the Drone Manufacturing and Sales Company Limited (*Drone Co* or *Drone* for short).

Drone was started and is wholly owned by Jane Marshall. Her brother Phil is a qualified and experienced bookkeeper, and works part-time as Drone's bookkeeper. Drone's reporting period and income-tax year coincide, and run from midnight on a 30 June to midnight on the following 30 June.

The example event consists of two transactions:

1. Drone taking control of the printer from the supplier, the ThreeDee Company, on 13 March 2016, and thereby incurring a debt
2. Drone paying the supplier in full for the printer on 31 March by bank transfer, and thereby discharging the debt incurred on 13 March.

6.2.1 Representing the example event excluding consumption tax

Figure 6.1 shows the bill Drone received on taking control of the 3D printer. The bill assumes that no value added tax was charged. The figure 6.2 balance chart represents Drone taking control of the printer (the acquisition core transaction), and also explains how balance charts represent transactions. In figure 6.2 the transaction is represented by two postings. (A *posting* is 'one of the two or more records of a transaction which increase or decrease the balance of the ledger account to which that posting is made'.) That figure 6.2 represents two postings illustrates that the term *double-entry bookkeeping* was entirely appropriate when introduced into the English language about 300 years ago. The term however became less appropriate once trading (buying and selling) transactions started to be taxed because, as you'll see later in this chapter, to record such transactions requires more than two postings.

INVOICE No: 000241

Date: 13 March 2016

ThreeDee Company, ThreeDee's address, contact details and any required identification numbers	**Credit customer:** Drone Co Ltd Drone's address and any other relevant details

Quantity	Description of Goods Supplied	Unit price ($)	Total ($)
One	Makebot brand 3D printer	7,368	7,368
	Less 5% discount if payment received within 30 days		(368)
		Total	7,000

Payment due 30 days after the date of this invoice

Figure 6.1 The invoice raised by ThreeDee Co which Drone received when Drone took control of the Makebot brand 3D printer.

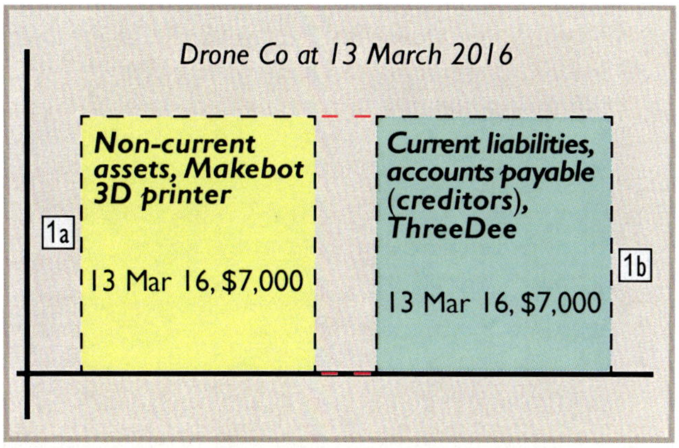

Figure 6.2 A balance chart whose two boxes represent the transaction of Drone taking control of the printer, and Drone's resulting simultaneous incurrence of a debt owing to ThreeDee Co.

This figure's caption has two parts. The first part explains balance charts in general; the second part explains the transaction that this balance chart represents.

Balance charts in general

The balance chart boxes pictured in earlier chapters represented account balances. Balance charts can also include boxes which represent, as here, the postings for one or more transactions. All the balance charts in this book have the following features:

- A vertical y axis drawn to an appropriate monetary scale, and an x axis drawn horizontally to the right from y = $0.
- Boxes in two bars (an assets bar on the left and a sources bar on the right). The boxes in each bar are stacked above the x axis and/or hang below the x axis. The vertical length of a box side (its height or depth) represents an amount of money. When the box heights and depths aren't all drawn >

> to the same monetary scale, the y axis is labelled *nts* meaning 'not to scale'.

- Whether a box represents an account balance or a posting, the name of the relevant account is printed in bold italic type just below the top of the box. It's usually unnecessary to include in the account name the names of the related higher-level control accounts. Therefore this figure's green box could be named just *accounts payable (creditors), ThreeDee*, or even just *ThreeDee*. The brackets in the preceding sentence signify that '*creditors*' is a synonym for '*accounts payable*'.
- Chapters 2 and 3 clarify in which bar and on which side of the x axis the positive balances of different accounts are located. Therefore a box which represents a posting which would increase an account's positive balance should be located in the same bar and on the same side of the x axis as the box which would represent that positive account balance.
- Balance chart boxes always represent positive amounts. If the account balance is negative or the posting would decrease a positive balance of that account, its representing box should be located in the same bar but on the opposite side of the x axis to that of a box representing a positive balance of or a positive posting to that same account.
- When a balance chart represents a series of transactions, the later the date of the posting or the account balance, the further its box is above or below the x axis.
- The date and amount of a posting, or the date on which an account had the stated balance and the amount of that balance, are printed in Roman text halfway down the vacant space in the box below the account name.
- Although unnecessary for comprehension, each box has a fill whose colour corresponds to the category of the related account. Yellowish tones are used for assets balances and postings, greenish tones for liabilities balances and postings, and bluish tones for equity balances and postings
- Boxes which represent postings made on the balance date have black dashed outlines and black text within. The outlines of boxes representing > earlier postings have black unbroken outlines and black text within. The outlines of boxes representing account balances are always unbroken unless the account balance results from a single posting made on the balance date.
- A reference number, usually with a reference letter, within a square outline is located alongside each box and vertically halfway between the account name and the date and amount line. The boxes representing the two or more postings for a transaction will have the same reference number but different reference letters. In the balance chart's caption the first of the paragraphs which explains a balance or a posting starts with the same reference number and letter (if there is a reference letter) within a square outline. The reference numbers for posting and account balances usually start afresh from 1 in each chapter.
- When a balance-signifying line (usually magenta in colour) connects to a box with a dashed outline, the line is dashed: otherwise the line is full.

This balance chart in particular

[1a] Drone intends to use the printer to produce economic benefit past the end of the next annual reporting period. Therefore when Drone takes control of the printer, it's acquiring a non-current asset.

[1b] By acquiring the printer Drone becomes liable to pay the supplier, ThreeDee, $7,000 within the agreed 30 days of 13 March 2016.

6.3 VALUE ADDED TAX

Figures 6.1 and 6.2 ignore the value added tax which should have been charged. This section introduces value added tax.

The first value added tax was introduced in France in 1954 and is called there *taxe sur la valeur ajoutée* or *TVA*. By 2016 value added taxes were being levied in more than thirty countries including Japan and China, but not the United States. The UK's consumption tax is called *Value Added Tax* or *VAT*, and this name most clearly explains how value added taxes work.

A typical value added tax has four components:

1. **the value-added-tax rate** This book will assume a rate of 20%. Some national value added taxes have a single rate; some have different rates for sales of different types of taxable supplies (sales of goods and services subject to value added tax)

2. **amounts of value added tax charged on an entity's value-added-taxable outputs** Only certain types of entity (called in this book *value-added-tax-registered entities*) are required to and can charge value added tax on their outputs of taxable supplies. The amounts of value added tax charged by value-added-tax-registered selling entities are later reported to and payable to the taxing authority by the due dates as prescribed in the relevant tax law

3. **amounts of value added tax charged to importers on those imports which would have had value added tax charged on them had they been produced within the country** These amounts of value added tax are typically collected by the nation's customs authority and transferred by it to the taxing authority

4. **amounts of value added tax charged on an entity's imports and by suppliers on an entity's purchases and acquisitions of taxable supplies** If the importing and/or buying entity is value-added-tax registered, the entity is then entitled to have the amounts of value added tax it's been charged on its inputs reimbursed to it by the taxing authority.

The tax law related to value added tax can be complicated:

- Not all types of entity may be able to be value-added-tax registered. Members of the general public, for example, cannot be.

- Not every type of supply will necessarily attract value added tax, or the rate charged may be 0%.

- For some types of taxable supply a value-added-tax-registered entity may be able to have the value added tax it's been charged on its inputs reimbursed by the taxing authority even though the entity can't charge value added tax on the entity's sales of that supply or on the entity's sales of supplies which incorporate those inputs.

For many value-added-tax-registered entities the amounts of value added tax paid balance the amounts reimbursed as table 6.1 illustrates. Therefore the effective payers of value added tax are members of the general public and those entities which aren't registered for value added tax.

Value-added-tax-registered entities are effectively tax collectors, and do incur associated costs. These costs comprise the interest costs incurred because of the intervals between paying for taxable supplies and receiving the related cash reimbursements from the taxing authority; there are also additional bookkeeping costs.

Description	Cash flows	
	Net of tax	Tax @ 20%
Purchase of a supply by Drone	(1,000)	(200)
Purchase additional raw materials and components	(100)	(20)
Additional labour	(200)*	
Reimbursement of tax to Drone		220
Sale of supply by Drone	2,000	400
Drone pays tax to taxing authority		(400)
Totals	700	0

Amount of value added tax collected by the taxing authority through Drone's addition of $900 of value is $400 – $220 = $180

* Employee wages and salaries don't attract consumption tax

Table 6.1 The cash flows resulting from Drone buying a supply for $1,000 plus 20% value added tax, processing it for resale by adding raw materials, components and labour, and then selling it for a $700 profit.

Drone made a profit, but Drone's payments of value added tax equalled the reimbursements of value added tax Drone was entitled to claim.

Were the supply sold by Drone to an entity not registered for value added tax, the taxing authority wouldn't have had to reimburse $400 to the buyer from Drone. The taxing authority would have thereby collected from Drone and kept the full amount of value added tax payable on Drone's sale.

6.3.1 Representing the example event with value added tax charged

Figures 6.3 to 6.5 illustrate how value added tax at the example rate of 20% would be charged and reimbursed to Drone in the example acquisition event.

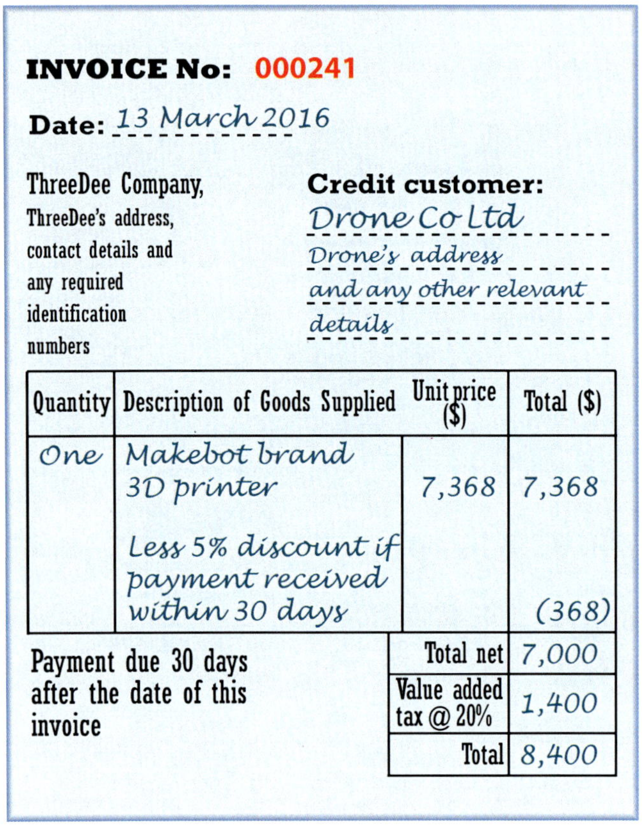

INVOICE No: 000241

Date: 13 March 2016

ThreeDee Company,
ThreeDee's address,
contact details and
any required
identification
numbers

Credit customer:
Drone Co Ltd
Drone's address
and any other relevant
details

Quantity	Description of Goods Supplied	Unit price ($)	Total ($)
One	Makebot brand 3D printer	7,368	7,368
	Less 5% discount if payment received within 30 days		(368)
Payment due 30 days after the date of this invoice		Total net	7,000
		Value added tax @ 20%	1,400
		Total	8,400

Figure 6.3 The invoice raised by ThreeDee Co which Drone received when Drone took control of the Makebot brand 3D printer. The seller, ThreeDee, has added value added tax of 20% x $7,000 = $1,400 to the $7,000 net price.

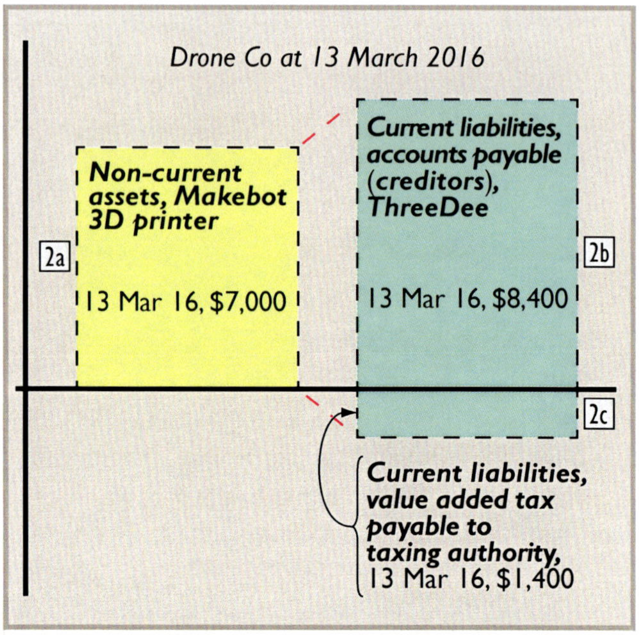

Figure 6.4 A balance chart which represents Drone taking control of the 3D printer on which the seller, ThreeDee, charged 20% value added tax.

2a The cost of the printer to Drone is $7,000. The cost is not $8,400 because Drone will have the $1,400 reimbursed by the taxing authority. Also the cost of the printer to Drone doesn't include the $368 discount because Drone will pay ThreeDee within 30 days, and thereby be entitled to accept the discount.

2b Drone has incurred a debt to ThreeDee of the net price plus the amount of value added tax charged.

2c Drone recorded the value added tax charged on its acquisition as a debit to a value-added-tax-payable current liabilities account. Alternatively the amount could have been posted as a debit to an accounts-receivable (debtors) account located above the x axis in the assets bar.

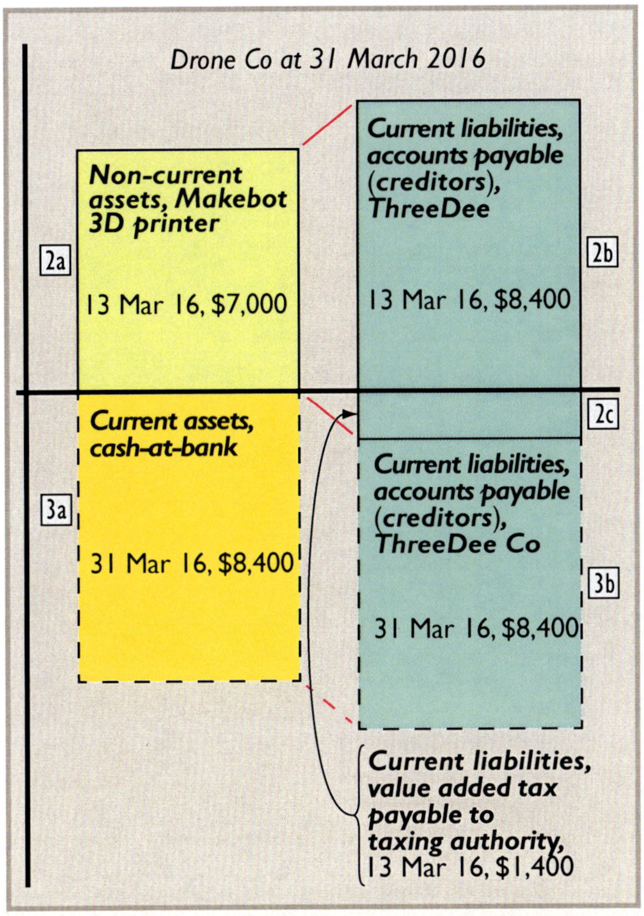

Figure 6.5 A balance chart which represents the two-transaction event of Drone taking control of the printer on 13 March, and paying ThreeDee for it by bank transfer on 31 March.

[2a], [2b] and [2c] These postings were explained in the caption to figure 6.4.

[3a] Entities should keep a current assets, cash-at-bank ledger account for each bank account. When an entity has money in a bank account, its amount should be recorded as a positive balance of the appropriate cash-at-bank account. In a balance chart this balance is represented by a box above the x axis in the assets bar. A withdrawal from an entity's bank account is therefore represented by a box below the x axis in the assets bar.

[3b] Box [2b] represents Drone's debt to ThreeDee. A reduction to a debt is represented by a box below the x axis in the sources bar.

6.4 BALANCING ACCOUNTS

Adding postings and account balances can make a balance chart undesirably tall and/or result in a confusing number of boxes. However the height of such a chart and its number of boxes can usually be reduced by balancing the chart's accounts. An account's balance is the total of all the postings (whether debits or credits) made to that account from when that entity was started to the balance date. To balance an account, to its most recent account balance (if there is one) debit all subsequent debit postings and credit all subsequent credit postings. For example, figure 6.6 is figure 6.5 with the accounts-payable (creditors) account balanced. In manual book-keeping accounts are balanced regularly as explained on page 51.

Observant readers will have noticed that figure 6.6 doesn't balance on 13 March, but does on 31 March. This is because posting [2b] in figures 6.4 and 6.5 which ensured balance at 13 March has been effectively been re-dated to the 31 March balance date.

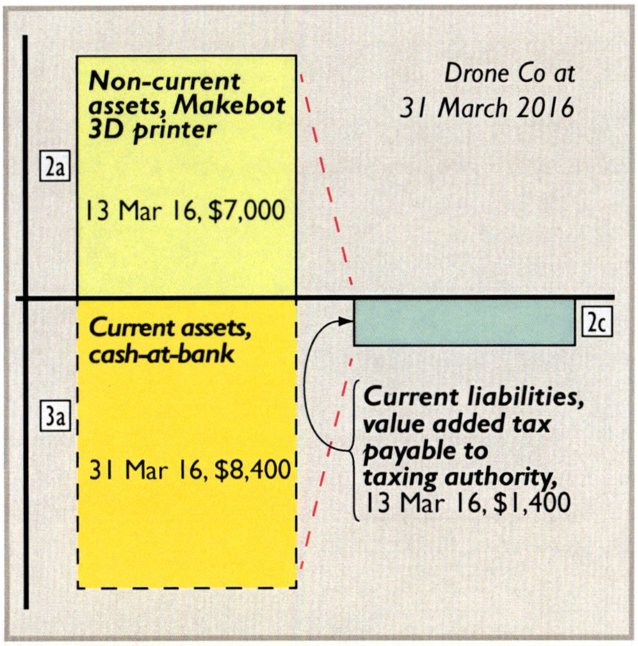

Figure 6.6 Figure 6.5 after balancing the accounts-payable (creditors), ThreeDee account. Posting-representing boxes [2b] and [3b] in figure 6.5 have cancelled each other leaving a balance of zero, and don't therefore appear in this chart.

6.5 ADDING BALANCING ACCOUNT BALANCES

Equations 5.c to 5.f on pages 26 and 27 can be summarised as:

- In a balance chart the total of the debit postings and account debit balances must always equal the sum of the credit postings and account credit balances.
- In a balance chart which represents one or more transactions and any account balances, the net heights of the assets and sources bars must always be equal.

It's essential when adding postings or account balances that balance (having equal net bar heights) is retained. For example, figure 6.7 focuses on and represents Drone paying its $8,400 debt to ThreeDee. The three postings represented are correct, but if balance charts whose net bar heights aren't equal are allowed, the important checking facility of the equal-net-bar-heights imperative is lost. To enable that facility, it may be necessary to add one or more balancing account balances. Figure 6.8 shows this, and then balances at both 13 March and 31 March.

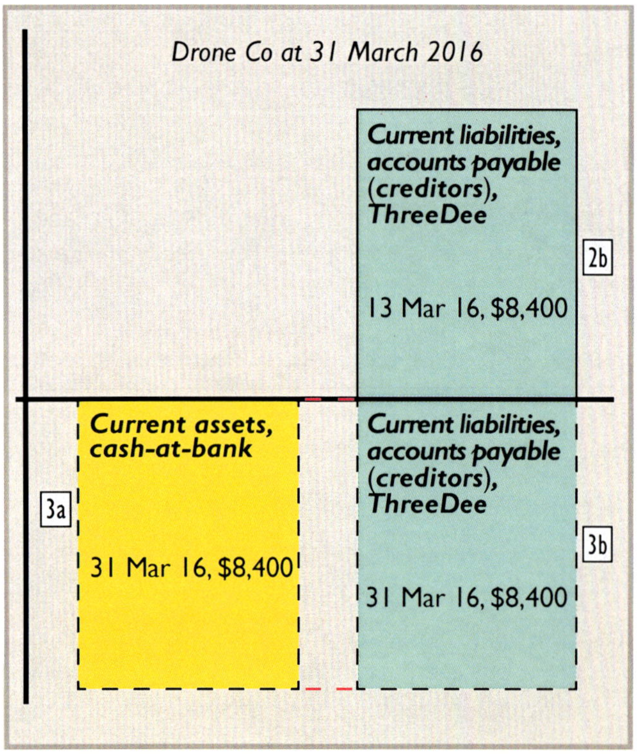

Figure 6.7 A balance chart (derived from figure 6.5) which doesn't balance on 13 March, and which focuses on Drone discharging its debt to ThreeDee.

[2b] Represents Drone's debt. However because there is no balancing debit account balance or posting dated 13 March, the net-bar-heights imperative stated on page 27 is violated.

[3a] and [3b] These represent the payment of the debt. Boxes [2b] and [3b] then sum to zero, confirming that the debt was paid.

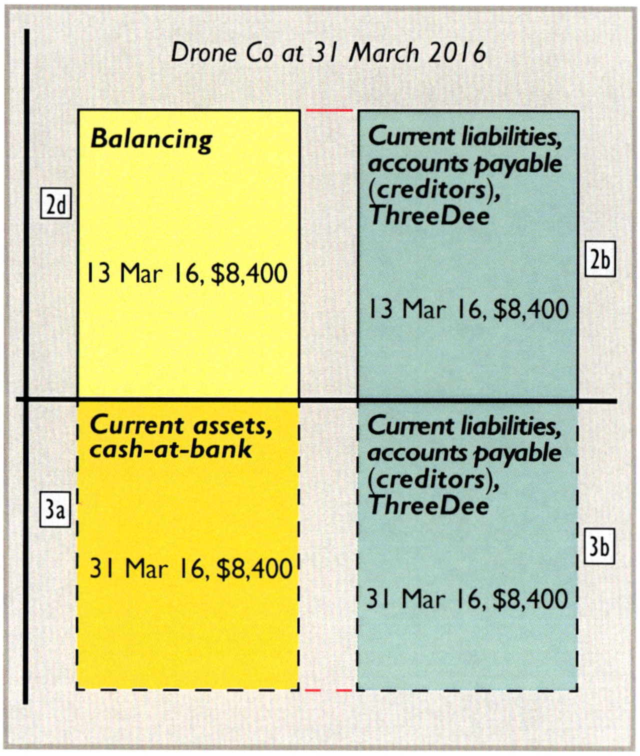

Figure 6.8 Figure 6.7 with a balancing account balance [2d] added to restore balance on 13 March. There's no need to name balancing account balances more specifically.

As figures 6.4 to 6.8 illustrate, balance charts can be drawn so as to focus only on the transactions and account balances deemed relevant.

6.6 RECORDING (MEASURING) THE EXAMPLE EVENT

Figure 6.9 explains the accounting cycle in more detail than does figure 4.1 on page 19. Figure 6.9 also shows that in manual bookkeeping transactional data is usually first recorded (entered) into one or more journals (day books), and then transcribed (posted) from the journals into the ledger accounts housed in ledgers. Manual journals and manual ledgers are typically books with ruled but otherwise blank pages in which respectively entries and postings are written in ink so that they can't be erased.

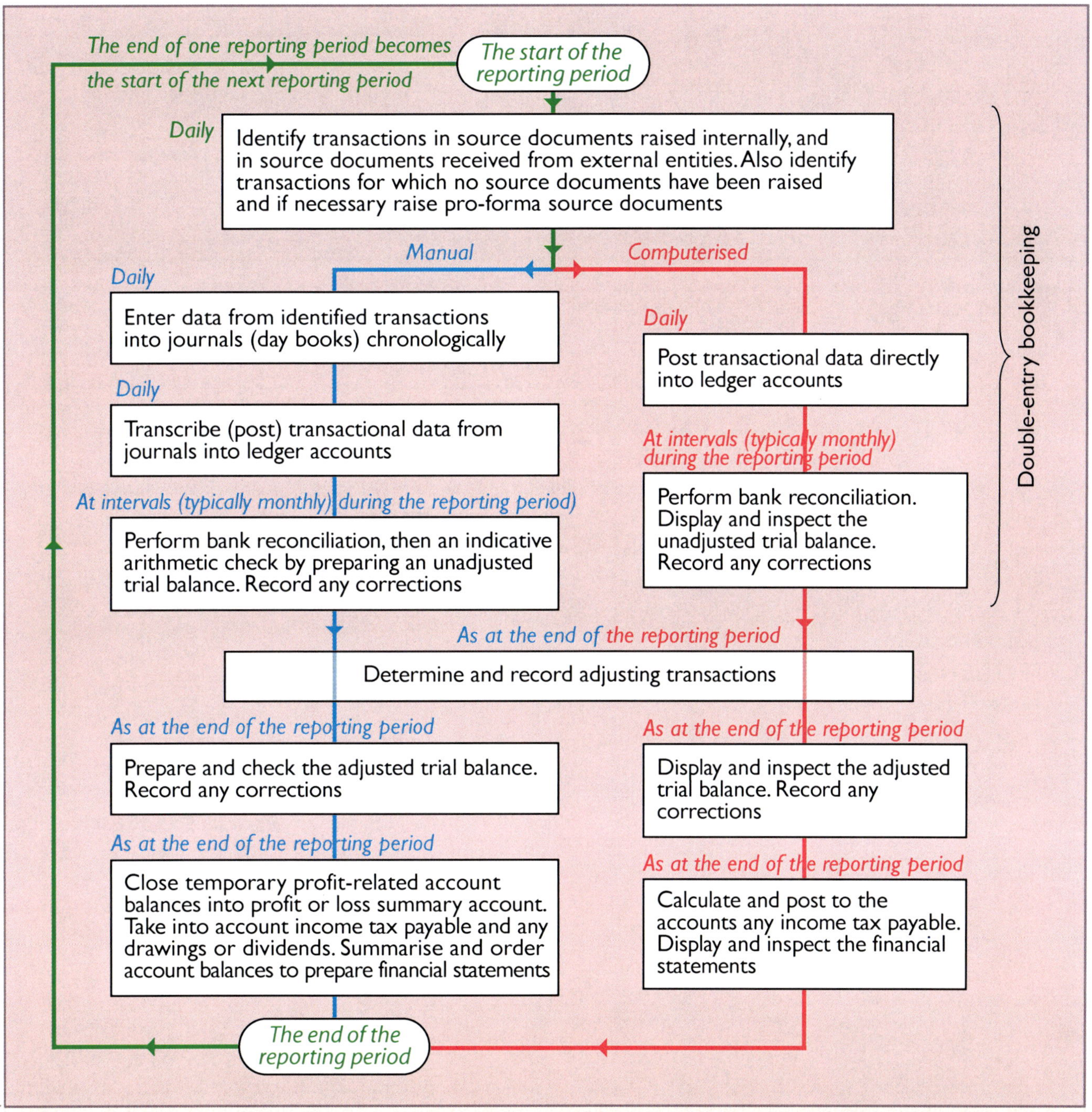

Figure 6.9 The accounting cycle shown in more detail than in figure 4.1. In computerised bookkeeping the manual bookkeeping step of entering the data for each transaction into a journal is omitted, and the data is instead posted directly into the ledger accounts. The activities performed by some bookkeepers extend further 'down' the accounting cycle than the bracket on the right-hand side indicates.

6.6.1 Recording the example event manually

Were Phil keeping Drone's journals and accounts manually, figure 6.10 shows the manual journal entries, and figures 6.11 to 6.14 the related postings to the manual ledgers for the example two-transaction event shown graphically in figure 6.5. The column headings *debit* and *credit* in these figures are explained on pages 25 to 27.

Accounting period 2015-16 — Journal — 107

Date D	Date M	Details of transaction	Folio	Debit ($)	Credit ($)
13	3	3D printers original cost, Makebot 3D printer	1-6370	7,000.00	
		Value added tax payable to taxing authority	2-4990	1,400.00	
		Accounts payable, ThreeDee	2-2065		8,400.00
		Acquiring 3D printer from ThreeDee, bill 000241			
31	3	Accounts payable, ThreeDee	2-2065	8,400.00	
		Cash at bank, BundyBank	1-0020		8,400.00
		Paying ThreeDee's bill 000241 for 3D printer			

Figure 6.10 The two entries in Drone's manual journal which record the event of Drone acquiring the Makebot 3D printer. The number of the ledger account which will receive a particular posting is written in the folio column. (A folio is a single rectangular piece of paper folded vertically in half. In manual bookkeeping, the vertical leg of a T account (see figure 6.11) typically ran down the fold. Hence *folio number* continues to be used instead of *page number* for the location of a ledger account.)

The first entry records: Drone taking control of the printer, Drone becoming liable to pay the supplier, and Drone becoming able to require that the taxing authority reimburse to Drone the amount of input value added tax charged by the supplier.

The second entry records Drone paying the 3D printer's supplier ThreeDee.

The later journal entry recording Drone's receipt of the $1,400 reimbursement from the taxing authority isn't shown.

Recording postings to accounts

Figures 6.11 to 6.14 show the postings which would have been made to record the two transactions shown in figure 6.5 were Phil, Drone's bookkeeper, keeping Drone's books of account manually.

The name of the account receiving the posting is at the head of the page. Then:

- If the amount to be recorded in the posting were being debited to the account named at the head of the page, the record should be written along the next free, left-hand, half-width line. And vice versa were the amount a credit.
- The date written into the details cell should be the date on which the transaction occurred.
- If the transaction is being recorded by two postings, the account name written into the details cell should be that of the other account which should simultaneously receive a posting to fully record the transaction.
- If the transaction is being recorded by three or more postings, and the amount is being debited, the account name written into the details cell should be that of the account which should simultaneously receive the largest credit. And vice versa were the amount a credit.

Account name: *Accounts-payable (creditors), ThreeDee* 2-2065

Date	Details	Debit ($)	Date	Details	Credit ($)
			13 Mar 16	Makebot 3D printer	8,400.00
31 Mar 16	Cash-at-bank	8,400.00			

Figure 6.11 The postings made to the accounts-payable (creditors), ThreeDee account from the two journal entries in figure 6.10.

This format of ledger page is called a *T account* as indicated by the mauve bands.

Account name: *Non-current assets, 3D printers, Makebot* 1-6370

Date	Details	Debit ($)	Date	Details	Credit ($)
13 Mar 16	ThreeDee	7,000.00			

Figure 6.12 The posting which recorded Drone acquiring the 3D printer non-current asset.

Account name: *Current liabilities, value added tax payable* 2-4990

Date	Details	Debit ($)	Date	Details	Credit ($)
13 Mar 16	Accts-payable, ThreeDee	1,400.00			

Figure 6.13 The posting which recorded the right to claim a reimbursement of the amount of value added tax paid by Drone resulting from Drone's purchase of the 3D printer.

Account name: *Cash-at-bank (bank account at BundyBank)* 1-0020

Date	Details	Debit ($)	Date	Details	Credit ($)
			31 Mar 16	ThreeDee	8,400.00

Figure 6.14 The posting which recorded the transfer of $8,400 from Drone's bank account at BundyBank to ThreeDee's bank account.

6.6.2 Recording the example event with accounting software

When using accounting software a transaction's postings are posted directly into the accounts. Figure 6.15 shows the postings made directly to the accounts-payable (creditors), ThreeDee ledger account during March and April 2016. Computer display equivalents of figures 6.12 to 6.14 aren't shown.

When using accounting software there won't be any arithmetical errors, unbalanced postings can't be input, and trial balances and financial statements can be generated at the click of a mouse. Another advantage of accounting software is that when a transaction is recorded, the balances of the receiving ledger accounts are updated and simultaneously so are the balances of all the control accounts into which the balances of the receiving ledger accounts directly and indirectly feed.

Drone Manufacturing and Sales Company Limited
Account name: Accounts-payable (creditors), ThreeDee

Date	Details	Debit ($)	Credit ($)	Balance ($)
13 Mar 16	Acquire Makebot 3D printer, invoice 000241		8,400.00	8,400.00
31 Mar 16	Pay invoice 000241	8,400.00		0.00
17 Apr 16	Replacement UUP injector, invoice 000783		370.00	370.00
22 Apr 16	New Felicks hopper, invoice 000821		475.00	845.00
30 Apr 16	Pay invoices 000783 and 000821	845.00		0.00

Figure 6.15 The postings which recorded Drone's transactions with supplier ThreeDee during March and April 2016. The first two postings record Drone incurring the debt resulting from Drone's acquisition of the 3D printer, and Drone later discharging that debt. The April postings record later transactions. The right-hand column of the three money columns records a running balance.

Chapter 7
RECORDING DIFFERENT TYPES OF EVENT

Section 6.1 on page 28 explains that financial events consist of one or more transactions. This chapter uses balance charts to explain how bookkeepers record different types of event in an entity's ledger accounts. The account-keeping entity for these example events is Drone.

In this chapter it's assumed that Drone and the other entities mentioned are operating in a country which levies value added tax at 20%, but doesn't levy sales tax.

7.1 RECORDING TRANSACTIONS

To record a financial event transaction using double entry a bookkeeper must analyse any relevant source documents and if necessary seek information elsewhere to decide:

- the transaction's date
- the identities of the two or more ledger accounts which will receive postings to record the transaction
- the amount of each posting, and whether it's a debit or a credit.

How a bookkeeper decides these parameters is explained in the next three subsections.

7.1.1 Transaction dating

Under accrual accounting the date of a transaction is the date on which the transaction happened. Many transactions record a transfer of control of an asset. If the date of the transfer of physical possession and of the transfer of control differ, the transaction date is when control is transferred.

Under accrual accounting, when the date of the transfer of control for the asset differs from that of the, say, single related payment, the event's transfer of control is recorded by a *core transaction*, and the payment by a separate *payment transaction*. Under cash accounting the same event would be recorded as one transaction whose date was when the payment was received or sent.

7.1.2 Deciding on the ledger accounts

To decide the two or more ledger accounts which should each receive a posting to record a transaction, the bookkeeper needs to be familiar with the entity's chart of accounts and the relevant principles, concepts, accounting standards and laws introduced in chapter 5. Experience is also a great help. The example transactions explained in this chapter will clarify which account categories are involved in most of the common types of transaction. Once the bookkeeper identifies the type of transaction, for example a credit sale or the reduction in the unit carrying amount of an asset, the ledger accounts which should receive the postings are usually obvious; if not, attempting to sketch the balance chart for the transaction will usually reveal them.

7.1.3 Deciding on the amount and sign of each posting

How the terms *debit* and *credit* relate to postings and account balances was explained in section 5.5 (pages 25 to 27). Having decided on the ledger accounts which will each receive a posting to record a transaction, the amount and sign (whether a debit or a credit) of each posting will usually be obvious. If not, knowing that the total of a transaction's debit postings must equal the total of that transaction's credit postings will help (equation 5.e on page 27). Again, sketching the balance chart for the transaction will usually reveal the unknowns.

7.1.4 Recording expenses in accrual accounting

Many events involve the incurrence of an expense. This subsection explores the complexity of expenses.

On page 3 an *asset* was defined as 'something controlled by the entity whose cost or value can be measured reliably and from which economic benefits are expected to flow to the entity'. An expense is then a decrease in economic benefits during the reporting period in the form of an outflow or a depletion of an asset or the incurrence of a liability as figure 7.1 illustrates. Incurring an expense therefore decreases the amount of an entity's equity. However a distribution to an entity's owner or owners is not regarded as an expense.

An expense should be recognised (understood and recorded) simultaneously when:

1. A cost is incurred to earn a specific income. (A *cost* is the 'amount of cash or cash equivalents paid or the fair value of the other consideration given to purchase or acquire an asset'.) That cost and that income are then matched. Matching involves the recognition of an income and of expenses that result directly and jointly from the same event. One such cost is the fall in the carrying amount of an asset when all or part of that asset is sold.

2. A cost is incurred from which an economic benefit is expected to arise. The economic benefit can either be expected to be received only during the current reporting period, or over several reporting periods. The association between the cost and the related economic benefit doesn't have to be direct or indirect.

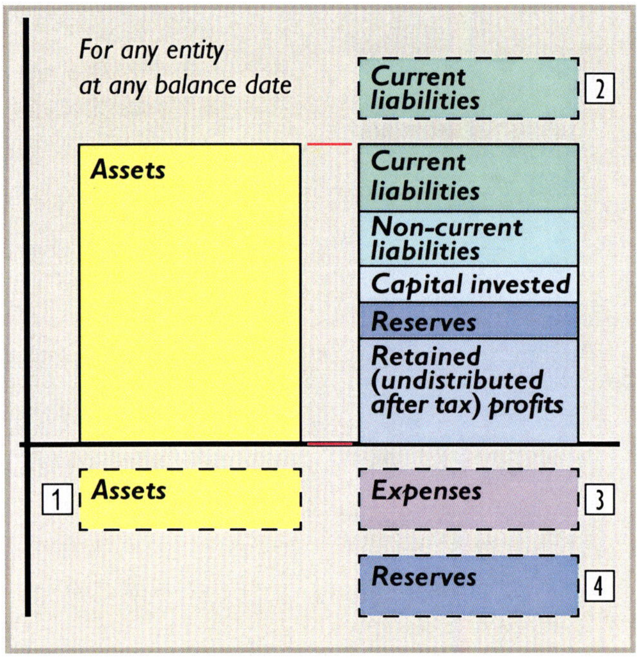

Figure 7.1 Posting an expense. So as to not violate the balance sheet equation, to balance the reduction in the carrying amount of an asset [1] or the incurrence of a liability [2], a posting of an equal amount is debited to an expenses account [3].

In certain circumstances (explained in chapter 9) a fall in the value of an asset [1] is balanced by a debit posting to a reserves account [4].

3. There is or is expected to be within the current reporting period a depletion of the fair, market or some other relevant and approved value of an asset while the asset remains controlled by the entity.

4. The depletion or consumption of an asset is expected to occur over more than one reporting period. That expense should then be recognised in the accounts during each of those periods by a systematic and rational allocation.

5. The subject of an expenditure is unlikely to be wholly consumed within the reporting period, but its amount is sufficiently small that assuming that the subject were wholly consumed within that period will not materially affect the reliability of the entity's accounts and financial statements.

6. A liability is incurred without the carrying amount of an asset being reduced.

7. As at the end of an reporting period, an expense has been incurred, but its actual amount is not yet known. An estimate should then be used.

But an expenditure isn't an expense if it results in the acquisition or purchase of an asset, or an improvement in an asset, or an extension to the life of an asset. Therefore while normal maintenance is an expense for a machine used for manufacturing, reconditioning isn't an expense and its cost should be recorded as increasing the carrying amount of the machine.

7.2 EXAMPLE EVENTS

The credit acquisition of a non-current asset has already been explained in chapter 6. The financial events which will be explained in the remainder of this chapter are:

- purchasing inventory (stock) on credit, subsection 7.2.1
- selling inventory on credit, subsection 7.2.2
- raising a credit note, subsection 7.2.3
- declaring a debt bad, subsection 7.2.4

- making a cash sale and later banking the cash, subsection 7.2.5
- recording an acquisition as an expense, subsection 7.2.6
- recording a liability without an asset being recognised, subsection 7.2.7
- repaying a loan principal and paying interest, subsection 7.2.8
- recording a continuous expense, subsection 7.2.9
- paying an employee, subsection 7.2.10.

7.2.1 Purchasing inventory on credit

On 2 April 2016 Drone purchased batteries on credit from Bird Batteries. Drone intended to resell the batteries, not use them within the company. The credit purchase event is explained in figures 7.2 and 7.3.

Unsold goods on hand are called *stocks* in some countries, and *inventories* in others, even though outside accounting an inventory is a detailed list of items, not the items themselves.

INVOICE No: 004345

Date: 2 April 2016

Bird Batteries Company,
Bird's address and
other relevant details

Credit customer:
Drone Company Limited
Drone's address and
other relevant details

Quantity	Description of Goods Supplied	Unit price ($)	Total ($)
20	Rosella brand drone batteries	84.00	1,680.00
	Less 5% payment discount		(80.00)
		Total net	1,600.00
		Value added tax @ 20%	320.00
		Total	1,920.00

Payment due 30 days after the date of this invoice

Figure 7.2 The invoice source document raised by Bird Batteries for Drone's purchase on 2 April 2016 of Rosella brand drone batteries.

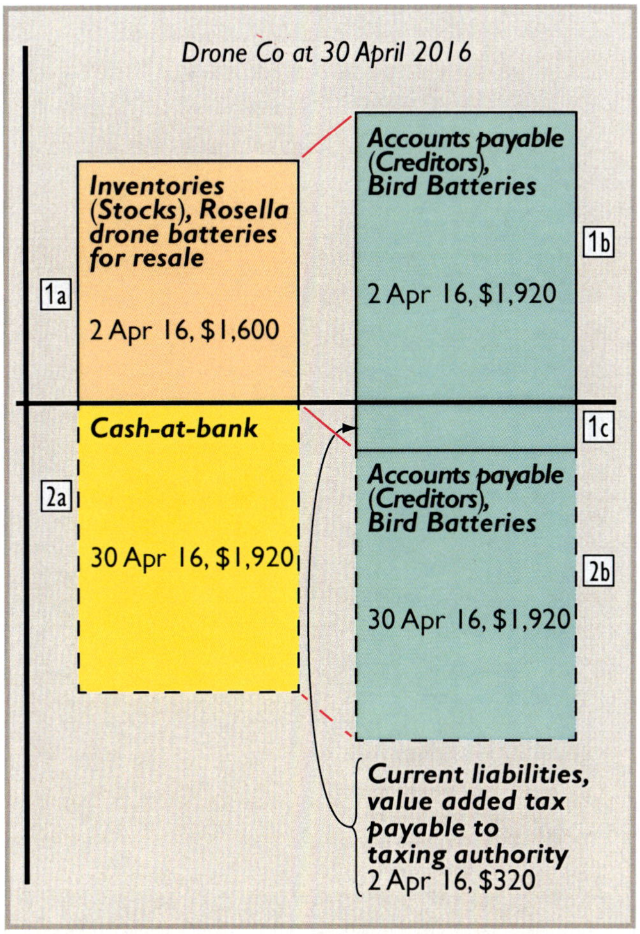

Figure 7.3 The event of Drone purchasing Rosella brand drone batteries on credit from Bird Batteries, and becoming entitled to claim the reimbursement of the amount of input value added tax charged by Bird.

1a The batteries' carrying amount is the cost of the batteries excluding value added tax because the value added tax charged will be later reimbursed by the taxing authority. This $1,600 cost is debited to Drone's batteries inventories account because the batteries are intended for resale, not for internal consumption by Drone. Because Drone intended to pay Bird Batteries within 30 days, Drone took the $80 discount. This discount reduced the cost of the batteries to Drone; it wasn't recorded as a separate revenue to Drone.

1b By purchasing the batteries on credit, Drone incurred a debt of the price of the batteries less the discount plus the value added tax charged.

1c Drone keeps only one value-added-tax ledger account called value added tax payable ('to the taxing authority' is understood). This account is >

> a current liabilities account. Any amount of input value added tax charged by a supplier is debited to this account, and is represented by a box below the x axis in the sources bar. This is because Drone is entitled to have these amounts of value added tax reimbursed by the taxing authority.

Instead of keeping one value-added-tax-payable ledger account, an entity registered for value added tax could keep two ledger accounts: a value-added-tax-payable account would be used to record the amounts of value added tax charged by the entity on its sales of taxable supplies; and a current assets, value-added-tax-receivable account would be used to record the amounts of value added tax which the entity is entitled to have reimbursed by the taxing authority. To determine its net value-added-tax situation, the entity would have to calculate the difference between these two account balances.

[2a] Drone paid the full amount of the bill on 30 April by transferring $1,920 from Drone's bank account with BundyBank into Bird Batteries' bank account.

[2b] The reduction in Drone's debt to Bird Batteries. Amounts [1b] and [2b] then cancel one another.

7.2.2 Selling half the Rosella batteries on credit

On 8 April Drone sold half the batteries it had purchased on 2 April for resale. The buyer was the company AirSpy. The event is represented and explained in figures 7.4 and 7.5.

Drone Manufacturing and Sales Company Limited
Drone's address and other relevant details

Invoice No: D003461

Date: 8 April 2016

Credit customer: AirSpy Company
AirSpy's address and other relevant details

Quantity	Description of Goods Supplied	Unit price ($)	Total ($)
10	Rosella drone brand batteries	120.00	1,200.00

Payment due 30 days after the date of this invoice

Total net	1,200.00
Value added tax @ 20%	240.00
Total	1,440.00

Figure 7.4 Drone's invoice for its credit sale to AirSpy of half the Rosella brand batteries purchased on 2 April.

Drone's retail price for an item is the item's cost marked-up by 50%.

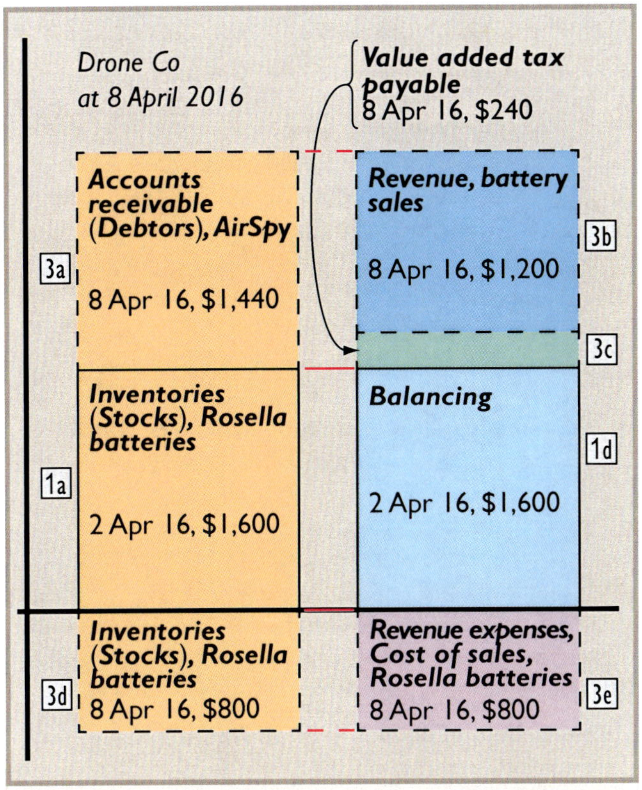

Figure 7.5 On 8 April Drone sold on credit half the batteries purchased on 2 April.

When a value-added-tax-registered entity sells a taxable supply, the entity becomes liable pay the amount of value added tax it must charge the buyer to the taxing authority by the due date. The amount of this current liability is credited to a value-added-tax-payable ledger account.

[1a] Drone's Rosella battery inventory before the sale (also shown in figure 7.3).

[1d] A balancing account balance added so that the assets and sources bar net heights balanced as at 2 April.

[3a] As shown on Drone's invoice in figure 7.4, the credit provided to the buyer AirSpy was $1,440.

[3b] The revenue earned by Drone from the sale was $1,200.

[3c] The value added tax Drone charged on the sale was $1,200 x 20% = $240. Drone therefore owed the taxing authority this amount.

[3d] The carrying amount of Drone's Rosella batteries inventory was reduced by the cost of the inventory sold. >

> [3e] A reduction in an entity's assets (here of an inventory) is an expense, here a cost of sales expense.

7.2.3 Raising a credit note

Figure 7.5 represents the core transaction of Drone's credit sale of Rosella drone batteries to AirSpy on 8 April. On 15 April AirSpy returned half of the batteries to Drone because they were faulty. Drone and AirSpy agreed on 17 April that Drone would provide a credit note (a negative invoice) which would halve AirSpy's debt. Figure 7.6 shows the credit note. Figure 7.7 represents the postings Phil made in Drone's accounts to record the sale, the return to Drone of the faulty batteries, the batteries' scrapping by Drone, the raising of the related credit note, and AirSpy's payment for the faultless batteries AirSpy kept.

Drone Manufacturing and Sales Company Limited

Drone's address and other relevant details

Credit Note No: CN0094

Date: 17 April 2016

Customer: AirSpy Company
AirSpy's address and other relevant details

Description of Goods Credited	Total ($)
5 Rosella drone batteries at $120 each (original invoice no. D003461 dated 8 April 2016)	600.00

Total net	600.00
Value added tax @ 20%	120.00
Total credited	720.00

Figure 7.6 The credit note Drone raised which halved the amount AirSpy owed Drone.

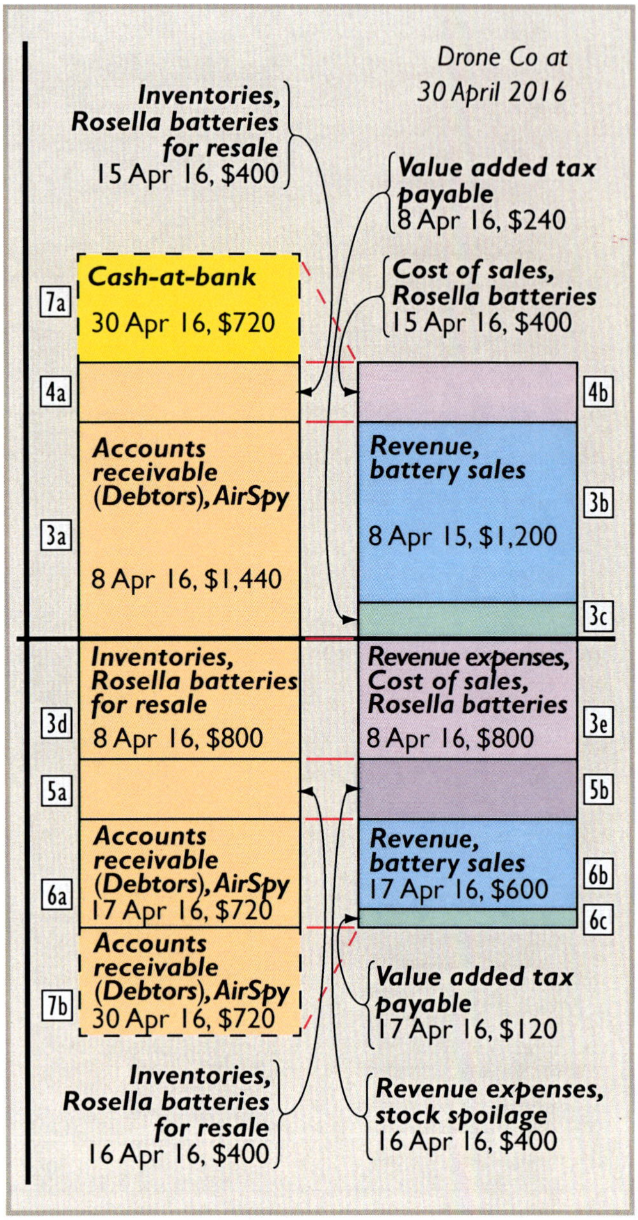

Figure 7.7 The postings which represent Drone's credit sale of batteries on 8 April, the return on 15 April of half the batteries because they were faulty, Drone scrapping the returned faulty batteries on 16 April, Drone raising a credit note on 17 April, and AirSpy paying its debt on 30 April.

Account balances [1a] and [1d] included in figure 7.5 could also have been included here, but aren't.

[3a] to [3e] These five postings represent the sale and are explained in the caption to figure 7.5.

[4a] AirSpy returned half the batteries to Drone on 15 April. This increased Drone's inventory of Rosella batteries by $400. >

> [4b] The expense of the batteries sold had to be reduced by half because of the return.

[5a] The returned faulty batteries were inspected and deemed worthless on 16 April, and were then scrapped. This reduced the carrying amount of Drone's stock of Rosella batteries.

[5b] The reduction in the carrying amount of an asset is an expense.

[6a] After confirming that the returned batteries were indeed faulty, on 17 April Drone raised the figure 7.6 credit note which reduced AirSpy's debt by half.

[6b] Raising the credit note reduced the revenue earned by the 8 April sale by half.

[6c] By raising the credit note, Drone was entitled to claim a reimbursement of the related amount of value added tax from the taxing authority.

[7a] The receipt of AirSpy's payment into Drone's bank account at BundyBank on 30 April.

[7b] The receipt of AirSpy's payment discharged AirSpy's debt.

[3a], [6a] and [7b] Their amounts sum to zero, confirming that on 30 April AirSpy fully discharged its debt to Drone related to the credit sale.

7.2.4 Declaring a debt bad

On 9 April Drone sold half its remaining stock of ten batteries to a company called ConU on 30 day's credit. Five weeks later ConU hadn't paid. Phil investigated and learned that other ConU suppliers weren't being paid and that ConU's owner had been imprisoned. Jane and Phil on 21 May agreed to declare ConU's debt bad (uncollectable). Figure 7.8 shows the two related single-transaction events.

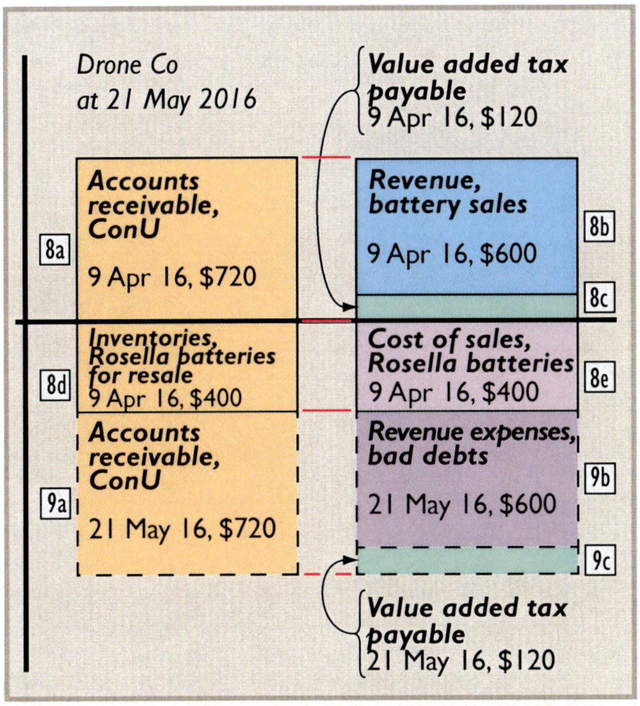

Figure 7.8 Selling inventory, and later declaring the resulting debt bad.

This and later balance charts won't include the synonyms *stocks*, *debtors* and *creditors* for respectively *inventories*, *accounts receivable* and *accounts payable*.

[8a] to [8e] These five postings represent Drone's sale of the five batteries to ConU.

[9a] Declaring ConU's debt bad cancelled the debt. To record this cancellation Phil credited the amount of the debt to ConU's accounts-receivable account.

[9b] Writing-off a debt is recorded as an expense, not a reduction in revenue.

[9c] The $120 value added tax can be claimed back by Drone from the taxing authority.

7.2.5 Making a cash sale and later banking the payment

Figure 7.9 represents Drone's retail sale of one Rosella battery on 20 April. The customer immediately paid with cash. Because Drone is located in a remote rural village, Jane or Phil can't every day bank the cash and any cash equivalents such as cheques that Drone has received. Until they're banked, Phil debits their amounts to an undeposited funds account.

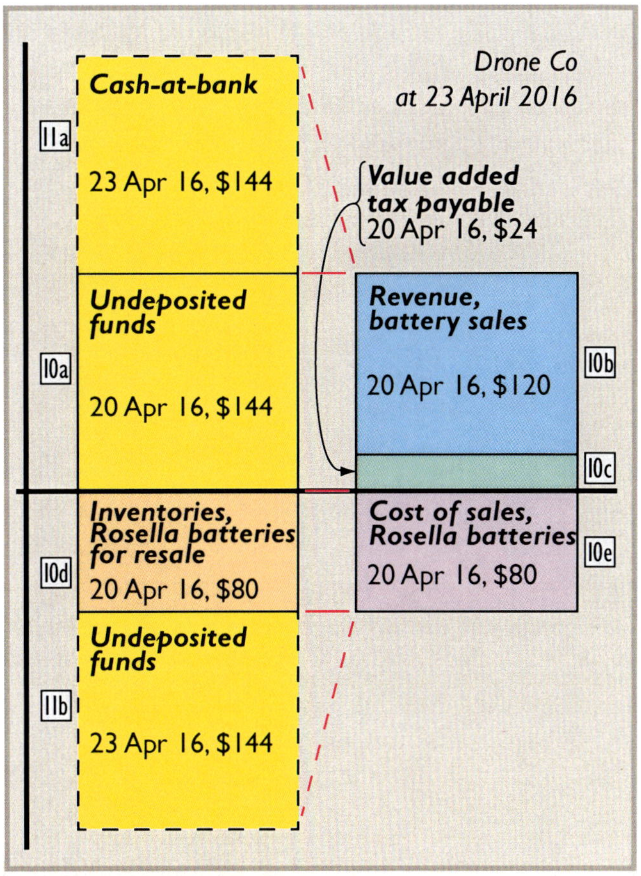

Figure 7.9 A cash sale on 20 April and the delayed banking of the proceeds on 23 April.

A cash sale could be recorded as a credit sale with same-day payment. The postings would then be similar to those above except that [10a] and [11b] would be respectively a debit and a credit to an accounts-receivable account. However the preferred practice is to record each cash sale by issuing a receipt, a source document which records the seller receiving payment for the related sale (and for the buyer, that the buyer has paid for and received the related supply).

[10a] Because the buyer's cash wouldn't be banked until a date later than its receipt, Phil debited its amount to an undeposited funds account.

[10b] Through the sale Drone earned a revenue.

[10c] Drone was liable to pay to the taxing authority the amount of value added tax Drone added to the battery's $120 net price.

[10d] and [10e] The reduction in the asset inventory was a cost of sales expense. >

> 11a and 11b On 23 April Phil deposited the $144 cash plus other cash and cash equivalents received since the previous banking into Drone's bank account at BundyBank. 11b records Drone ceasing to control the $144 cash; 11a records its banking. Postings 10a and 11b cancel each other.

7.2.6 Recording an acquisition as an expense

On 21 April 2016 Phil purchased an item of office equipment, an inexpensive calculator, using Drone's credit card. That purchase transaction is represented in figure 7.10. Drone later paid off the credit card balance which included the $24 for the calculator purchase, but this isn't shown.

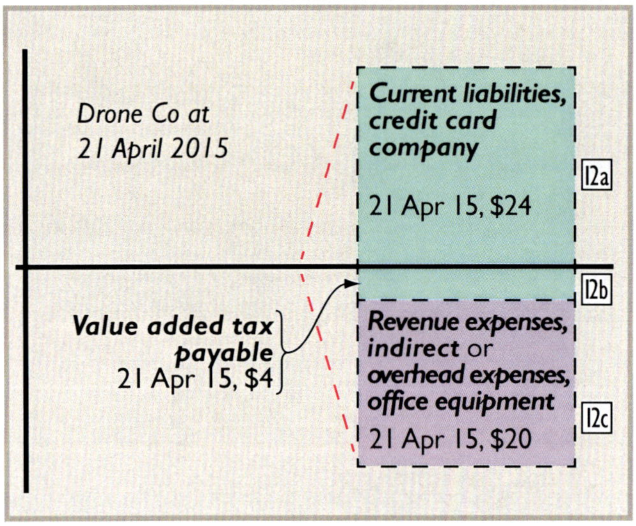

Figure 7.10 Incurring an expense using a credit card.

12a Drone's debt to the credit card company is the cost of the calculator plus the value added tax.

12b The value added tax charged by the seller is recorded as a debit to value added tax payable.

12c Although the calculator should be usable for some years, the bookkeeping cost of treating it as a non-current asset and recording its falls in carrying amount over its life would exceed its original and insignificant cost. Therefore recording the calculator's purchase as an expense would not affect the reliability of Drone's financial statements.

7.2.7 Recording a liability without an asset being recognised

When goods are sold with a warranty, future expenditures are likely to be incurred if the goods don't perform and last as they should. Figure 7.11 shows how to account for such warranty expenses.

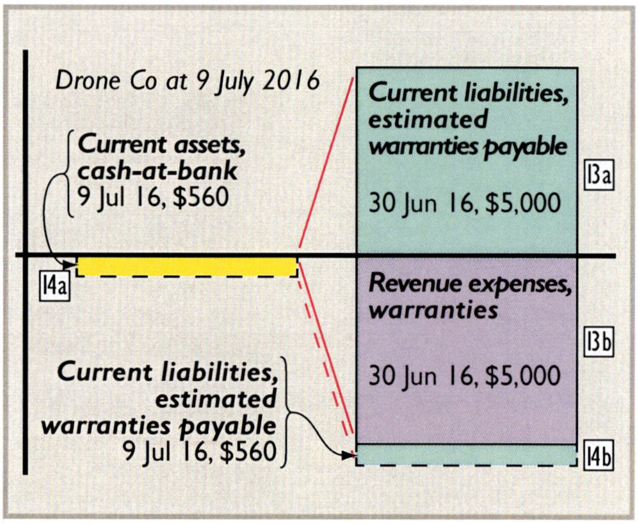

Figure 7.11 Accounting for warranties.

13a Represents the posting made as on 30 June 2016 of the current liability incurred because of the sales of goods with warranties during the 2015–16 reporting period. From past experience and based on the total sales of warranted goods during 2015–16, Drone was able to reliably estimate that liability as $5,000.

13b To balance the box 13a liability, an expense is simultaneously recognised in 2015–16. The postings 13a and 13b match the estimated warranty expense to the sales revenue so that both are recorded as occurring within the same reporting period.

14a On 9 July 2016 Drone spent $560 to fix a faulty drone sold during 2015–16 with a warranty.

14b The expenditure recorded in box 14a simultaneously reduced the $5,000 estimated liability.

7.2.8 Repaying a loan

Figure 7.12 illustrates that repaying a loan usually involves both repaying the loan principal, and paying amounts of interest on the outstanding amounts of loan principal. The figure 7.12 balance chart also clarifies the difference between a present obligation to pay (a liability), and a future commitment to pay which isn't a liability yet. Figure 7.12 assumes that no value added tax was involved.

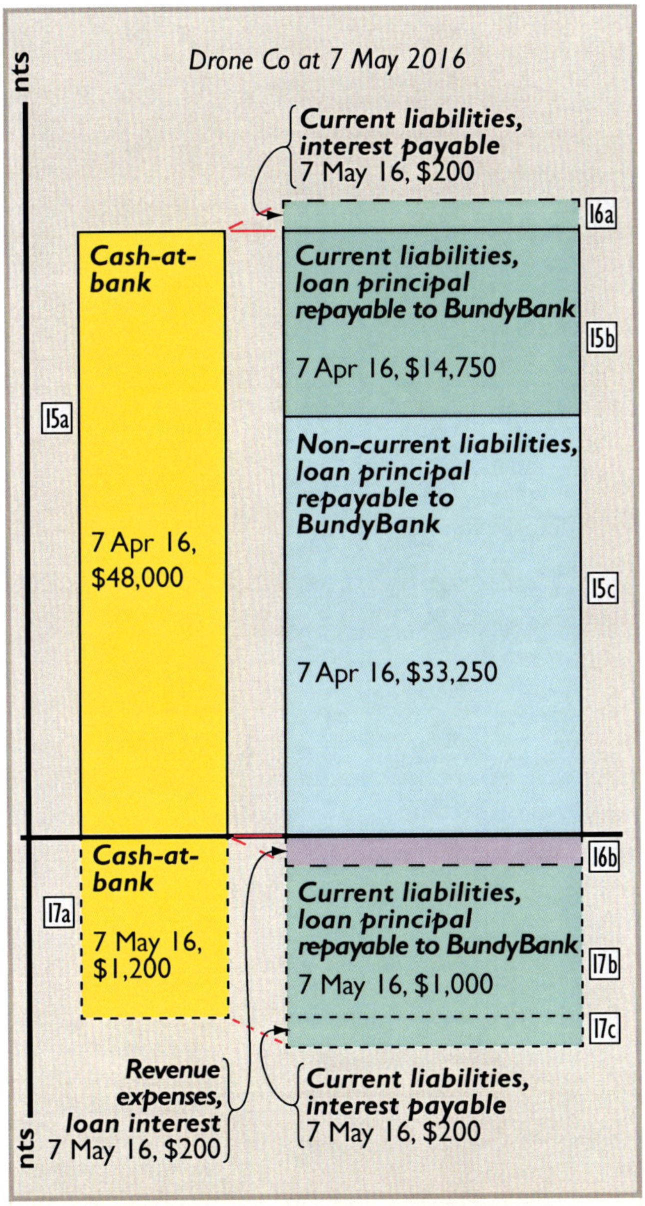

Figure 7.12 Drone borrowed $48,000 from BundyBank on 7 April 2016, and made the first repayment of principal and the first payment of interest on 7 May 2016. >

> Under the loan agreement, Drone had to make 48 principal repayments of $1,000 on the seventh of each calendar month starting on 7 May 2016. At the interest rate applying during April and May 2016, Drone's first monthly interest payment was $200.

[15a] On 7 April 2016 BundyBank deposited the loan principal of $48,000 into Drone's bank account at BundyBank.

[15b] and [15c] By receiving the loan principal, Drone incurred a present obligation (a liability) to repay the $48,000. The amount of the principal repayable to 30 June 2017 was 14.75 months x $1,000 = $14,750. (30 June 2017 is the end of Drone's next annual reporting period, and liabilities which are due to be paid by that date are classified as current liabilities.) The amount of the principal repayable after 1 July 2017 was $48,000 – $14,750 = $33,250, and this was therefore recorded as a non-current liability.

[16a] Drone had made a future commitment (which is not a liability) to pay loan interest at a variable rate each month to BundyBank. By 7 May 2016 Drone had incurred a present obligation (a liability) to pay interest of $200.

[16b] The incurrence of liability [16a] was an expense.

[17a] On 7 May BundyBank automatically, and as it was entitled to, withdrew $1,200 from Drone's BundyBank bank account. Drone thus thereby paid the current liabilities recorded in postings [16a] and part of [15b].

[17b] $1,000 of Drone's $1,200 7 May payment was a repayment of the loan principal, and reduced the amount of the loan principal current liability.

[17c] $200 of Drone's $1,200 7 May payment paid for the interest incurred between 7 April and 7 May 2016, and thus cancelled liability [16a].

7.2.9 Recording a continuous expense

Supplies such as insurance and the leasing of property are consumed continuously but are typically invoiced by the supplier in advance. Two situations can arise:

1. The entity expects or knows that the amount of the supply billed to it will all be consumed by the entity within the current reporting period. When recording a bill for such supplies, the debit posting should be made to an expenses account.
2. The entity expects or knows that its consumption of the supply billed will extend past the end of the current reporting period. When recording such events, the debit posting which records the supply should be made to an assets account as shown in figure 7.13.

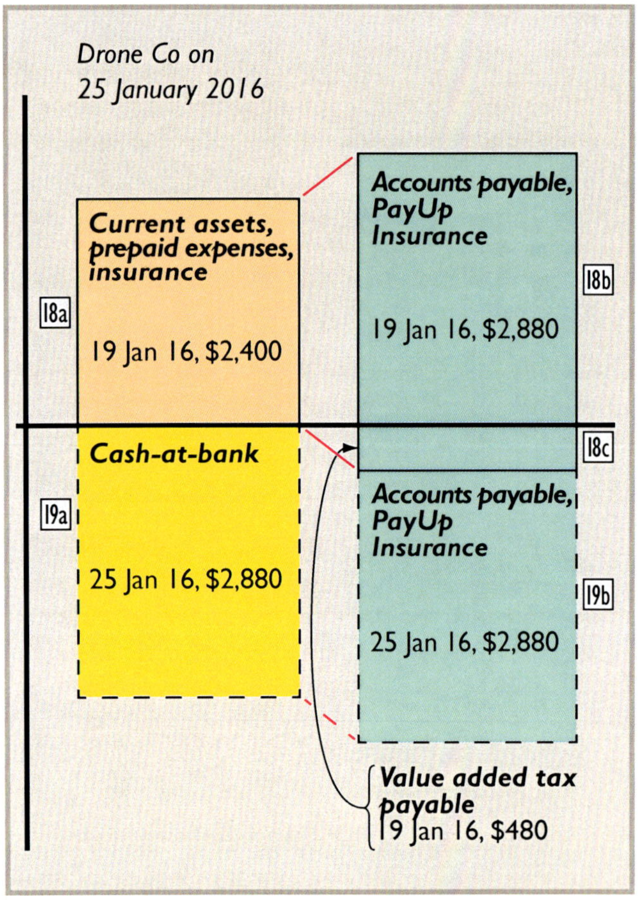

Figure 7.13 On 25 January 2016 Drone paid the bill dated 19 January for $2,400 plus 20% value added tax of $480 for a fire and business liability insurance policy. The 12-months insurance term started on 1 February 2016. >

> 18a PayUp Insurance's bill was dated 19 January. The bill date is the date usually used as the transaction date when recording the credit to an accounts-payable account. The insurance cover extended past Drone's 30 June 2016 reporting date (a *reporting date* is the 'end date of a reporting period'). Therefore Phil recorded the insurance cover as a prepayment current asset. Had the insurance term been five months or less, Phil would have debited the insurance cover facility to an expenses account.

Because the insurance cover was recorded as a prepaid expenses asset, as at the end of the then current reporting period, 30 June 2016, Phil later made the adjustment explained in figure 8.4 on page 53. This adjustment converted the amount of insurance cover consumed to 30 June 2016 into an expense incurred during 2015–2016.

18b Until paid, Drone's debt defined in PayUp's bill was a current liability.

18c It's assumed that the only tax on the insurance premium is value added tax at 20%. Because Drone uses accrual accounting, by becoming indebted to PayUp, Drone became entitled to a value-added-tax reimbursement of $480.

19a Drone paid for the insurance by bank transfer.

19b Drone's debt for the 12-months of insurance was cancelled by Drone's payment.

7.2.10 Paying an employee

Figure 7.14 illustrates how paying an employee's entitlements and wages or salary is recorded.

Because Phil is Drone's bookkeeper his salary payments are recorded by credits to a cash ledger account, and debits to an indirect-revenue-expenses ledger account. Were Phil instead directly engaged in manufacturing goods for sale, the debits would be posted to an inventories, work-in-process ledger account.

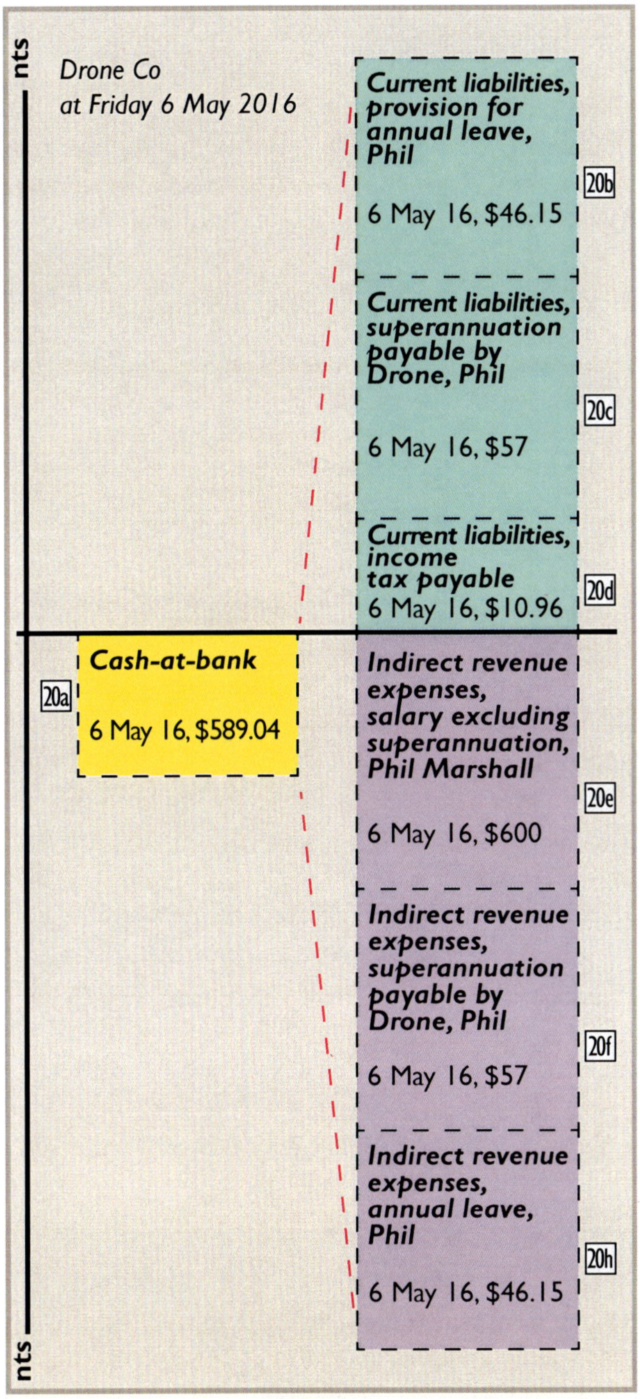

Figure 7.14 Drone pays Phil's weekly salary. >

> 20e Phil's part-time salary is $600 per week gross paid weekly in arrears (on Fridays).

20c and 20f Phil's $600 salary excludes the 9.5% superannuation contribution which is paid by the employer. Superannuation per week paid by Drone = 9.5% x $600 = $57. Drone will by the due dates pay those amounts of superannuation contributions into Phil's superannuation fund. It's assumed here that no tax is payable on this employer superannuation contribution.

20d Phil's income-taxable income = 52 x $600 = $31,200 p.a. On that income-taxable income Phil would be required to pay income tax of $570 p.a. = $10.96 p.w. The taxing authority requires that Phil's employer, Drone, deduct that $10.96 from Phil's weekly salary and forward these amounts of income tax on Phil's behalf to the taxing authority as specified by the tax law.

20a Per week Phil receives $600 – $10.96 tax = $589.04 cash.

20b and 20h Phil isn't entitled to long-service leave and if sick is paid as if at work. Phil has four weeks annual leave paid at $600 p.w. This is equivalent to 4 x $600 = $2,400 p.a. = $2,400/52 = $46.15 p.w. The liability of having to pay Phil while on annual leave is of uncertain timing and is therefore recorded by a provision and a balancing revenue expense. (A *provision* is 'a liability of uncertain timing or amount'.)

Chapter 8

END-OF-PERIOD TASKS

This chapter explains the bookkeeping/accounting tasks usually performed as at the ends of calendar months and as at the ends of reporting periods. The explanations assume accrual accounting and that value added tax applies.

8.1 TASKS TYPICALLY PERFORMED MONTHLY

This section explains five tasks which when bookkeeping was manual were typically performed at regular intervals, in many entities monthly, during reporting periods.

8.1.1 Bank reconciliation

An entity may have several bank accounts. Each should have its own current assets ledger account in the entity's chart of accounts. A bank's customer accounts are written from the bank's point of view. Since the bank owes a customer the amount the customer has on deposit with the bank, that amount is recorded by the bank as a current liability. A debit posting in a bank customer entity's cash-at-bank ledger account should therefore appear as a credit posting in the bank's related bank statement, and vice versa.

For a given interval, the postings recorded in an entity's cash-at-bank ledger account may not exactly mirror the postings in the corresponding bank statements because:

- **A deposit into or a withdrawal from a bank account can be recorded in an entity's cash-at-bank account and in the corresponding bank statement at different dates** For example, there can be a significant interval between the date an entity mails a cheque to pay a bill (the payment's transaction date as recorded by the buying entity) and the date the cheque clears after being presented by the seller and thus appears in a bank statement.
- **A posting which is first recorded in a bank statement won't appear in the entity's corresponding cash-at-bank ledger account unless copied over from the bank statement** Bank statements are the source documents for most bank fees and charges, and for amounts of bank interest directly transferred into or out of an bank account. Bank statements are also important source documents for standing-order payments, problem cheque payments, and money transfers directly into and from a bank account.
- **Omissions** Amounts which the bank has omitted to post to the bank's account for the entity, or amounts which the entity has omitted to post to the corresponding cash-at-bank ledger account.
- **Posting errors by the bank or by the entity** For example, an amount is posted as $2,010.00 instead of $2,001.00.

To resolve any such differences, the bank statements and the entity's corresponding cash-at-bank ledger accounts should be regularly reconciled (brought into agreement) with each other. There isn't a statutory reconciliation period, but many entities reconcile as at the end of each calendar month. Reconciliation is necessary whether the entity uses manual or computerised bookkeeping. Most accounting software has a bank reconciliation facility.

The steps in a bank reconciliation won't be detailed here.

8.1.2 Review accounts receivable and accounts payable

Entities which sell on credit need to frequently review their debtors' accounts, chase monies overdue, and reassess which customers should continue to be offered credit and on what terms.

Over time an entity may find that the amount of accounts receivable which become bad (uncollectable) in reporting periods later than the one in which the debts originated can be reliably forecast. That forecast may be a percentage of the credit sales during the originating reporting period or a percentage of the balance of the accounts-receivable control account as at the end of the originating reporting period. This forecast is then posted as an allowance and a simultaneous expense as at the end of the originating reporting period as shown in figure 8.1. Figure 8.2 then shows how a customer debt which is declared bad in the reporting period after the originating reporting period is debited against the allowance for doubtful debts. (Subsection 7.2.4 on pages 44 and 45 shows how a debt which is declared bad during the originating reporting period is recorded.)

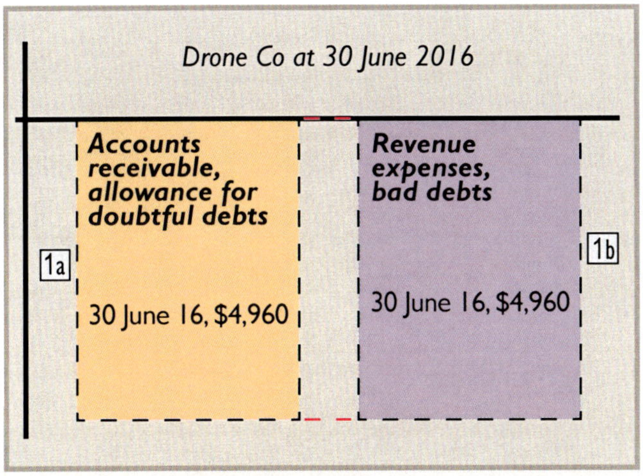

Figure 8.1 Recording an allowance for doubtful debts.

Drone had found that about 0.8% of each year's total credit sales became uncollectable after the end of that year. Drone's total credit sales for the annual reporting period 2015–16 were $620,000. Drone therefore estimated that $620,000 x 0.8% = $4,960 would be uncollectable after 30 June 2016.

1a Phil credited the estimated amount of bad debts to a contra account to the accounts-receivable control account thus reducing the carrying amount of the accounts-receivable current asset.

1b The reduction in the carrying amount of an asset is an expense. To conform to the matching principle of accrual accounting, the $4,960 was recorded as an expense in the annual reporting period in which the related sales were made. Because the $4,960 was considered to be a reliable estimate, it was debited to an expenses, not a to a provisions account. (A *provision* is an 'expense whose amount or timing is uncertain'.)

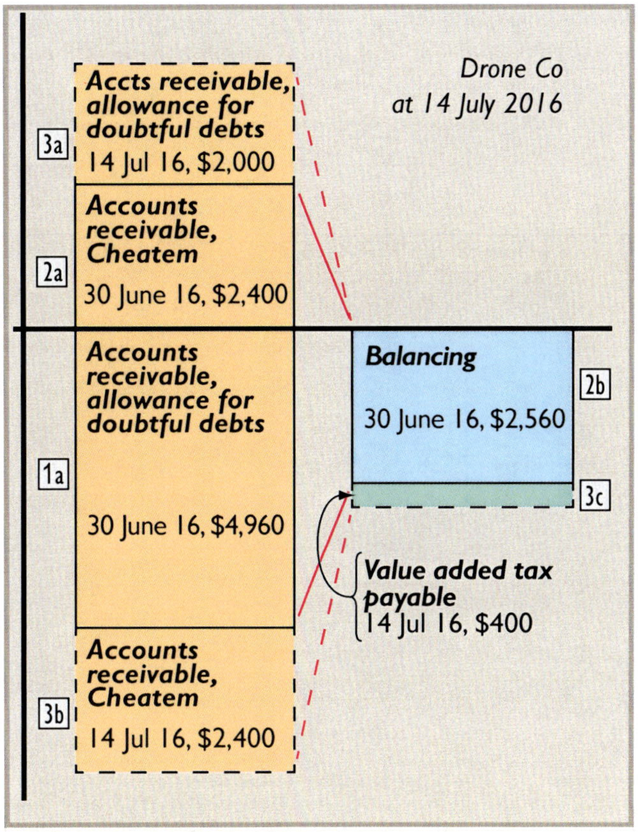

Figure 8.2 Offsetting a bad debt against an allowance for doubtful debts.

By 14 July Jane and Phil were certain that Cheatem Co which on 13 May 2016 had bought a drone on credit for $2,400 ($2,000 net plus $400 value added tax) wouldn't pay its debt. Jane and Phil therefore agreed to declare the debt bad.

1a This balance is 1a in figure 8.1, and is the estimated debts from credit sales during 2015–16 which will be declared bad after 30 June 2016.

2a The debt from Drone's 13 May 2016 sale to Cheatem as at 30 June 2016.

2b The balancing account balance required on 30 June 2016 to balance 1a and 2a.

3a Declaring a debt bad cancels the debt. $400 of Cheatem's debt will be recovered by Drone from the taxing authority. Therefore this posting consumes $2,000, not $2,400, of the allowance for doubtful debts.

3b This posting cancels Cheatem's debt.

3c Because Cheatem's debt was declared bad, Drone will be able to have the value added tax component reimbursed by the taxing authority.

Similarly the accounts payable accounts need to be regularly reviewed, and any necessary steps taken to ensure that the entity remains liquid (has sufficient cash to pay bills, wages, etc. as they fall due).

8.1.3 Calculate account balances

In manual bookkeeping the balance of each of an entity's accounts is calculated at regular intervals. With computerised bookkeeping running balances are generated automatically. (The right-hand money column of figure 6.15 on page 38 shows a running balance.) An entity's accountant should still however check the account balances at appropriate intervals to guard against fraud or error.

8.1.4 Write-off small amounts

Over time the number of insignificant account balances which are unlikely to change is likely to grow. Bookkeeping efficiency is increased if these balances are closed to zero, for example by the balances being transferred to an expenses, rounding account. In computerised bookkeeping the closed to zero (but not deleted) accounts can then be rendered inactive. The entity's accountant should supervise and check that any such closing is performed in accordance with the entity's relevant policies.

8.1.5 Perform a trial balance

In manual bookkeeping, typically after performing the bank reconciliation described on page 50, bookkeepers perform an arithmetical check of ledger account balances called a *trial balance.* The check utilises equation 5.c on page 26, and is shown graphically in figure 8.3.

If a trial balance's two totals aren't equal there must be at least one error in the postings or in the totalling. And even if the two totals are equal some ledger account balances may still be incorrect because:

- not all the entity's transactions have been posted
- amounts have been posted to the wrong accounts
- one or more transactions' debits were posted as credits and vice versa
- other self-cancelling errors have been made.

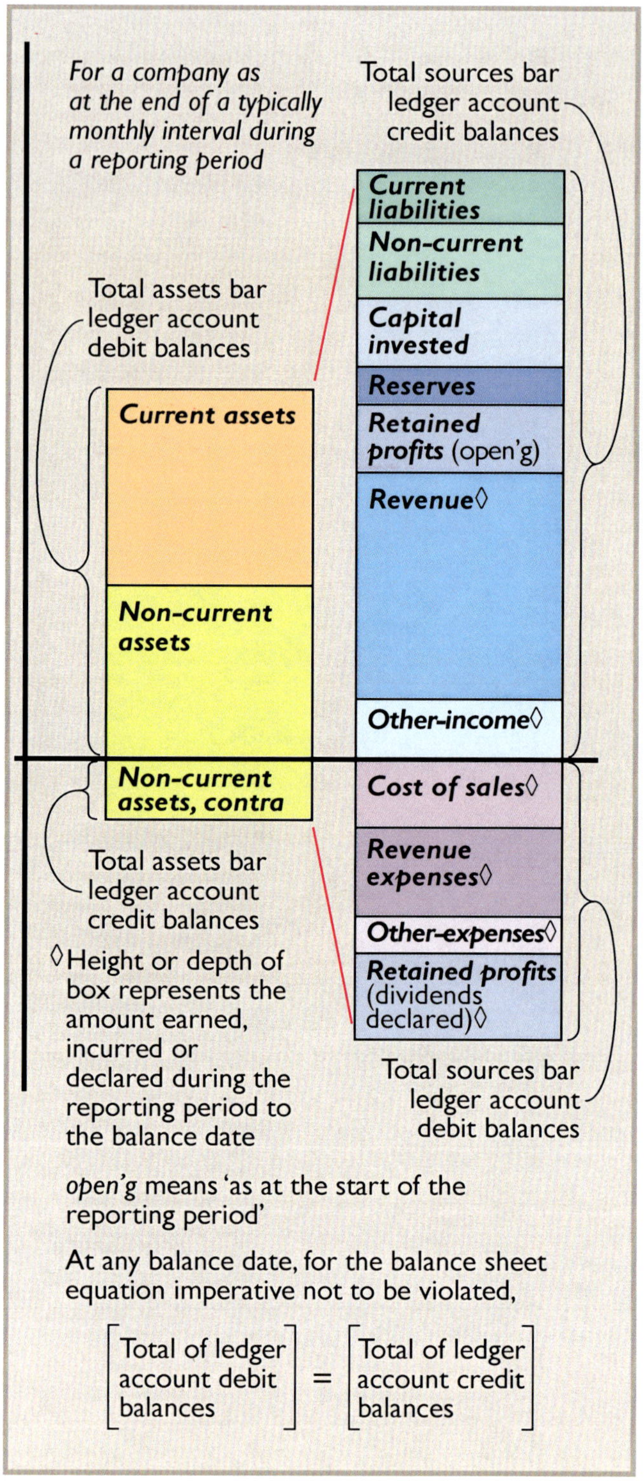

Figure 8.3 A balance chart showing a trial balance, here for a company.

In many entities a bank reconciliation is performed as at the end of each calendar month irrespective of whether the entity's bookkeeping is manual or computerised. A trial balance should then be performed (only a mouse click is needed to do so in computerised bookkeeping), and appropriately checked.

Bookkeeping software doesn't permit the postings for a transaction to be input unless balanced. Therefore although in computerised bookkeeping the trial balance arithmetical check is redundant, trial balances should still be checked to pick up any non-arithmetical errors.

8.2 INTRODUCING END-OF-REPORTING-PERIOD TASKS

Even if an entity's bookkeepers have assiduously recorded the entity's transactions and performed the tasks explained in section 8.1 during the whole of a reporting period, any financial statements prepared from the resulting accounts might still not comply with the objectives of accrual accounting described in section 5.4.2 on pages 24 and 25. Such non-compliance will occur if any of the carrying amounts of the assets controlled by the entity should have been updated as explained in chapter 9. Non-compliance will also occur unless adjustments for deferrals and accruals are made. Deferrals will be explained next, then accruals.

8.3 DEFERRALS

To *defer* is to 'delay'. In accounting a deferral is an event in which the earning of an income or the incurrence of a expense is delayed. Delayed relative to what? Answer, the related receipt or payment of cash. Therefore there are two types of deferral; they're usually called *prepaid expenses* and *unearned incomes*.

8.3.1 Prepaid expenses

A prepaid expense deferral is an event in which the entity records the supplier's bill and/or pays in full for the supply, before the related supply is all consumed.

When the entity records the earlier of the bill or the payment for a supply which is expected to provide benefits beyond the end of the current reporting period, the debit posting should be made to an assets account. Then, as at the end of that reporting period, the portion of the supply used during that period should be transferred to an expenses account as shown in figure 8.4.

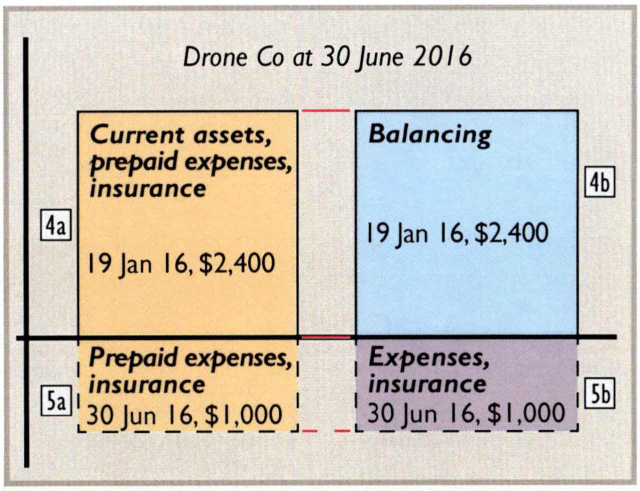

Figure 8.4 An end-of-reporting-period adjustment to a prepaid (deferred) expense.

Figure 7.13 on page 48 records that on 19 January 2016 Drone paid PayUp Insurance's bill for 12-months insurance. The insurance term began on 1 February 2016. This figure 8.4 chart shows the related end-of-reporting-period adjustment.

[4a] The insurance term extended past 30 June 2016, the end of the 2015–16 reporting period. Therefore the insurance cover was recorded as creating a current asset prepaid expense (posting [18a] in figure 7.13).

[4b] A balancing account balance to achieve balance as at 19 January.

[5a] Five months of insurance cover was consumed to 30 June 2016. This cover cost $1,000.

[5b] The reduction in the carrying amount of an asset recorded in [5a] is an expense.

8.3.2 Unearned incomes

An unearned income is an event in which the related cash is received by the entity or an invoice is raised by the entity before the related income is earned.

If the entity raises the invoice before the related income is earned, when the invoice is recorded as a debit to the specified buyer's accounts-receivable account, the balancing credit should be posted to a liabilities, revenue-invoiced-in-advance account. If the credit posting were instead made incorrectly to an income account, then the entity would overstate its profit for the reporting period (and have to pay more income tax).

If the cash is received before the entity has raised the related invoice, when recording this receipt the balancing credit is usually posted to a liabilities, revenue-received-in-advance account.

Figure 8.5 illustrates how to account for an unearned income.

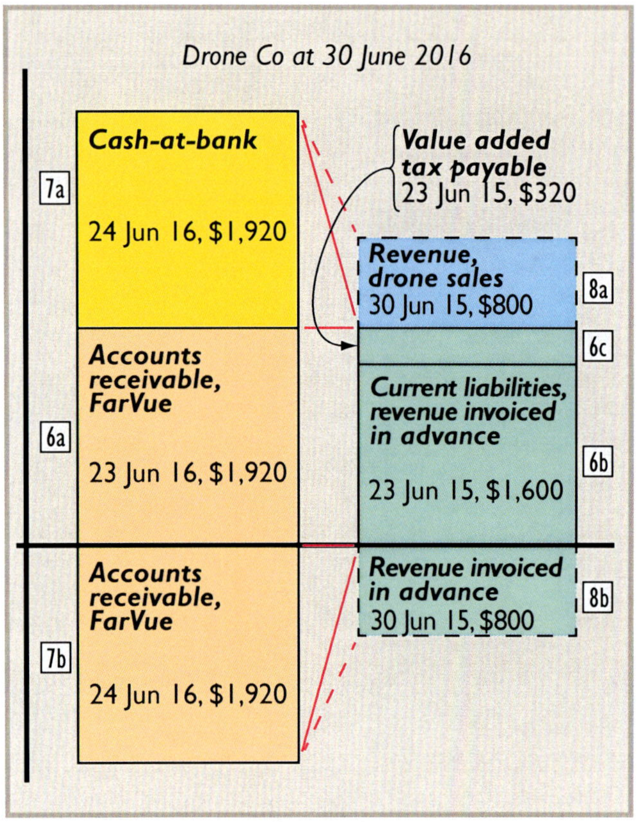

Figure 8.5 The adjustment for and payment of a deferred (unearned) income.

On 23 June 2016 Drone quoted $1,600 net plus $320 value added tax to manufacture a drone for the new customer FarVue Co. The work would take two weeks. FarVue required an immediate start. Because Drone wasn't able to check FarVue's credit rating before starting the work, FarVue agreed to pay in advance. Drone therefore invoiced FarVue for the full amount on 23 June, and FarVue paid in full by bank transfer on 24 June. By 30 June Drone had completed half the work.

[6a] Records Drone's invoiced amount including tax.

[6b] The revenue referred to in Drone's invoice had not been earned on 23 June, and was therefore recorded as a revenue invoiced in advance.

[6c] The value added tax charged by Drone. >

> [7a] Drone's receipt of FarVue's cash payment for the full amount quoted.

[7b] Records FarVue's payment of Drone's invoice.

[8a] By 30 June Drone had earned revenue of $800.

[8b] To balance [8a] $800 has to be debited to the revenue-invoiced-in-advance account.

8.4 ACCRUALS

To *accrue* is to 'accumulate naturally'. In accounting the earning of an income or the incurrence of an expense usually and therefore 'naturally' precedes its recording in the accounts. Until an amount of income earned or expense incurred is recorded in the accounts, it's an accrual. There are therefore two types of accrual:

1. **an accrued income**: an income earned but unrecorded in the accounts because no invoice has been raised by the entity and no related cash been received from the buyer
2. **an accrued expense**: an expense incurred but unrecorded in the accounts because no supplier's bill has been received nor has any related cash been paid out by the entity.

If an income is earned or an expense is incurred and the related invoice or bill or payment is recorded within the same reporting period, no end-of-reporting period adjustment will be needed. But if an accrual event's duration crosses the end of one or more reporting periods, an adjusting transaction should be recorded as at the end of each of those periods. Two adjusting transactions are explained next.

8.4.1 An accrued income

The representations of the accrual event explained in figures 8.6 and 8.7 include postings to inventories accounts. The total of an entity's current asset inventories may include some or all of the costs of:

- finished goods purchased for resale without any additional processing by the entity. These finished goods can include raw materials and components. For resale includes being provided as part of a service

- materials and components intended for processing by the entity into finished goods for sale
- work in process (or progress) of being manufactured for sale. The cost of a particular quantity of work in process on a particular date includes:
  a. the cost of the materials and components used including freight-in costs, plus
  b. the cost of the direct labour used, plus
  c. the overhead costs directly attributable to that work in process, and commonly called *factory overhead*
- finished goods already manufactured by the entity for sale.

Figure 8.6 shows the end-of-reporting-period adjustments for an accrued income event, the manufacture of a special drone, whose duration of manufacture spans two reporting periods. Figure 8.7 then shows the other transactions used to record the complete event.

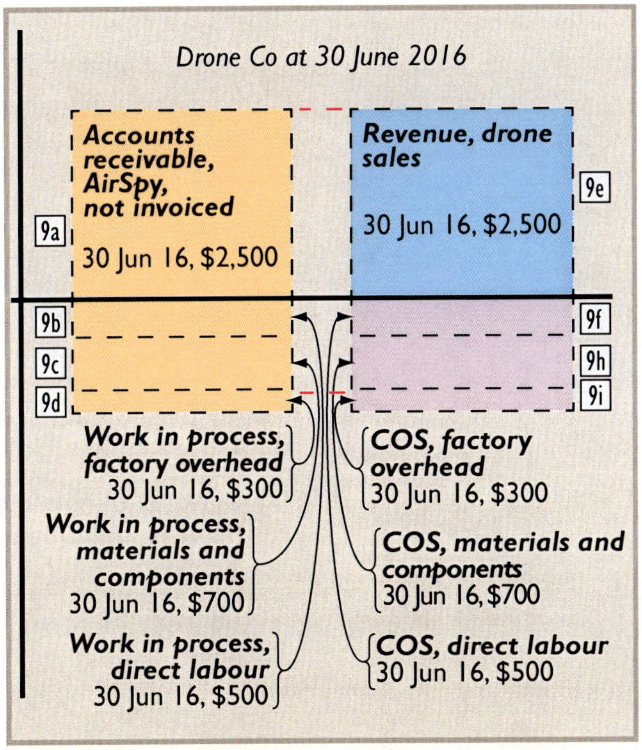

Figure 8.6 A balance chart representing an accrued income. >

\> In early June 2016 Drone was asked by customer AirSpy Co to start immediately to manufacture a special drone. Because AirSpy was a trusted and valued customer, Jane decided that Drone would invoice the quoted net price of $5,000 plus $1,000 value added tax when the job was completed in late July. The $5,000 consisted of $3,000 of estimated manufacturing costs plus $2,000 profit before income tax.

By 30 June 2016 Drone had half completed AirSpy's drone, but had neither invoiced AirSpy for the work done nor received any payment from AirSpy.

So that Drone's financial statements as at 30 June 2016 would include this accrued income and thus be true and fair, Phil recorded the eight-postings adjusting transaction represented in this balance chart.

[9a] The cost of the work done by Drone on AirSpy's drone to 30 June was $1,500, and Drone's allowed profit on that work was an additional $1,000. Those amounts exclude value added tax. Because AirSpy hadn't been invoiced by 30 June, this $1,500 + $1,000 debit was posted to an accounts-receivable, AirSpy, not-invoiced account.

[9b] to [9d] These three credit postings total $1,500. They decreased the balance of Drone's inventories, work-in-process accounts in which the work done had been recorded. The balances of those inventories, work-in-process accounts aren't shown.

[9e] As at 30 June Drone had earned revenue of $2,500. No credit to value added tax payable was recorded because at 30 June Drone hadn't yet raised an invoice for the work done for AirSpy.

[9f] to [9i] The credits to work in process recorded in [9b] to [9d] reduced Drone's assets. Therefore simultaneously to keep the net bar heights equal, $1,500 must be debited to one or more expenses accounts. The cost-of-sales accounts which received the postings could alternatively have been called *cost-of-manufacturing accounts*.

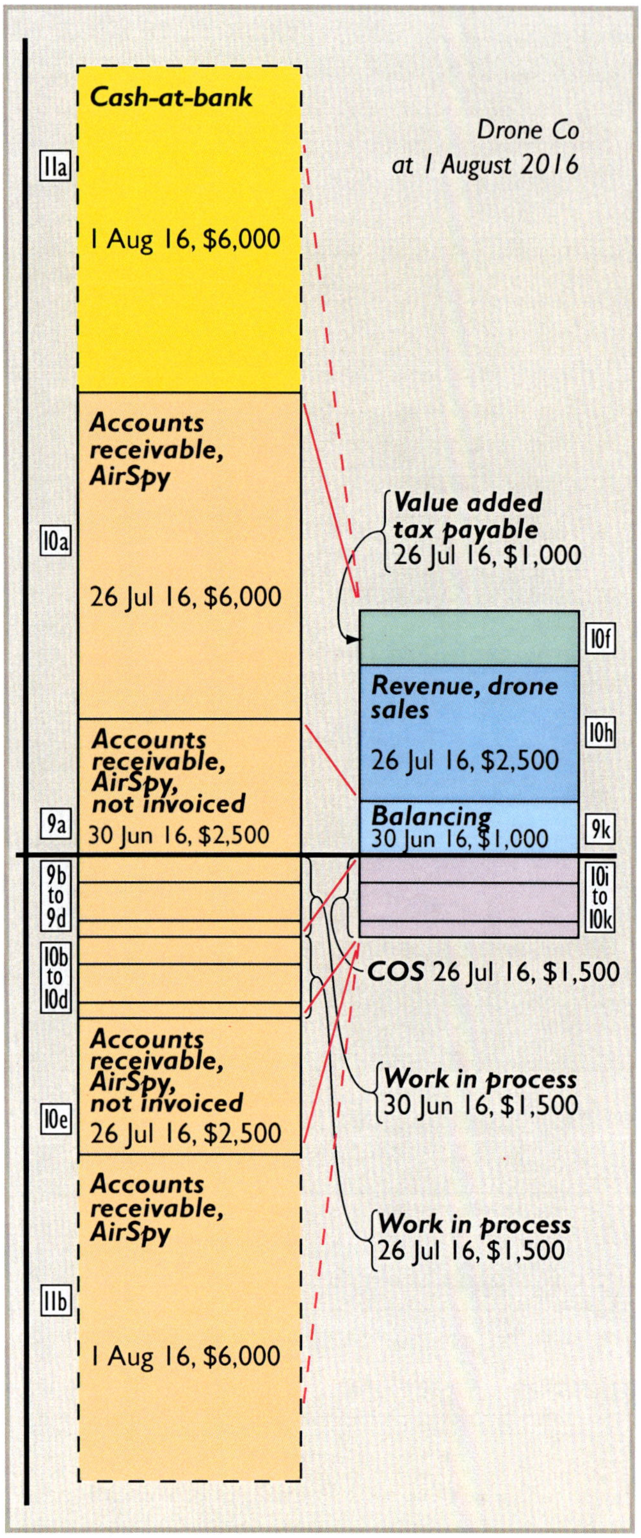

Figure 8.7 The postings from figure 8.6 plus the later postings related to Drone's job for AirSpy.

9a to 9d These amounts have been explained in the caption to figure 8.6. Because of the accounting practice of closing the profit-related accounts as at the end of each reporting period, > postings 9e to 9i in figure 8.6 don't appear in this figure 8.7 balance chart.

9k A balancing account balance required so that the net bar heights balanced as at 30 June 2016.

10a On 26 July Drone completed the drone and raised an invoice for the quoted amount.

10b to 10d These three credit postings total $1,500, the cost of the work done on the drone during July. These three postings decreased the balances as at 26 July of Drone's inventories, work-in-process accounts. The balances of those inventories, work-in-process accounts aren't shown.

10e This posting cancelled the $2,500 AirSpy debt-not-invoiced in 9a.

10f Drone was liable to pay to the taxing authority by the due date the value added tax charged on the invoice to AirSpy.

10h Between 1 July and 26 July Drone had earned additional revenue of $2,500 by completing the drone for AirSpy.

10i to 10k The decreases in assets recorded in 10b to 10d give rise to expenses.

11a Records the $6,000 payment from AirSpy being received into Drone's bank account on 1 August.

11b Cancels AirSpy's debt recorded in 10a.

8.4.2 An accrued continuous expense

An accrued expense is one consumed before the supplier's bill is recorded and before the entity pays the supplier for the related supply. If the duration of the event extends past the end of a reporting period, an adjusting transaction should be recorded as at the end of that period. Figure 8.8 shows such an adjusting transaction.

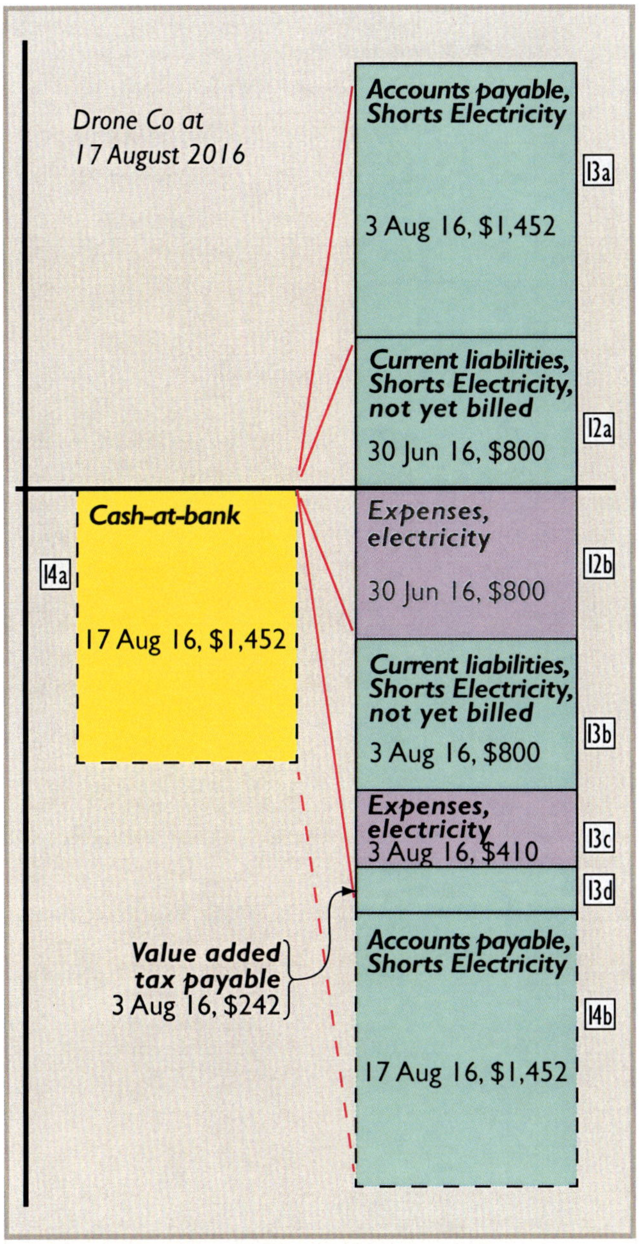

Figure 8.8 The postings for an accrued continuous expense involving an external entity.

Shorts Electricity supplied electricity to Drone, and billed Drone in arrears every three months for the electricity used. By 30 June Drone had consumed two month's of electricity during the billing period which started on 1 May. Phil estimated the net cost of that electricity consumed as $800.

On 3 August Drone received Shorts' bill dated 3 August for $1,452 including $242 value added tax for electricity used during May, June and July. Drone paid the bill by bank transfer on 17 August.

To match the estimated electricity consumption expense to the correct reporting period Phil made postings 12a and 12b as at 30 June 2016. As at 3 >

> August Phil recorded Shorts' bill, and using his estimated cost of electricity consumed during May and June determined and recorded the cost of the electricity used during July. Phil then recorded Drone paying its electricity bill on 17 August. The postings for these three transactions are explained below

12b The estimated electricity consumed was an expense. (Because all Drone's expenses accounts are closed at as at each 30 June, this posting would not normally appear in a balance chart whose balance date was after 30 June 2016. This balancing box therefore has a grey outline and grey text.)

12a As at 30 June 2016 Drone owed Shorts an estimated $800 excluding value added tax. What account should be credited? The choice depends on the exact definition of *accounts payable* used by the entity. Drone's definition is that a credit to an accounts-payable ledger account only records an amount billed to Drone, not a debt incurred which hasn't yet been billed. Phil therefore credited the $800 to a not-yet-billed account.

Some bookkeepers post accruals to a current liabilities, accruals account

13a Records Shorts' electricity bill. When recording a bill the transaction date used should ideally be when the debt was incurred. In this case it would be 31 July. However, unless there would be a significant error, for convenience the date on the bill is usually accepted.

13b Because the supplier's bill had been received, the estimated liability recorded in 12a was cancelled by this posting.

13c The $410 increased the total expense of the electricity used for May to July inclusive to the correct amount. Even if Phil's estimate of electricity used in May and June had been less accurate, the effect on the financial statements would not have been significant. Were an estimate so different from the later actual that the entity's estimate-based financial statements were unreliable, revised financial statements would have to be prepared and reported.

13d Drone was entitled to claim back the value added tax charged on Shorts' bill.

14a and 14b Record Drone paying Shorts' bill.

Chapter 9

MORE END-OF-PERIOD TASKS

When an entity first purchases a current asset or acquires a non-current asset, the asset's cost is recorded as the asset's carrying amount in the accounts. Over time an asset's unit fair, or other appropriate value can increase, or more likely decrease. If an entity's accounts and financial statements are to present through time a true and fair picture of an entity's financial positions and of the changes in its financial position, the carrying amounts of the entity's assets will need to be updated (more commonly called *adjusted*) as at the ends of reporting periods, and as at other appropriate times.

An *accrual* was defined on page 54 as an 'expense incurred or an income earned for which no related bill, invoice, cash payment or cash receipt has been recorded'. This definition means that a change to the carrying amount of an asset while controlled by an entity is not an accrual.

Adjusting the carrying amounts of accounts-receivable current assets has already been explained on pages 43 to 45. This chapter will explain why, when and how the carrying amounts of some common types of asset should be adjusted. This chapter won't however attempt to explain how to account for changes in the values of financial assets (IFRS 9 *Financial Assets* is an accounting standard which is particularly mind-numbing). This chapter also explains closing accounts and the adjusted trial balance.

9.1 ADJUSTING INVENTORIES

This section will explain how to account for and adjust the carrying amounts of inventories intended for sale.

The unit fair or other relevant defined value of an inventory current asset can change through time due to obsolescence, deterioration, outmoding, etc. An entity can also become aware that the number of units of an inventory recorded as being controlled by the entity is wrong because of earlier theft, spoilage or misrecording. Therefore accounting standards which comply with IAS 2 *Inventories* allow the carrying amounts of an entity's inventories to be adjusted. Unless it's appropriate to adjust the value of an inventory earlier, such adjustments are usually made as at the end of reporting periods.

9.1.1 What an inventory is

To be recorded as inventory (*trading inventory* would be a more meaningful term) goods must be:

- for sale in the ordinary course of the entity's activities
- on hand, that is controlled by the entity, and being processed for sale (and then called *work in process* or *work in progress*), or
- intended be consumed during processing for sale or in providing a service to an external entity.

Therefore the office stationery which an entity keeps for its own use isn't trading inventory, and purchases of such stationery are recorded by crediting a cash or accounts-payable account and debiting an expenses account.

9.1.2 The cost of an inventory

The cost of an inventory is:

- its purchase price plus any related duties and taxes, but for a value-added-tax-registered entity excluding any reimbursable value added tax charged,
- less any discounts received, less any allowance (a price reduction negotiated after purchase, typically because the quantity or quality of inventory received by the buying entity was less than ordered), and less the amount of any return (a *return* is the 'agreed cost of inventory returned to the supplier'),
- plus the cost (including direct labour costs and factory overhead) of any conversion from raw materials and components to produce the finished good for sale,
- plus all other costs incurred to bring the inventory to its present condition and location (these include freight-in, the cost of delivering the inventory to the entity), and

- plus any directly incurred borrowing costs.

The cost of an inventory may be determined from the actual costs incurred, or by other methods such as the standard cost method provided that the cost so determined approximates actual cost. (In the standard cost method, carefully predetermined measures of what cost components should cost are used in determining an inventory unit's carrying amount.)

Costs which should not be included in the costs of inventories, but should be instead recorded as expenses in the reporting period in which they are incurred, include:

- abnormal wasted amounts of materials, labour or other production costs
- storage costs unless incurred during production of inventories
- administrative overheads
- selling costs.

9.1.3 Accounting for inventories

Accounting for inventories can be complicated because:

- The number of different types of inventory stocked by an entity can be considerable.
- Different types of inventory may sold differently; for example, by number, weight, or volume, or in packages which contain a known number of units.
- The trading in some types of inventory is accompanied by significant and unavoidable waste; for example, perishable fruit and vegetables.
- The cost of purchasing or converting additional interchangeable units of an inventory is likely to change through time, as is an inventory's unit selling price.
- Inventory transactions may involve freight costs, allowances, discounts and returns.
- As new batches of interchangeable units are purchased or converted and added to an existing inventory, the batches to which any particular sale of units belongs may not be identifiable. Also interchangeable units may not be sold in any particular order.
- A particular value of an unit of inventory may change through time, especially if the stock has deteriorated or become outmoded or obsolete.
- Accounts record in monetary units, but recording for inventories may also require the numbers of units purchased, sold, returned, scrapped, etc. to be recorded.
- The number of inventory units recorded as being in stock may differ from the number of units in stock as determined by a *stocktake* (a 'physical count of the stock'). Such 'book' versus 'physical' discrepancies may be due to misrecording, losses, theft, etc.

To account for trading inventories and the associated complexities, two particular methods have been developed:

1. **the perpetual system** under which all inventory trading and other inventory-related transactions and stock records are fully recorded. This method is used to record all inventory-related transactions in this book
2. **the periodic system** which is suited to low-value inventory units. It requires less record-keeping effort (credits to inventory asset accounts due to sales aren't recorded), but doesn't allow the entity to access the monetary totals of the units in stock at any date without performing a stocktake. (The periodic system isn't explained in this book.)

Equation 9.a below defines how to determine the carrying amount of an inventory:

$$\begin{bmatrix}\text{Carrying}\\\text{amount}\\\text{of an}\\\text{inventory}\end{bmatrix} = \begin{bmatrix}\text{Average}\\\text{carrying}\\\text{amount}\\\text{of a unit}\\\text{of that}\\\text{inventory}\end{bmatrix} \text{x} \begin{bmatrix}\text{Number}\\\text{of units}\\\text{in stock}\end{bmatrix}$$

In equation 9.a the average carrying amount of an inventory's unit can change through time because:

- the unit is one of an inventory of interchangeable units, and the original cost of units added to the inventory varies through time, and/or
- the net amount that the entity expects to realise from the sale of units of that inventory in the ordinary course of business changes through time.

Determining the carrying amounts of an inventory whose interchangeable unit original cost varies through time

Drone sells drone batteries. Drone's cost of buying the batteries from its wholesale supplier varies through time. Drone sells its drone batteries in no particular order. How does Drone determine the carrying amount of the battery inventory at a specified instant, and the carrying amount of the batteries sold in a particular sale?

To record a sale of interchangeable inventory units the then current carrying amount of the units sold has to be credited to the inventory's current-assets account and debited to an expenses COS account. The selling entity may also want to relate an inventory unit's sale price to the then current inventory unit carrying amount. Accounting standards based on IAS 2 *Inventories* permit the use of one of the two methods below to calculate the current carrying amount (sometimes confusingly called the *cost*) of an interchangeable inventory unit:

1. **FIFO (first-in, first-out)** This assumes that units are sold in the same order in which they were purchased or otherwise added to the inventory.
2. **Weighted-average cost** The carrying amount of the units sold in a sale is the average cost of all the units in stock immediately before the sale. This method is illustrated in figure 9.1.

Adjusting inventory unit carrying amounts because the net amount expected to be realised changes

IAS 2 requires that inventories be measured at the lower of the then carrying amount and the then net realisable value. This comparison is performed and any related transaction posted as at the end of each reporting period and at other appropriate times. The *net realisable value (NRV)* is the 'estimated selling price in the ordinary course of business less the estimated costs of completion (costs of getting the inventory to a saleable state), and less the estimated costs necessary to make the sale'. Net realisable value is thus the net amount that the entity expects to realise from the sale of the inventory in the ordinary course of business.

A reduction in the carrying amount of an inventory is recorded by a credit to the inventory's current asset

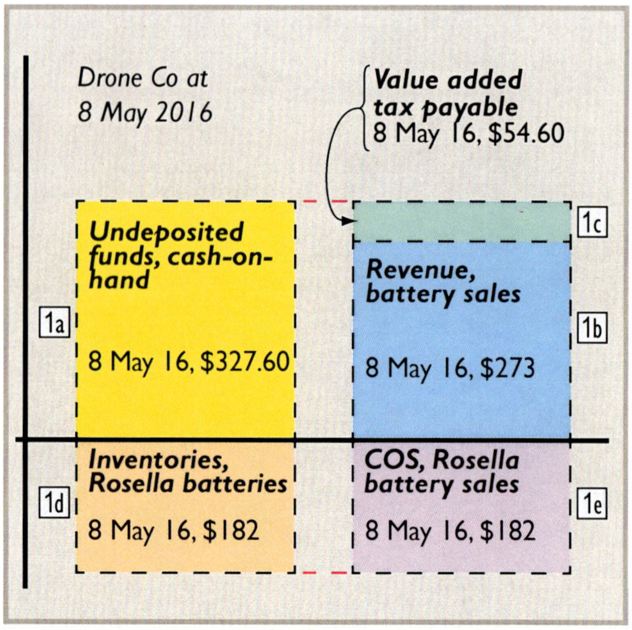

Figure 9.1 Drone's 8 May cash sale of two drone batteries with the related COS (cost of sales) calculated using the weighted-average cost method.

Immediately before this sale, Drone's inventory of Rosella brand drone batteries consisted of the four batteries remaining after the sale on 20 April shown in figure 7.9 which were purchased at $80 each (see figure 7.3 on pages 41 and 42), and 20 purchased in early May at $93.20 each net. The weighted-average cost of these batteries was therefore:

$$[(4 \times \$80) + (20 \times \$93.20)] \div 24 = \$91 \text{ each}$$

Therefore the COS of the two batteries sold was 2 x $91 = $182.

Drone's retail mark-up was 50%. Therefore the two batteries' net sale price was $182 x 150% = $273. The value added tax charged at 20% was 20% x $273 = $54.60.

Rather than record a cash sale as a credit sale in which the entity records first an invoice and then the same-day payment of that invoice by a debtor, entities typically record cash sales by issuing receipts. Phil thus recorded the transaction using the five postings explained below.

1a Drone's receipt of the $327.60 in cash from the customer.

1b Drone's revenue from the cash sale. >

> [1c] The amount of value added tax charged by Drone which is then payable by Drone to the taxing authority by the due date.

[1d] The fall in the Rosella inventory resulting from the sale.

[1e] A reduction in the carrying amount of an asset is balanced by a simultaneous expense.

account and a debit to an expenses account. If earlier an inventory unit's carrying amount had been decreased because the unit net realisable value fell below the then unit carrying amount, but the unit's net realisable value later increases, such increases are recorded by debits to the inventory's current-asset account and credits to an expenses, cost of sales account, not by credits to a revenue account. However, an inventory unit's carrying amount cannot be increased above its original cost.

The accounting is relatively simple if the inventory consists of only one unit whose original cost is then a specific original cost. But many inventories consist of multiple interchangeable units which are purchased at original costs which vary through time and are sold at prices which also vary through time. FIFO or weighted-average cost should then be used to determine the carrying amounts or amount of the units in stock which can then be compared with the then net realisable value of a unit as shown in figure 9.2.

Another permitted method to determine a unit's carrying amount is the *retail inventory method*. In that method a unit's carrying amount is its unit retail price multiplied by an appropriate percentage.

Adjusting the number of units in stock

Under the perpetual system the number of units of an inventory in stock should be available from the accounts and/or from the stock control records. However that number needs to be confirmed by regular stocktakes. If there is a discrepancy it should be investigated, and if confirmed a correcting transaction recorded as illustrated in figure 9.2.

For inventories recorded using the periodic system, because when a sale is recorded a credit isn't posted to

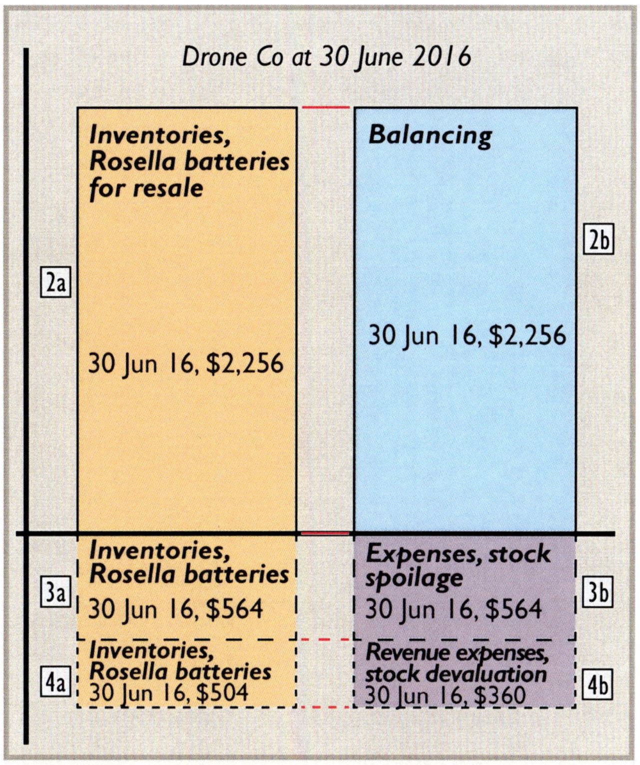

Figure 9.2 Two end-of-reporting-period inventory adjustments under the perpetual system.

Drone's records showed 24 Rosella brand drone batteries in stock at 30 June 2016. A stocktake on that date confirmed that 24 batteries were in stock, but that six had been damaged by rats. The weighted-average cost of the 24 batteries was $94 each. Also, in June 2016 an improved and cheaper substitute battery had just been widely released. Jane and Phil agreed that the 18 unspoiled batteries remaining in stock could be sold at $99 each retail, that the selling costs were $25 each, and that therefore the carrying amount of each battery should be reduced to its NRV of $74.

[2a] The carrying amount of the undamaged plus damaged batteries at 30 June 2016 before the two adjustments was 24 batteries x $94 = $2,256.

[2b] Required to balance balance [2a].

[3a] and [3b] These postings record the 6 x $94 = $564 fall in carrying amount of the batteries caused by rats, and the resulting expense.

[4a] and [4b] These postings record the fall in carrying amount of the 18 undamaged batteries due to the availability of cheaper and improved substitutes. This devaluation equalled 18 x ($94 – $74) = $360.

the inventory's current-asset account, the number in stock can only be determined from a stocktake. Then:

$$\begin{bmatrix}\text{Number}\\\text{of units}\\\text{'sold'}\end{bmatrix} = \begin{bmatrix}\text{Number}\\\text{of units}\\\text{in stock}\\\text{at start}\\\text{of period}\end{bmatrix} + \begin{bmatrix}\text{Number}\\\text{of units}\\\text{added}\\\text{during}\\\text{the}\\\text{period}\end{bmatrix} - \begin{bmatrix}\text{Number}\\\text{of units}\\\text{from}\\\text{end-of-}\\\text{period}\\\text{stocktake}\end{bmatrix}$$

Equation 9.b

This number 'sold' might then be adjusted using assumptions or knowledge of wasteage, theft, etc.

9.2 ADJUSTING TANGIBLE NON-CURRENT ASSET CARRYING AMOUNTS

Buildings, machinery and vehicles are examples of tangible (meaning 'touchable') non-current assets. Most tangible assets have a value related to their physical substance. However there are exceptions such as available-for-sale company shares which the entity intends to retain long term. These are regarded as tangible because they're not as intangible as more obviously intangible assets such as patents and trademarks.

The values of tangible non-current assets can rise and can fall. Such a rise or fall is recorded as:

- an amount of *depreciation*. To *depreciate* a non-current asset is to 'model its gradual fall in value during the duration through which that asset is expected to be available for use'. A resulting fall in value during a period is an amount of depreciation.
- an *impairment loss* which is the 'amount by which the carrying amount of an asset exceeds its recoverable amount'. (An asset's *recoverable amount* is the 'higher of the asset's fair value less costs to sell and its value in use'. An asset's *value in use* is the 'present value of the estimated future cash flows expected to arise from the continuing use of the asset and from its disposal at the end of its useful life'. Present value is explained on page 107.)
- a *gain*, an 'income that does not necessarily arise from the ordinary activities of the entity'. The term *gain* is commonly applied to an 'increase in the fair value of a non-current asset'. For example, if land is rezoned from rural to urban, the resulting increase in market value is a gain.

9.2.1 Valuing ppe non-current assets under accounting standards

IAS 16 *Property, Plant and Equipment* allows an entity to record the carrying amounts of its tangible property, plant and equipment (the common initialism is *ppe*) non-current assets under either of two models:

1. **Cost model** An asset's *carrying amount* under the cost model is its 'cost less any accumulated depreciation and any accumulated impairment losses'. Under the cost model there isn't a provision to revalue upwards (to record gains), but there is a requirement to depreciate where appropriate and to subtract impairment losses.
2. **Revaluation model** An asset's *carrying amount* under the revaluation model is its 'most recently determined fair value less any subsequent accumulated depreciation and any subsequent accumulated impairment losses'.

An entity is free to choose which model it will apply to a non-current asset, but must apply the same model to all the non-current assets in an entire class of property, plant and equipment. Typical classes include: land, buildings, machinery, and office equipment.

Falling in value is much more common than rising. The values of many ppe assets fall over time because, for example, such assets:

- deteriorate, becoming less safe and less productive
- can no longer be economically maintained
- become obsolete, and/or
- become outmoded.

If such falls in value are gradual and can be forecast with reasonable accuracy, they're recorded under accounting standards as depreciation.

9.2.2 Depreciation

Both the cost and revaluation models allow the modelling of depreciation. If a non-current asset's carrying amount were left unchanged until that asset was sold or scrapped and the asset's fall in value was only then recorded as an expense, that fall in value would reduce the profit only for the reporting period in which the sale or scrapping occurred. However the fall in value of most tangible non-current assets is gradual. It's therefore realistic to spread such a fall in value throughout the whole duration during which the asset is expected to produce economic benefit for the entity. This results in more-realistic smaller reductions to entity profit spread through the reporting periods during that duration, and thus smooths reported profits.

Figure 9.3 outlines the two most-common types of method used to calculate depreciation. Both types require the amounts of the relevant parameters to be decided. These parameters include:

- **Cost** A non-current asset's cost is its acquisition price including any duties and non-refundable amounts of tax, less any discounts and rebates, plus any costs required to bring the asset to the location and condition required for its intended use, plus, if the asset were formerly in use elsewhere, the initial estimate of any costs to dismantle and remove the asset and restore the site where it was. The acquisition price is the first-element cost; the other amounts above constitute the asset's second-element costs.
- **Start of useful life** The date from when the asset is first available for use.
- **Useful life** The period over which the asset is expected to be available for use.
- **Residual value** The estimated amount that the entity could currently realise from disposal of the asset in its anticipated condition as at the end of its useful life after subtracting the estimated disposal costs.

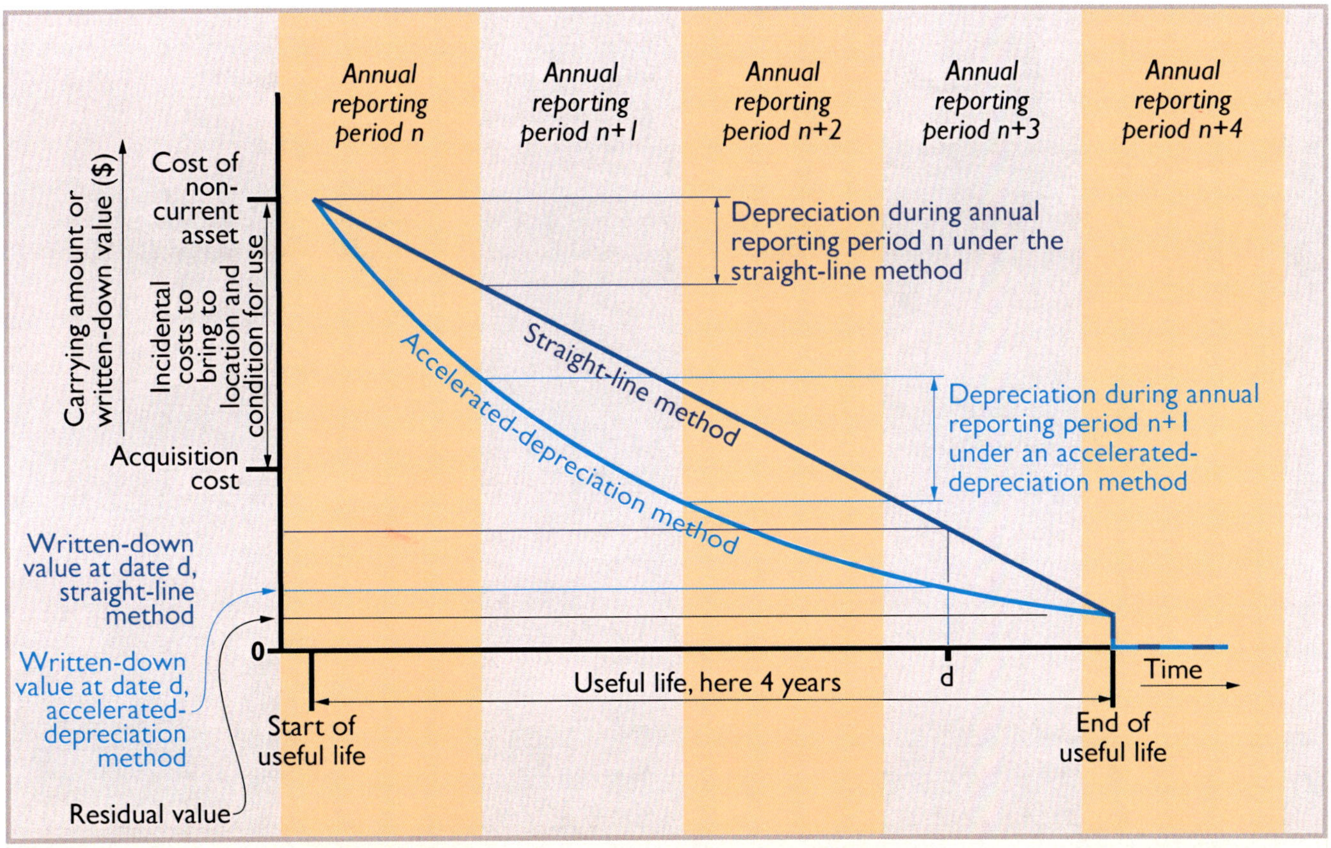

Figure 9.3 Two types of depreciation method. An entity should choose, subject to the accounting standards, the depreciation method, the useful life's start date and duration, and the residual value which most accurately represent the entity's intentions and expectations regarding the subject non-current asset. The reducing carrying amounts shown assume that no gains or impairments are recorded during the asset's useful life.

Annual reporting period	Straight-line method, depreciation calculation	Double-diminishing-balance-rate method accelerated depreciation calculation
2015–16	$\frac{\$6{,}600}{4} \times \frac{107}{365} = \$484$	$\frac{2 \times \$7{,}000}{4} \times \frac{107}{365} = \$1{,}026$
2016–17	$\frac{\$6{,}600}{4} = \$1{,}650$	$\frac{2 \times (\$7{,}000 - \$1{,}026)}{4} = \$2{,}987$
2017–18	$\frac{\$6{,}600}{4} = \$1{,}650$	$\frac{2 \times (\$5{,}974 - \$2{,}987)}{4} = \$1{,}494$
2018–19	$\frac{\$6{,}600}{4} = \$1{,}650$	$\frac{2 \times (\$2{,}987 - \$1{,}494)}{4} = \$747$
2019–20	$\frac{\$6{,}600}{4} \times \frac{258}{365} = \$1{,}166$	$\frac{2 \times (\$1{,}493 - \$747)}{4} \times \frac{258}{365} = \$528$ Use $346

Table 9.1 Two methods for calculating the depreciation during annual reporting periods for Drone's Makebot 3D printer. Because the printer's residual value is $400, the depreciation during 2019–20 using the double-diminishing-balance-rate method cannot be greater than $746 – $400 = $346. The calculations assume that no gains or impairments are recorded during the asset's useful life.

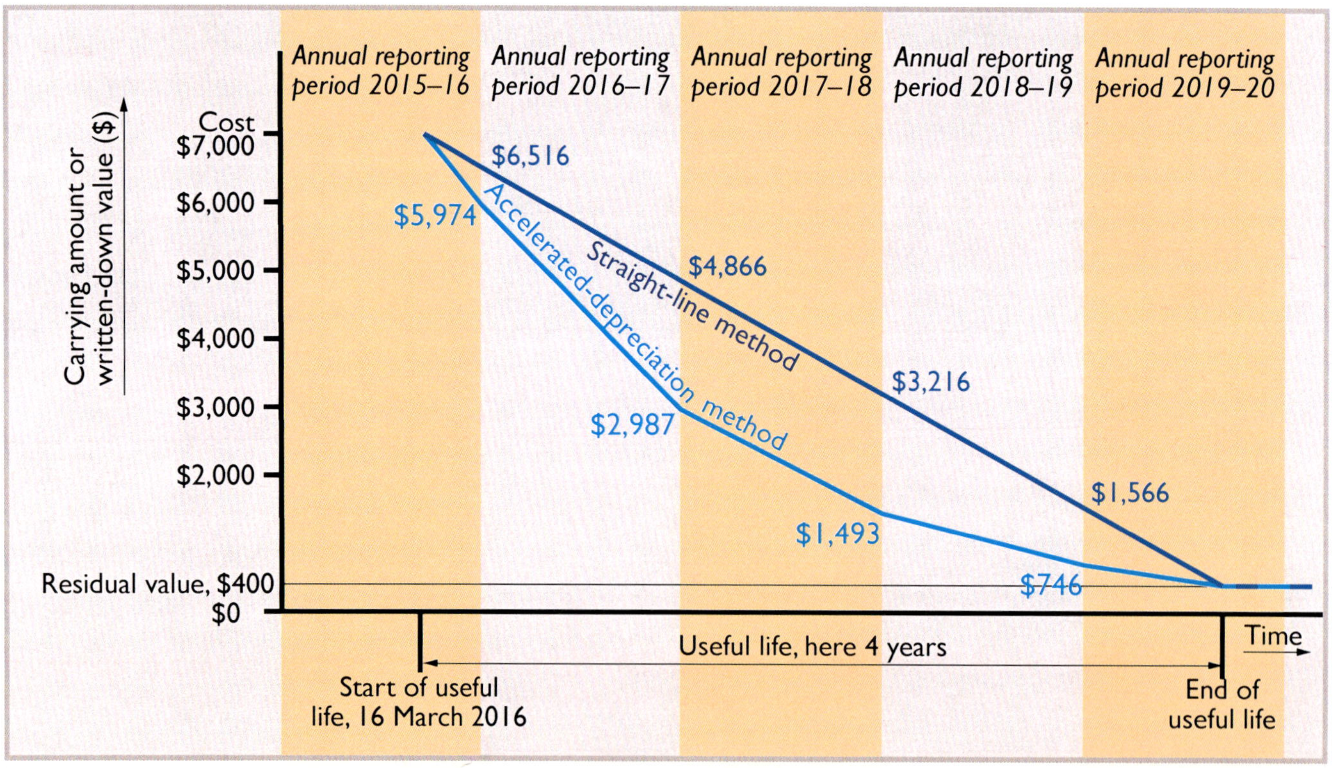

Figure 9.4 The depreciated carrying amounts of Drone's Makebot 3D printer during that printer's useful life determined using the amounts of depreciation calculated in table 9.1.

Table 9.1 and figure 9.4 show two depreciation calculations for Drone's Makebot printer which cost $7,000 excluding consumption tax on 13 March 2016 (figure 6.3 on page 32). The printer was ready for use on 16 March, and there were no additional delivery or installation expenditures needed for the machine to be ready to use. Jane assessed that the machine's useful life was four years, and that its residual value at the end of that four years would be $400. From 16 March to 30 June is 107 days.

Under the straight-line method the depreciation during any period during an asset's useful life is:

$$\frac{\text{Cost} - \text{Residual value}}{\text{Useful life in years}} \times \frac{\text{days in period}}{365}$$

Equation 9.c

The particular accelerated-depreciation method shown in table 9.1 and figure 9.4 is the double-diminishing-balance-rate method (one of the simplest of the several different accelerated-depreciation methods in use). Under this method the amount of depreciation during a period is:

$$\frac{2(\text{Cost} - \text{Accumulated depreciation})}{\text{Useful life in years}} \times \frac{\text{Days in period}}{365}$$

Equation 9.d

In this equation the accumulated depreciation subtracted is that to the beginning of the subject period. Also note that the residual value isn't subtracted from the cost, and therefore the equation shouldn't be used where the residual value is relatively large.

As shown in figure 9.5, to record a depreciation adjustment transaction, each calculated amount of depreciation reduces the carrying amount of the non-current asset, typically by being credited to a contra account for the asset. The balancing debit is posted to an expenses depreciation account.

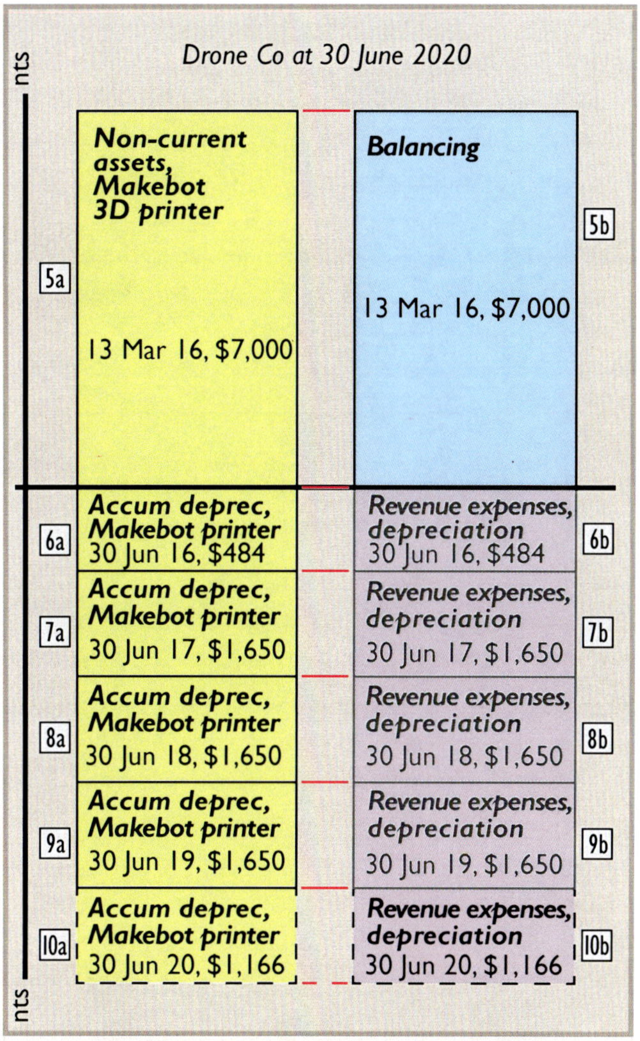

Figure 9.5 Recording depreciation, here for Drone's Makebot 3D printer. The amounts of depreciation are calculated using the straight-line method shown in the second column from the left in table 9.1.

[5a] The cost of the printer. This cost excludes the value added tax charged by the seller because that amount would be reimbursed to Drone by the taxing authority.

[5b] A balancing account balance.

[6a] The depreciation to 30 June 2016 was credited to an accumulated depreciation contra ledger account.

[6b] The depreciation in the carrying amount of the printer recorded in [6a] is balanced by a posting to a revenue expenses, depreciation account.

[7a] to [10a] plus [7b] to [10b] These postings record the amounts of depreciation and of the balancing >

> debits to revenue expenses during the four annual reporting periods 2016–2017 to 2019–2020. The revenue expenses, depreciation account to which postings [6b], [7b], [8b], and [9b] were made is closed as at 30 June of 2016, 2017, 2018, and 2019 respectively. To signify this, those postings have grey outlines and text. (Closing accounts as at the ends of annual reporting periods is explained on pages 67 and 72.)

9.2.3 Carrying amounts under the revaluation model

Only tangible ppe (property, plant and equipment) non-current assets whose fair values can be measured reliably can be accounted for under the revaluation model. Such assets must then be revalued sufficiently frequently that their carrying amounts at the ends of reporting periods don't differ materially from their then fair values.

Unlike the cost method, the revaluation method allows carrying amounts to decreased and to be increased (including to an amount greater than the asset's original cost). When a ppe asset is revalued to a fair value which is greater than the asset's current carrying amount, a gain transaction is recorded. When a ppe asset is revalued to a fair value which is less than the asset's current carrying amount, an impairment loss transaction is recorded. To record such changes in carrying amounts can involve making postings to reserves accounts.

The role of reserves accounts in revaluation

Reserves accounts were introduced on page 8 where it was explained that they are 'used to record amounts of profit which are unrealised and uncertain', and therefore should be reserved from being spent or being distributed to the entity's owners. Such changes in an entity's ppe assets' carrying amounts could be material for decision making and should therefore be recorded and reported in financial statements. (Recording and reporting changes in the carrying amounts of other types of tangible non-current assets and liabilities are not explained here.) Entities therefore report:

- income and expenses which have been realised or if unrealised are, like depreciation, deemed sufficiently reliable to be included in profit or loss statements, and
- unrealised equivalents of incomes and expenses (often called *gains* and *impairments*) in a statement grandly called the *statement of other comprehensive income*.

The realised income and expenses for a reporting period plus the unrealised gains and impairments for the same period then equal the comprehensive income for that period.

Recording ppe asset gains and impairments

How accounts are closed (their balances brought to zero) is explained in figure 9.6. To record ppe asset gains and impairments in conformance with IAS 16 *Property, Plant and Equipment* can involve account closures, is illustrated in figures 9.7 and 9.8, and requires that:

1. If no impairments have been previously recorded for the asset, a gain in carrying amount is recorded by debiting the amount of the gain to the assets bar account for the asset (for clarity an extra assets-bar upward revaluations account is used in figure 9.7). The same amount should be simultaneously credited to a reserves, OCI (other-comprehensive-income) temporary account for the asset.

2. If no gains have been previously recorded for the asset, an impairment is recorded by crediting the amount of the impairment to the assets bar account for the asset, or as in figures 9.7 and 9.8 to an assets bar, accumulated impairments, contra account. The same amount should simultaneously be debited to an expenses, loss-on-revaluation account. Such an impairment is thus reported in the profit or loss statement for the reporting period.

3. Revaluations of the asset can result in both gains and impairments while the asset is under the entity's control. Then:

   i. if immediately prior to recording a gain, earlier revaluations have resulted in a net impairment:

a. If the gain is less than the net earlier impairments, the amount of the gain is debited to an asset's account and credited to a revenue account, thereby partially reversing the balance of impairment expenses

b. If the gain exceeds the net earlier impairments, the amount of the gain is debited to an asset's account, an amount of the gain equal to the net impairment is credited to a revenue account, and the excess remaining gain is credited to a reserves, OCI, temporary account.

The financial statement called the *statement of comprehensive income* includes details of the other comprehensive income for the reporting period, which in turn includes any excess gains. The amounts of these excess gains usually have the amounts of income tax which would be payable were those excess gain realised subtracted. This is because the profit (or loss) for the period, also reported in the same statement, has itself had the income tax payable subtracted. As at the end of the reporting period, the reserves, OCI, temporary account is closed by debiting its balance to it, crediting the income tax on the gain to a provisional liability account, and crediting the remainder of the balance to a reserves, revaluation surplus, permanent account.

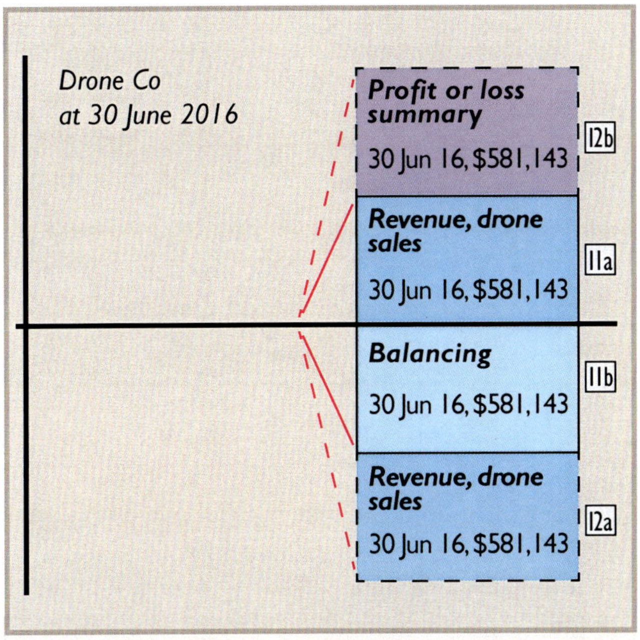

Figure 9.6 Closing a ledger account, here closing the balance of Drone's revenue, drone sales account into the profit or loss summary account.

11a Drone's last drone sale during the annual reporting period 2015–16 was on 27 June, and brought the total revenue from those sales to $581,143. This amount was therefore the balance of that account as at the end of Drone's 2015–16 annual reporting period.

11b This account balance was created to balance account 11a.

12a The debit posting required to close the drone sales account to zero balance.

12b The balancing credit posting to the profit or loss summary account which when its balance is positive is located above the x axis in the sources bar.

ii. if immediately prior to recording an impairment, earlier revaluations have resulted in a net gain, the reserves, revaluation surplus account for the asset should having a positive balance. The amount of the impairment should be credited to an asset's bar contra account for the asset. Then to balance:

a. If the amount of the impairment is less than the balance of the revaluation surplus account for the asset, the amount of the impairment should be debited to that revaluation surplus account and credited to an asset's bar contra account for the asset

b. If the amount of the impairment is greater than the balance of the revaluation surplus account for the asset, the amount of the impairment should be credited to an asset's bar contra account for the asset. And to restore balance an amount of the impairment equal to the balance of the revaluation surplus account should be debited to that account to bring its balance to zero. The excess impairment should then be recorded as an expense.

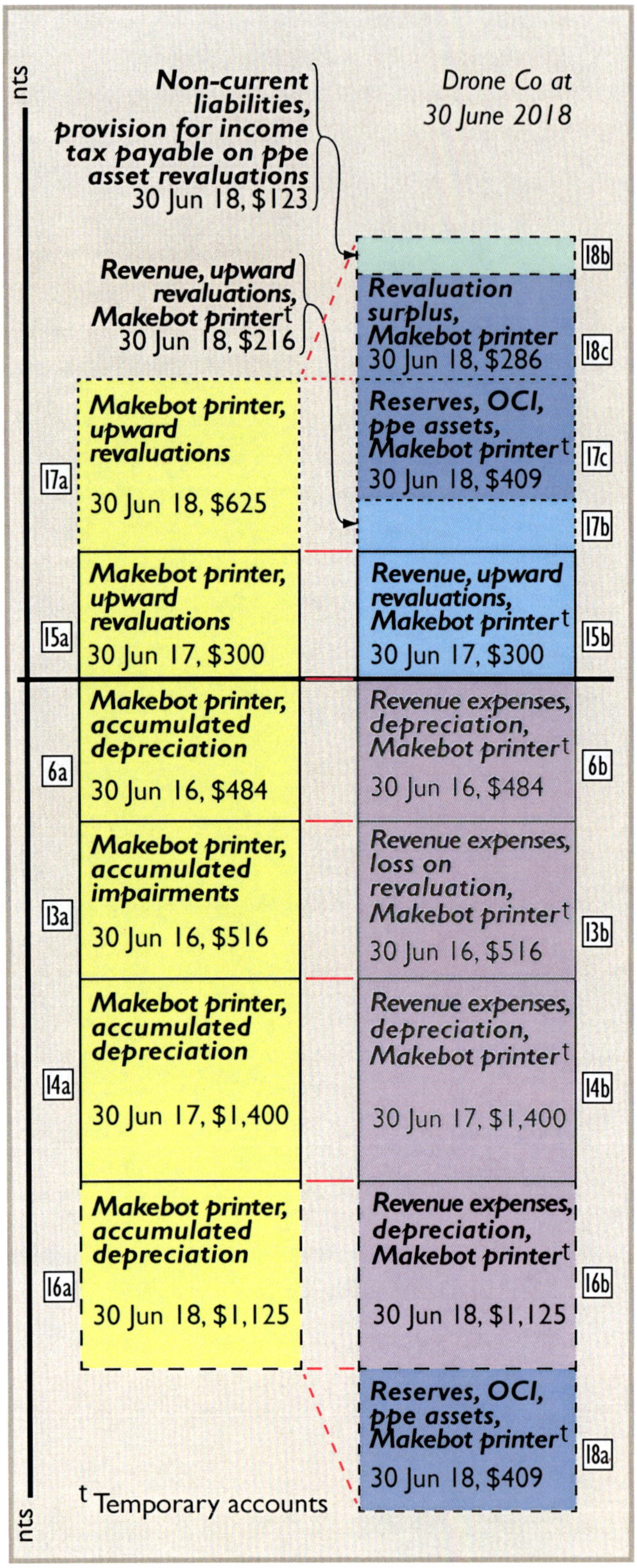

Figure 9.7 Recording depreciation, gains and impairments under the revaluation model for Drone's Makebot 3D printer.

The values of 3D printers was exceptionally volatile between 2015 and 2020. Therefore Drone > revalued its printers at the end of every reporting period in addition to depreciating them.

[6a] and [6b] These two postings were first shown in figure 9.5, and represent the printer's straight-line depreciation during 2015–2016. The carrying amount of the printer as at 30 June 2016 was therefore $7,000 – $484 = $6,516. The outline and text of [6b] (and [13b] and [14b]) are grey to indicate that the accounts which had received those postings had been closed before 30 June 2018.

[13a] At 30 June 2016, the Makebot printer's fair value was assessd as $6,000, an impairment of $516. In order to retain the original cost of the printer in the accounts, depreciation and impairments are in this figure and in figure 9.8 credited to separate contra ledger accounts.

[13b] As there haven't been any earlier revaluations which have resulted in a net gain, this simultaneous balancing posting is a debit to an expenses, loss-on-revaluation account for the printer. This impairment is therefore reported in the 2015–2016 reporting period's profit or loss statement.

[14a] and [14b] The useful life of the printer was unchanged at four years, as was its residual value at $400. Therefore the straight-line depreciation during 2016–2107 was ($6,000 – $400) ÷ 4 = $1,400. The printer's depreciated carrying amount as at 30 June 2017 was therefore $6,000 – $1,400 = $4,600.

[15a] The fair value of the printer as at 30 June 2017 was assessed as $4,900, an upward revaluation of $300 on the $4,600 depreciated value at that same date. To retain the original cost of the printer in the accounts, the amount of the gain was debited to a separate, non-current assets, accumulated upward revaluations ledger account for the printer.

[15b] The balance of the printer's expenses, loss-on-revaluation account before Phil, Drone's bookkeeper, recorded the $300 gain on 30 June 2017 was zero. This was because that account's $516 balance had been closed into Drone's profit or loss summary account as at 30 June 2016. Phil, however, after inspecting the postings in the printer's, expenses, loss-on-revaluation account knew that the printer's net impairment as at 30 June 2017 was $516. The whole of the $300 gain >

> was therefore used to indirectly and partially reverse that net impairment (recorded in 13b by being posted as a revenue which would be reported in the profit or loss statement for 2016–2107.

16a and 16b The depreciation during 2017–2018 was ($4,900 – $400) ÷ 4 = $1,125, and the printer's depreciated carrying amount as at 30 June 2018 was therefore $4,900 – $1,125 = $3,775.

17a The fair value of the printer as at 30 June 2018 was assessed as $4,400, an upward revaluation or gain of $4,400 – $3,775 = $625.

17b By inspecting the printer's loss-on-revaluation account, Phil knew that the net impairment to 30 June 2018 was $516 – $300 = $216. Therefore $216 of the $625 gain was used to offset that earlier loss-on-revaluation expense by being credited to a revenue account.

17c The remaining $625 – $216 = $409 was posted to a reserves, OCI, temporary ledger account for the printer.

18a, 18b and 18c Each of Drone's ppe non-current assets whose carrying amount is being determined under the revaluation model has a reserves, OCI, temporary ledger account to which that asset's net unrealised gains are posted. Each of these OCI ledger accounts is closed as at the end of each reporting period. To close the printer's reserves, OCI, temporary ledger account $409 is debited by posting 18a. That posting is balanced by postings 18b and 18c to permanent accounts.

An entity's realised and unrealised profits should both be reported on the same after-tax basis in the statement of comprehensive income. Assuming an income tax rate of 30%, the income tax payable were the $409 realised would be 30% x $409 = $123. This $123 is credited to a liabilities, provisions, income-tax-payable permanent ledger account for all Drone's ppe assets. (A *provision* is a 'liability of uncertain timing and/or amount'.) Simultaneously box 18c represents $409 – $123 = $286 being credited to a reserves, revaluation surplus, permanent ledger account for the printer.

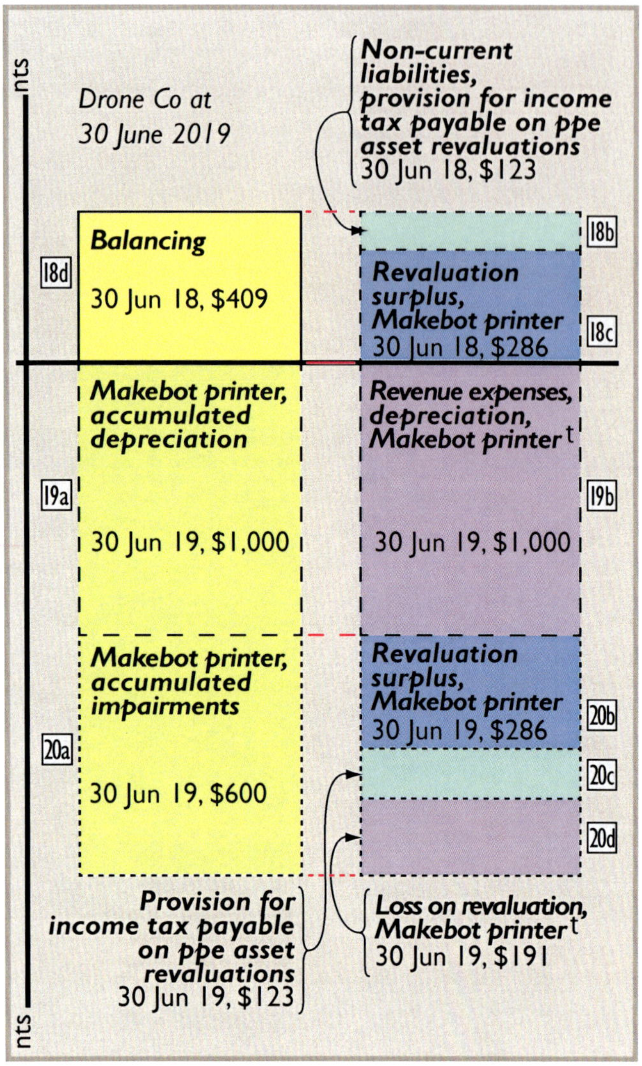

Figure 9.8 Recording depreciation, gains and impairments under the revaluation model for Drone's Makebot 3D printer continued.

18b and 18c These postings were shown in figure 9.7.

18d An account balance to balance 18b and 18c.

19a and 19b The straight-line depreciation of the printer during during 2018–2019 was ($4,400 – $400) ÷ 4 = $1,000, and the printer's carrying amount as at 30 June 2019 was therefore $4,400 – $1,000 = $3,400.

20a The fair value of the printer as at 30 June 2019 was assessed as $2,800, an impairment of $3,400 – $2,800 = $600.

20b, 20c and 20d As at 30 June 2019, but before recording the impairment, there was a net gain in the printer's carrying amount of $286 recorded in the printer's revaluation surplus account 18c. There was also a related $123 provision for income tax payable 18b. The $600 had to first be applied to reverse the 18c net gain and the related provision for income tax payable using postings 20b and 20c. The remaining ($600 – $286 – $123) = $191 was then debited to the to the expenses, loss on revaluation temporary account 20d.

9.3 WRITING-DOWN

Whether a non-current asset is being valued under the cost or the revaluation model, accounting standards which comply with IAS 36 *Impairment of Assets* require that an entity shall assess as at the end of each reporting period whether there's an indication that the asset may be impaired. If so, the entity must estimate the asset's recoverable amount. The *recoverable amount* is the 'higher of the asset's fair value less costs of disposal and the asset's value in use'. The *value in use* is the 'present value of the future cash flows expected to be derived from the asset'. If the recoverable amount is less than the carrying amount, the asset is impaired, and its carrying amount must be reduced to the recoverable amount.

9.4 INTANGIBLE ASSETS

An intangible non-current asset has a value without having an identifiable physical substance, or has a value unrelated to its physical substance (for example, a patent licence is typically worth far more than the worth of the paper and ink which comprises its physical substance). Many intangible non-current assets are a right to receive payments.

Intangible assets can be *identifiable* or *unidentifiable*. Intangible identifiable assets can be individually identified and sold, and include:

- brand names and trademarks
- intellectual property such as patents, copyrights, and registered designs
- rights to franchise fees
- in-house software

- mining, quarrying, and tipping rights and information
- research and development expenditures which are a necessary component of some intangible assets and can therefore be intangible assets themselves.

Goodwill is an example of an intangible, unidentifiable non-current asset. It includes customer loyalty, the entity's reputation, the entity's location, and the loyalty, knowledge and skills of its staff. The market value of an entity can be several times the amount of that entity's net assets (total assets minus total liabilities) because investors believe that components of the entity's goodwill are undervalued or not valued at all in the company's balance sheet. For example, figure 13.3 on page 110 shows that the company JB Hi-Fi Limited's market value was about six times the value of its net assets on 30 June 2015.

Goodwill may be internally generated, or it may be acquired when an entity is bought; it can't be isolated from an entity and sold separately.

9.4.1 Accounting for intangible non-current assets

Accounting for intangible non-current assets has many similarities to accounting for tangible non-current assets. IFRS 3 *Business Combinations*, IAS 36 *Impairment of Assets* and IAS 38 *Intangible Assets* are the most relevant IFRS accounting standards. National accounting standards that comply with them require that:

- The generation of an internally generated intangible asset must be classified into a research phase and a development phase. The costs of the research phase must be debited to expenses. If the costs of the development phase can be reliably measured and if the entity can reliably demonstrate that economic benefit will ensue, the development costs must be debited to an assets account. Because the carrying amount of such an asset may later be able to be reduced through amortisation and/or impairments, the effect of thus recognising an intangible asset is to push the profit-reducing effects of the related expenditures forwards to later years. (*Amortisation* is 'depreciation for intangible non-current assets'.)
- Internally generated brands, mastheads and similar can't be recognised as intangible assets.
- If an intangible asset is acquired, it should be initially valued at cost.
- After initial recognition, intangible assets may be valued under the cost model or the revaluation model (page 62).
- Under the cost model, the asset's carrying amount is its cost less any accumulated amortisation and less any accumulated impairment losses. Under the revaluation model the asset's carrying amount is its fair value at the most recent revaluation less any subsequent accumulated amortisation and less any subsequent accumulated impairment losses. Revaluations of fair value must be made with reference to an active market, and be made sufficiently often that at the end of each reporting period the asset's carrying amount doesn't differ materially from its fair value.
- The useful life of an intangible asset can be finite or indefinite. If finite, the asset can be amortised. If indefinite the recoverable value shall be compared with its carrying amount annually and whenever there's an indication that the asset may be impaired.
- If the useful life of an intangible asset is indefinite, it shall be reviewed each reporting period to see whether the indefinite useful life assessment can continue to be supported.

9.5 ADJUSTED TRIAL BALANCE

After making the postings for any end-of-reporting period adjustment transactions, the adjusted ledger account balances are in manual bookkeeping arithmetically checked by performing the adjusted trial balance calculation shown graphically in figure 9.9.

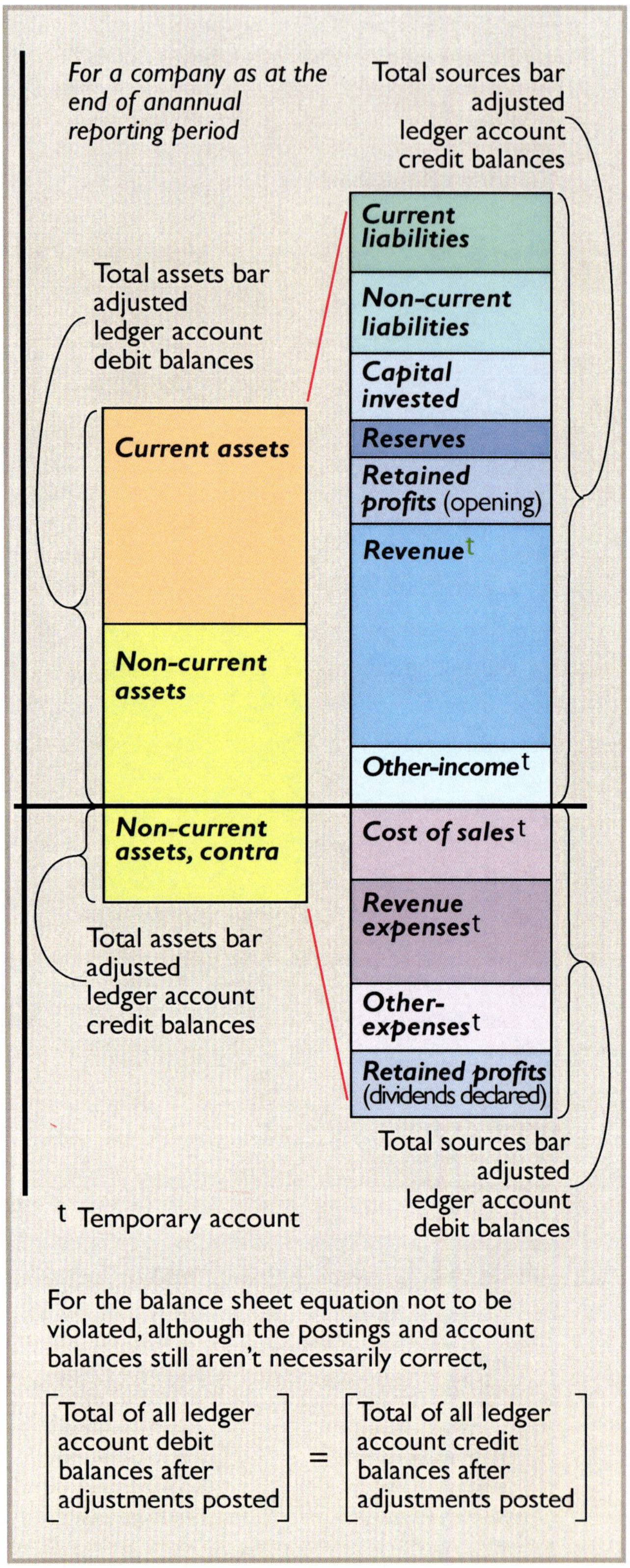

9.9 A graphical representation of an adjusted trial balance. The balances of the ledger accounts totalled are those current on the recording date after the adjusting transactions of the types introduced in chapter 8 and earlier in this chapter have been posted.

9.6 CLOSING LEDGER ACCOUNT BALANCES

Figure 9.6 shows how the balance of a ledger account is closed. As explained on pages 10 to 13, an entity's income and expenses for a reporting period are posted into temporary income and expenses ledger accounts. In manual bookkeeping the resulting temporary account balances are then closed as at the end of each reporting period into a temporary profit or loss summary account. That temporary account balance is then closed into the retained profits permanent account as shown in figures 3.4 and 3.5. For income-tax-paying entities, the temporary account closings described above don't directly produce a measure of the retained profit or loss for the reporting period because the income tax payable as at the end of the period must be subtracted. Amounts of other comprehensive income should similarly be reported net of the income tax which would be payable were the amounts realised as at the end of the reporting period.

Income tax is the subject of the next chapter.

Chapter 10

INCOME TAX

The successful movement to harmonise the IFRS and national accounting standards is mentioned on page 23. There is little evidence of a similarly successful push to harmonise the tax law of nations, in part because this is an area in which nations compete. This chapter's explanation of income tax is based upon that which applies in Australia, and is, I hope, relevant to you the reader.

IAS 12 *Income Taxes* is the applicable international accounting standard, but it will not be referred to in this chapter's explanations.

Income tax was first introduced in December 1798 in Great Britain at a rate of 0.83% to pay for the war against France. Income tax is now levied at much higher rates on individuals and other specified types of entity in the majority of countries.

Income-tax payers are those 'individuals and other types of entity which are levied for income tax'. Such entities have to report their income-taxable income to the taxing authority as at the end of each income tax year, and pay any income tax owing. (An *income tax year* was defined on page 6, and is 'one of the successive 12-months periods for which an income-tax payer is required to lodge a tax return'.) Income tax calculations are therefore simpler if an entity's annual reporting periods and income tax years coincide, and this is assumed in this chapter.

This chapter introduces income tax without attempting to cover its many complexities by:

- outlining which entities can be liable to pay income tax
- showing how income tax is calculated and reported
- discussing how companies, shareholders, partners and sole traders are taxed.

10.1 IDENTIFYING TAXPAYERS

Those legal entities which are liable to pay income tax typically include:

- **individuals**
- **private and public companies** A company is a separate legal entity and therefore able to be taxed
- **superannuation funds**
- **special entities** These are other types of entity which have special income tax arrangements

Entities which are not usually income-tax payers include:

- **those entities which serve some social, community or philanthropic purpose** These typically include: charities, educational institutions, societies, associations and clubs associated with the arts or sport, and hospitals and health insurers
- **government authorities**
- **sole traders and partnerships** These entities aren't separate legal entities and therefore can't be assessed for income tax. Instead these entities' incomes flow-through to their owner individuals. These individuals are then liable to pay income tax on their incomes from all sources as described on pages 76 and 77.
- **trusts** It's the beneficiaries of trusts who usually pay the income-tax .

10.2 CALCULATING INCOME TAX

As at the end of an income tax year an income-tax-paying entity calculates any income tax payable on its activities during that income year using equation 10.a:

$$\text{Income tax payable} = \text{Taxable income} \times (\text{income tax rate} + \text{levies and surcharges}) - \text{Tax offsets}$$

Equation 10.a

In equation 10.a taxable income is calculated using equation 10.b below

Taxable income = Assessable income + grants − Deductions

Equation 10.b

As equations 10a and 10b show, there can be up to seven variables involved in calculating an entity's income tax payable: the income tax rate, the assessable income, and any grants, deductions, offsets, levies and surcharges. These variables are introduced below.

10.2.1 Income tax rate

The percentage rate of income tax may be fixed for some types of income tax payer (typically companies). For individuals the tax rate is typically higher for higher ranges (brackets) of taxable income. The rates for different types of taxable income may be different; for example, investment income might be taxed at a lower rate than non-investment income.

Levies and surcharges are typically temporary increases to the income tax rate.

10.2.2 Assessable income

In equation 10.b *assessable income* is the only income excluding grants which is income-taxable under the tax law. The tax law may specify types of income which aren't assessable; for example, an entity's earlier overpayments of income tax which the taxing authority has refunded during the income tax year for which the assessable income is being determined. Therefore although an entity's assessable income is determined in much the same way as revenue and other-income, the two amounts aren't necessarily equal.

10.2.3 Grants

Taxable income can be increased by grants which also increase the income tax payable.

10.2.4 Deductions

Deductions are 'costs or outgoings incurred in gaining or producing assessable income, or carrying on a business for gaining or producing assessable income which are allowable under the tax law'. Costs or outgoings usually can't be deducted to the extent that they're: of capital or of a capital nature, private or domestic, incurred in gaining or producing income which isn't income-taxable, or non-deductible under the tax law. However, the amounts of non-income taxes which an entity is obliged to pay are usually deductible.

Non-deductible losses or outgoings of capital or of a capital nature are not incurred to produce income, and are typically non-recurring. When such outgoings are incurred to bring an asset into existence, that asset will be of a lasting nature, and relate not to the operations of the entity, but to its establishment, organisation, enlargement, extension or protection.

The amounts of an entity's allowable income tax deductions in equation 10.b aren't necessarily the same as the amounts of its expenses determined according to a nation's accounting standards. For example, the costs of entertaining suppliers and customers are expenses under accounting standards, but may not be allowable deductions under the tax law. Similarly, the deductions resulting from the declines in value of assets claculated under the tax law may be different and more prescribed than the determinations of depreciation, etc. under the accounting standards.

The differences between the amounts of expenses and the amounts of deductions for the same period reflect the different purposes of a nation's accounting standards and its tax law. The former are designed to attempt to ensure that an entity's financial statements present a true and fair financial picture of that entity, the latter are ideally designed to raise the revenue forecast in the national budget, support the implementation of government policies, and minimise the costs and argument involved in tax collection.

Tax losses

When an income-tax payer's total deductions exceed that taxpayer's assessable income plus any grants for an income tax year, that taxpayer incurs a *tax loss*, a negative taxable income. (Tax offsets don't reduce assessable income and therefore don't contribute to tax losses.)

Generally a national taxing authority only makes an income tax refund payment to a taxpayer when that taxpayer has paid too much income tax, not when a taxpayer's taxable income is negative. Instead a taxpayer's tax loss is typically carried forward to use in future income tax years as an extra deduction from assessable income.

10.2.5 Tax offsets

Tax offsets (sometimes referred to as *rebates*) are direct reductions to the income tax payable, not to taxable income.

10.3 TAX RETURNS

Typically within a specified period after the end of its income tax year every income-tax payer must complete and lodge with the taxing authority an income tax return and pay any income tax owing. The taxpayer is usually held responsible for the accuracy of the return. There are penalties for incorrect and late returns, and for failing to lodge a return. An entity must therefore ensure that its accounting system properly records tax-related amounts.

10.4 COMPANY INCOME TAX

An entity which is a company is a separate legal and taxable entity and is therefore required to pay by the due date the income tax owing for each income tax year calculated according to the tax law. A company's retained profit for a reporting period is then the accounting profit for that period less the income tax payable for the period less the dividends declared during the period.

10.5 TAXING DIVIDENDS

A company can pay an owner wages or a salary, reimburse expenses incurred by an owner while working for the company, and pay an owner for goods and services supplied by the owner to the company. Payments may also be made to the owners of a company by way of dividends. A dividend is a distribution of cash, the company's own shares or other assets to eligible owners. Although typically a dividend is a distribution of after-tax profits to owners (also called *shareholders* or *stockholders*), the accounting standards and prudence may limit the amount of a dividend.

10.5.1 Tax treatment of dividends

Because the taxable incomes of non-corporate businesses such as sole traders and partnerships are, as will be explained, taxed only once, some countries have what's called an *imputation scheme.* Such schemes prevent company dividends being taxed twice, first when the company pays income tax on that company's taxable income less offsets, and second when income tax is levied on the taxable income of each of that company's owners (shareholders) where that income includes the dividends received by the owner from that company during the subject income tax year.

Imputation and franking

To avoid dividends being double taxed they're usually *franked*, meaning 'exempted from' being taxed to some extent. In this context a *franked dividend* is a 'distribution on which the company has already paid an amount of income tax on behalf of the shareholder'.

For example, a shareholder received a dividend of \$10,000 during 2015–16, the dividend was franked at 30%, and the company income tax rate was a flat 30%. (When the franked percentage of the dividend and the company income tax rate are equal, the dividend is typically called *fully franked.*) Thus to pay the shareholder the \$10,000 cash, the company had to have earned a before income tax amount of

$$\frac{\$10{,}000}{(100\% - 30\%)} = \$14{,}286$$

The shareholder thus received $10,000 in cash on which income tax of $4,286 had already been paid by the company. The receipt of the dividend therefore increased the shareholder's taxable income by $14,286, but the shareholder also gained a tax offset of $4,286.

If the franked percentage is less than the company's income tax rate percentage, the dividend is *partly franked*. Dividends which don't provide any tax offset are described as *unfranked*.

10.6 TAXING PARTNERSHIPS

Figure 10.1 illustrates the method of accounting for partnerships in which a capital (equivalent to capital invested) account, and a current (equivalent to retained or undistributed profits) account is kept for each partner. Partners can withdraw cash from a partnership using drawings.

Partnerships aren't taxpayers, but are usually required to lodge tax returns. So that a partnership's profits are taxed, as at the end of each income tax year, the partnership's taxable income or tax loss for that income tax year is allocated (flows through) to each partner according to the relevant agreement made between the partners (the partnership agreement). Each partner's allocation is then notionally added to that partner's taxable incomes, tax losses and tax offsets from all other sources. Each partner's income tax payable is then calculated on that aggregate.

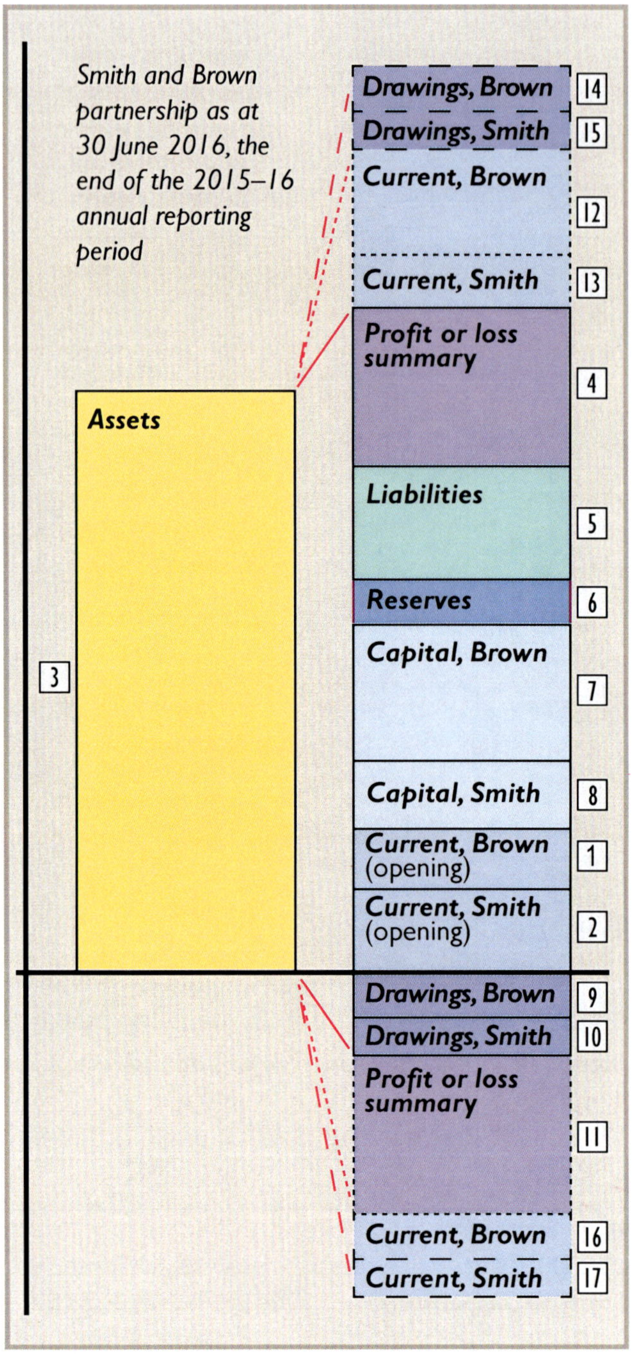

Figure 10.1 Accounting for a partnership, here between Smith and Brown.

1 and 2 These boxes represent respectively the balances of Brown's and Smith's current (retained profits) accounts as at the opening of the 2015–2016 annual reporting period.

3 to 10 These boxes represent the balances of these temporary and permanent accounts as at the end of the 2015–2016 annual reporting period.

Note that the balance of the profit or loss summary account 4 is determined according >

> to the accounting standards. This amount is not necessarily the same as the total of the partnership's taxable income or tax loss for 2015–2016 calculated according to the tax law, and which is notionally distributed to the partners and thus included in their individual taxable incomes.

[11] The debit posting required to close account balance [4] to zero.

[12] and [13] The credit postings which balance posting [11]. The Brown and Smith partnership agreement specifies that annual profits be split 2/3 to Brown, 1/3 to Smith. Therefore the amount of posting [12] is double that of [13]. This split reflects the partners' respective initial investments in the partnership shown in balances [7] and [8].

[14] and [15] These debit postings close the account balances [9] and [10] to zero.

[16] and [17] These debit postings balance postings [14] and [15].

After balancing as at 30 June 2016, the balance of Brown's current (retained profits) account is represented by the total of the box heights [1] + [12] – [16]. Similarly the balance of Smith's current (retained profits) account is represented by the total of the box heights [2] + [13] – [17].

10.7 TAXING SOLE TRADERS

One owner can own one or more different sole trader entities. These entities aren't income-taxable. For each income tax year for such an owner the assessable income plus grants minus the deductions for each entity is notionally aggregated with the owner's assessable income less deductions from other sources. The owner then pays income tax as an individual on his or her total taxable income adjusted for any available tax losses. Any tax offsets can also be utilised.

Chapter 11

FINANCIAL STATEMENTS

This chapter explains how financial statements are derived and what they report.

Financial statements are usually required to be produced and communicated at least annually, and may be required to be what may be called *general-purpose*, that is 'intended to meet the needs of users who are not in a position to require an entity to prepare reports tailored to their particular information needs'.

IAS 1 *Presentation of Financial Statements* states that a complete set of financial statements should include:

1. **a statement of profit or loss and other comprehensive income** for the reporting period. This statement may be allowed to be separated into a statement of profit or loss, and a statement of comprehensive income which begins with the profit or loss
2. **a statement of financial position** (**balance sheet**) as at the end of the reporting period
3. **a statement of changes in equity** is a detailed statement of the changes in capital invested, reserves, retained profits and, as will be explained, non-controlling interests during the reporting period
4. **a statement of cash flows** is a statement showing cash receipts and payments during the reporting period
5. **notes** which comprise a summary of the significant accounting policies applied in producing the financial statements, etc.

The financial statements 1 to 4 above may be required to list the previous reporting period's account balances alongside the current period's.

In this chapter's explanations I have chosen to use as examples the financial statements and related information published in the 2014–15 annual report of the Australian public (joint-stock) company Harvey Norman Holdings Limited (HVN). I show summarised and graphical versions of these statements in order to better explain particular features. Harvey Norman's annual reports can be viewed in full at <*www.harveynormanholdings.com.au/pdf_files/*>. Harvey Norman's annual reporting periods run from 1 July to the following 30 June.

I selected Harvey Norman as the example entity for this chapter because I wanted to use real, not fictitious, financial statements which were readily available. I thank Harvey Norman for permission to copy and use parts of its 2014–15 annual report in this book.

Non-controlling interests

Harvey Norman Holdings Limited is the majority shareholder in several other companies. The minority shareholders in such subsidiary companies have no control over those subsidiary companies, and are called *non-controlling interests* in the financial statements of the parent company.

The Australian accounting standards require that the financial statements of parent companies be consolidated to include the full amounts of the assets, liabilities, equity, income expenses and cash flows of both the parent company and its subsidiary companies.

Because amounts in a parent company's financial statements related to non-controlling (minority) interests are typically relatively tiny and not part of many company financial statements, they're printed in grey in this chapter.

11.1 STATEMENT OF PROFIT OR LOSS

Figure 11.1 explains how the profit or loss and balance sheet financial statements are derived. A profit or loss statement (also called an *income statement*) is essentially an expanded version of the profit equation,

Income – Related expenses = Profit (or loss)

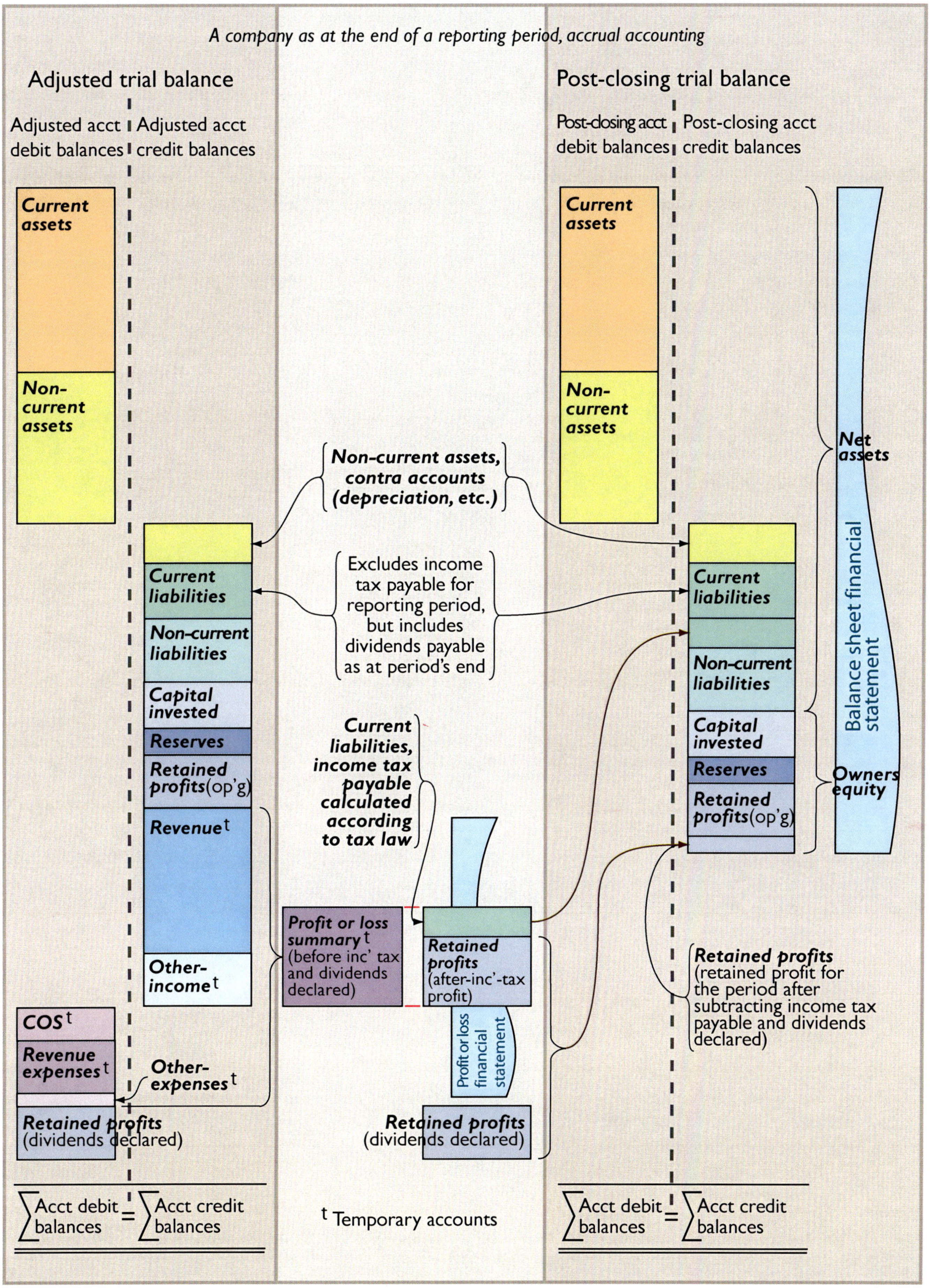
A company as at the end of a reporting period, accrual accounting
Adjusted trial balance
Adjusted acct debit balances
Adjusted acct credit balances
Current assets
Non-current assets
Non-current assets, contra accounts (depreciation, etc.)
Current liabilities
Non-current liabilities
Capital invested
Reserves
Retained profits(op'g)
Revenue t
Other-income t
COS t
Revenue expenses t
Other-expenses t
Retained profits (dividends declared)
Excludes income tax payable for reporting period, but includes dividends payable as at period's end
Current liabilities, income tax payable calculated according to tax law
Profit or loss summary t (before inc' tax and dividends declared)
Retained profits (after-inc'-tax profit)
Profit or loss financial statement
Retained profits (dividends declared)
Post-closing trial balance
Post-closing acct debit balances
Post-closing acct credit balances
Net assets
Owners equity
Balance sheet financial statement
Retained profits (retained profit for the period after subtracting income tax payable and dividends declared)
∑Acct debit balances = ∑Acct credit balances
t Temporary accounts

>

> **Figure 11.1** How the account balances of an adjusted trial balance are closed and then processed to produce a company's profit or loss and balance sheet financial statements. This balance chart assumes that there weren't any changes in reserves during the period, and that there weren't any non-controlling interests. Closing accounts in manual bookkeeping is detailed on pages 67 and 72.

Note that the total of the dividends declared during the reporting period is subtracted from the after-tax profit in calculating the retained profits as at the end of the period. Also the retained profits as at the end of a period equals the retained profits at the beginning of the period plus the retained profit (singular) for the period.

In the labels *acct* is a contraction for *account*, inc' is a contraction for *income*, and *op'g* is a contraction of *opening*.

As figures 11.2 and 11.3 show for a company, here Harvey Norman, the profit or loss statement records those changes to the ledger account balances during the reporting period which combine to yield the organisation's accounting profit after income tax. (Profit after income tax = Revenue + Other-income – (Cost of sales + Revenue expenses + Other-expenses + Income tax payable for that reporting period.)

Accounting standards may require that expenses and costs should be analysed either by:

- **nature** (what they are without reference to their functions within the business); or by
- **function**, what they are intended to achieve.

These alternatives were introduced on page 16. The expenses in Harvey Norman's statement of profit or loss shown in figure 11.2 are analysed by function.

Figure 11.2 A summary of HVN's profit or loss statement for 2014–15. The same reference number within a rectangular box is applied to a particular control account balance and its explanation in this caption.

	HARVEY NORMAN HOLDINGS LIMITED PROFIT OR LOSS STATEMENT FOR THE YEAR ENDED 30 JUNE 2015	CONSOLIDATED June 2015 $'000		CONSOLIDATED June 2014 $'000
	Sales revenue from sale of products	1,617,151		1,513,662
	Cost of sales	(1,126,894)		(1,064,892)
	Gross profit	490,257		448,770
1a	Non-sales revenues	1,047,432		993,155
	Other-income	53,854		40,469
1b	Distribution expenses	(18,744)		(15,114)
1b	Marketing expenses	(370,124)		(348,952)
1b	Occupancy expenses	(229,081)		(233,881)
1b	Administrative expenses	(447,198)		(427,604)
1b	Finance costs	(32,872)		(36,437)
	Other expenses from ordinary activities	(124,082)		(136,846)
1c	Share of net profit of joint ventures	8,659		17,501
	Profit before income tax	378,100		301,061
1d	Income tax payable	(109,186)		(88,823)
1e	**Profit after tax for the year**	268,914		212,238
	Attributable to:			
	Owners of the Parent	268,095		211,695
1f	Non-controlling interests	819		543
1h		268,914		212,238
1i	Basic earnings per HVN share	24.51cents		19.69 cents
	Dividends declared per share for the year	20.0 cents	1l	14 cents 1k
	Special dividend declared per share	14.0 cents	1m	

1a HVN is a retailer, a franchiser, and a property owner and developer. The non-sales revenues consist mainly of fees, rent and interest from franchisees; and rent, interest and dividends from other entities.

1b Expenses analysed and reported by function.

1c $8,659,000 is HVN's share of the total income less related expenses before tax earned by the joint ventures in which HVN was involved during 2014–15.

1d The income tax payable on HVN's activities during 2014–15 after subtracting any offsets and carried-forward tax losses.

1e The profit before tax less the income tax payable equals the profit after tax.

1f The amount of profit after tax attributable to non-controlling interests is repeated in the statement of changes in equity.

1h HVN owns the majority, but not all, of the shares in two companies. 100% of the income and expenses of those two companies are included in the amounts listed in this profit or loss statement. The $268,914,000 profit after tax includes all the profit after tax made by these two companies. $819,000 of this profit (stated in 1f) is claimable by the non-controlling (minority, non-HVN) interests in the two companies, and the profit after tax attributable to the HVN parent is $268,095,000.

1i The 24.51 cents was obtained by dividing $268,095,000 by 1,093,626,019 (the weighted average number of ordinary shares as at 30 June 2015).

1k The 14 cents of dividends per share is the interim dividend for 2013-14 of 6 cents per share declared on 28 February 2014 and paid on 5 May 2014, plus the final dividend for 2013–14 of 8 cents per share declared on 29 August 2014 and paid on 1 December 2014.

1l An interim dividend of 9 cents per share was declared on 27 February 2015. The $99,954,000 was paid on 4 May 2015. A final dividend of 11 cents per share was declared 2014–15 on 28 August 2015, with the $122.17m being paid on 1 December 2015.

1m A special dividend of 14 cents per share was announced on 25 November 2014 and paid on 30 December 2014.

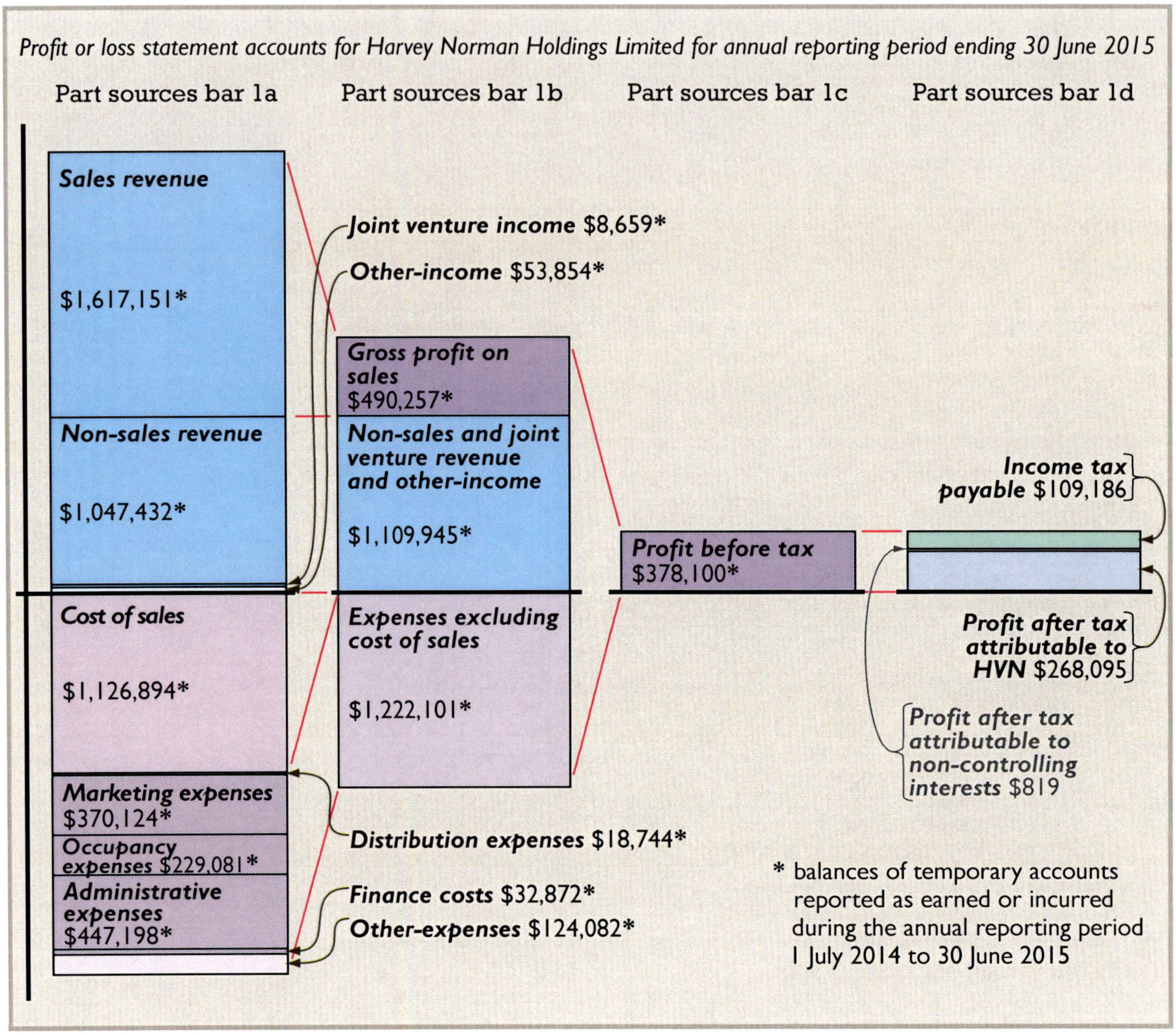

Figure 11.3 The calculation of Harvey Norman's profit after income tax for 2014–15. The amounts shown are in thousands of dollars. Thus $1,617,151 represents $1,617,151,000.

In part sources bars 1a, 1b and 1c the amounts of income, expenses and profit include 100% of the amounts of income, expenses and profit of two companies in which HVN owns the majority of shares and therefore the controlling interest.

Part sources bar 1a Sales revenue is revenue from sales of goods and associated services from stores HVN runs and to stores run by franchisees. Non-sales revenue is mainly franchise fees, rent and interest received.

Part sources bar 1b Gross profit is the accounting term for the period's sales revenue less the COS expenses of earning that revenue.

Part sources bar 1c The profit before tax includes HVN's share of the income received from joint ventures and 100% of the profit before income tax earned by the two companies in which HVN has majority controlling interests.

Part sources bar 1d The income tax payable is that payable on HVN's taxable income for 2014–15 adjusted for any tax losses and tax offsets.

The profit after tax of $212,238,000 comprises $268,095,000 attributable to the HVN parent plus $819,000 attributable to the non-controlling (minority) interests in the two companies in which HVN owns the majority of, but not all, the shares.

11.2 STATEMENT OF COMPREHENSIVE INCOME

A statement of comprehensive income (figures 11.4 and 11.5) reports both realised and unrealised income (profit), and starts by stating the after-income-tax profit or loss from the profit or loss statement for the reporting period in a single line. The statement then lists the entity's items of other comprehensive income. An item of other comprehensive income:

- isn't earned or expended through a business's ordinary activities (and isn't therefore a revenue or a revenue expense), nor is it earned or expended to earn other-income
- has a cost or value that can be reliably measured at the reporting date
- has yet to be realised, but when it is, its magnitude is likely differ from that stated at the previous reporting date, and any difference is likely to be due in part to factors outside the control of the entity
- is one accounting standards require:
  a. not be included in the profit or loss statement because it hasn't been realised and its amount when later realised is uncertain
  b. be recognised (recorded) in the statement of comprehensive income and in the balance sheet because there is a probability of an associated economic benefit flowing to or from the business. (An economic benefit results in an increase in owners equity which doesn't result from an increase in capital invested, and is balanced by an increase in assets or a decrease in liabilities.)

Accounting standards may describe five types of income and expense which must be recorded as other comprehensive income:

1. those arising from translating the financial statements of a foreign operation. For example, if the carrying amounts of assets owned in a foreign country remain unchanged when measured in the foreign currency, but the foreign currency declines in values relative to the home (functional) currency of the owning entity, that entity would suffer a translation loss
2. those arising from cash flow hedges. A *hedge* is a 'counterbalancing transaction entered into to protect against a severe loss'. For example, a trader may wish to buy something in the future which is priced in a foreign currency. To guard against the possibility of a substantial loss if the price of the something increases and/or the foreign currency increases in rate relative to the trader's home (functional) currency, the trader can hedge. For example, the trader could take out a futures contract to buy the something at a future date for an agreed price quoted in the trader's home currency. Assuming that the expectations are that the something's price in the foreign currency will rise and that the foreign currency will revalue upwards relative to the trader's home currency, the agreed price of the something in the futures contract will be higher than the price when the hedge is contracted, but at least for the trader the price will be known and is fixed.
3. those arising from revaluations of the non-current tangible assets of property, plant and equipment. (explained on pages 61 to 67), and from revaluations of intangible assets (explained on pages 67 and 68).
4. those arising from changes in the fair values of available-for-sale financial assets such as cash, shares, contracts or contractual rights
5. actuarial gains and losses on defined benefit plans. A defined benefit plan is one in which the employer promises a specifed lump sum and/or pension when an employee retires. The present value of the liability arising from a defined benefit plan is calculated using assumptions, for example on future interest rates. As it becomes necessary to update those assumptions, the resulting gain or loss is posted to other comprehensive income.

Accounting standards require that items of other comprehensive income be recorded in reserves accounts, not in income accounts, because when those items are realised in the future their amounts will probably be different.

A statement of comprehensive income should also report the amounts of tax which would have been payable had the amounts of other comprehensive income been realised on the reporting date.

	HARVEY NORMAN HOLDINGS LIMITED STATEMENT OF COMPREHENSIVE INCOME FOR THE YEAR ENDED 30 JUNE 2015	CONSOLIDATED June 2015 $'000	CONSOLIDATED June 2014 $'000
2a	**Profit after tax for the year**	268,914	212,238
	Items that may be reclassified subsequently to profit or loss		
2b	Foreign currency translation	(3,560)	28,529
2c	Net fair value gains on available-for-sale investments	1,302	829
2d	Net movement on cash flow hedges	4,699	3,857
2e	Income tax effect on net movement of cash flow hedges	(1,406)	(1,143)
	Items that will not be reclassified subsequently to profit or loss because these are valued in the balance sheet at original cost		
2f	Fair value revaluation of land and buildings	13,115	27,969
2h	Income tax effect on fair value revaluation of land and buildings	(2,055)	(8,624)
2i	**Other comprehensive income for the year (net of tax)**	12,095	51,417
2k	**Total comprehensive income for the year (net of tax)**	281,009	263,655
2l	Total comprehensive income attributable to:		
	Owners of the Parent	278,433	259,524
	Non-controlling interests	2,576	4,131
		281,009	263,655

Figure 11.4 A summary of Harvey Norman's statement of comprehensive income for 2014–15. The reference numbers within the square and rectangular boxes refer only to the amounts as at 30 June 2015.

This financial statement reports the realised profit and unrealised profit (other comprehensive income) for the annual reporting period 2014–2015. To report the amount of unrealised profit on the same basis as the realised profit (that is after subtracting income tax), the amounts of income tax which would be payable were the unrealised profits able to be realised on 30 June 2015 have been subtracted.

Amounts down to and including total 2h are for 100% of both HVN and the two companies in which HVN owns majorities, but not 100%, of the shares.

2a Restates the realised profit after income tax, amount 1e and 1h from figure 11.2.

2b This loss results from adverse changes in national currency rates. For example, the value of the non-current assets of one of the foreign companies in which HVN has a controlling, but not 100% interest, didn't change during 2014–15, but the foreign country's currency devalued against HVN's home (functional) currency, the Australian dollar. Then HVN would incur a foreign currency translation loss.

2c This gain resulted from revaluing available-for-sale investments such as shares at their fair values as at the reporting date.

2d This gain resulted from currency movements which were more favourable than those on which the hedges were based.

2e The income tax which would have been payable had 2d been realised.

2f This increase in reserves arises from revaluations of the carrying amounts of tangible ppe assets as described in subsection 9.2.2.

2h The income tax which would have been payable had unrealised income 2e been realised. >

> [2i] The total unrealised profit net of income tax for 2014–15.

[2k] The total of HVN's realised ([2a]) and unrealised ([2i]) after tax profits for 2014–15 . This amount includes 100% of the profit and the other comprehensive income earned by the two companies in which HVN has controlling interests. >

> [2l] Of the $281,009,000, $278,433,000 is attributable to HVN, and $2,576,000 is attributable to the non-controlling (minority) interests in the two companies in which HVN has the majority of the shares.

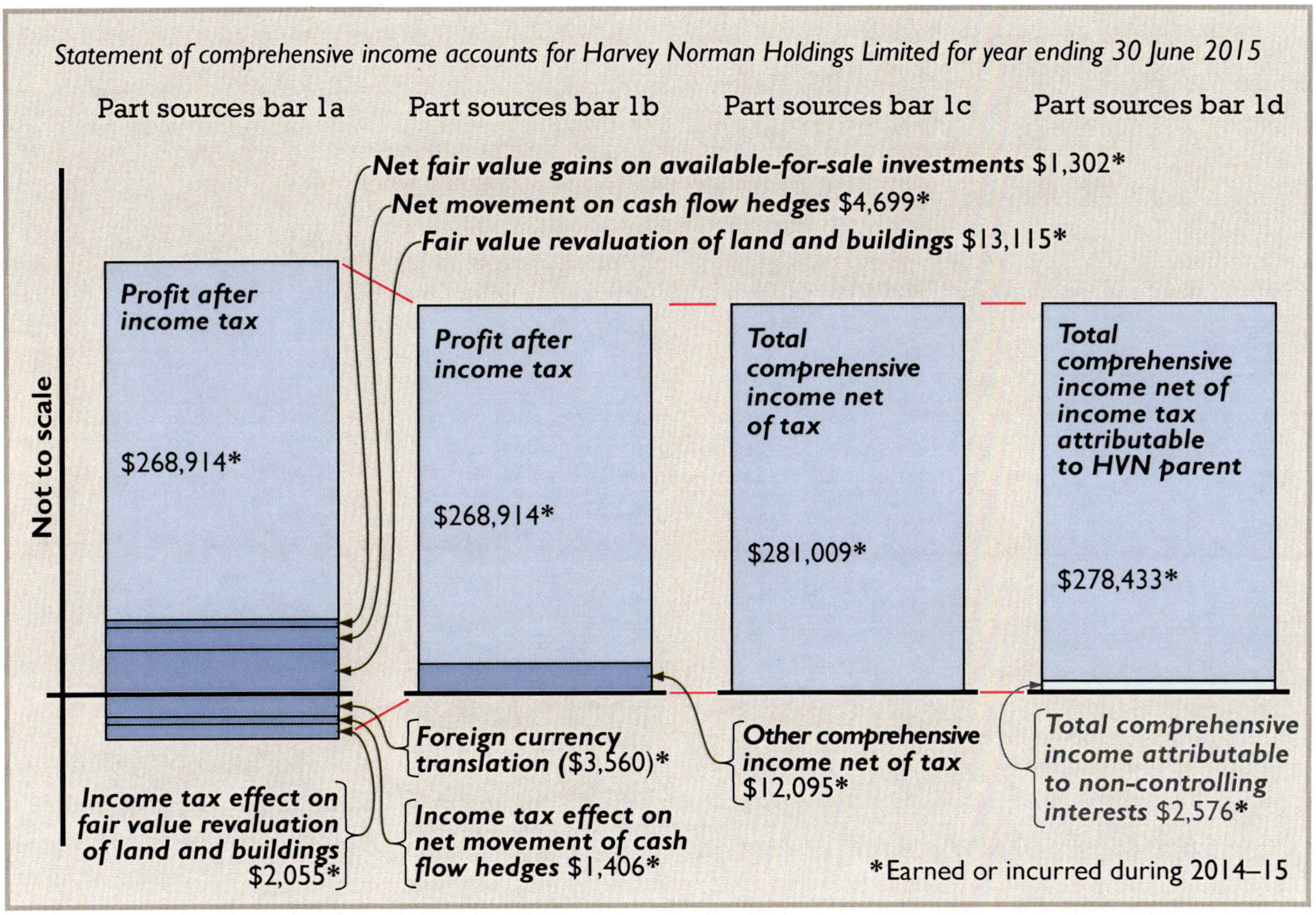

Figure 11.5 The calculation of Harvey Norman's total comprehensive income for 2014–15. The amounts in part sources bars 1a, 1b and 1c include 100% of the after-tax profit and other comprehensive income of the two companies in which Harvey Norman has a majority shareholding.

Part sources bar 1a The comprehensive income is the realised income including any adjustments (explained in chapters 8 and 9) less income tax payable for a period plus the unrealised income for the same period less the estimated income tax payable were those amounts of unrealised income realised at the end of the 2014–15 annual reporting period.

Part sources bar 1d The $2,576,000 of total comprehensive income attributable to the non-controlling interests in the two companies in which HVN has majority controlling interests consists of $819,000 of realised income ([1f] in figure 11.2) and $1,757,000 of unrealised income ([3b] in figure 11.6).

11.3 STATEMENT OF CHANGES IN EQUITY

The statement of changes in equity acts as a bridge between the statement of comprehensive income and the balance sheet. The statement of changes in equity (figures 11.6 and 11.7) isolates the changes in the entity's equity during the reporting period. These changes are of typically three types:

1. changes to capital invested (for a company its share capital)
2. changes to reserves already detailed in the statement of other comprehensive income
3. the change in retained profits. For a company this change equals the profit after tax less the dividends declared during the reporting period. (HVN uses *dividends paid* which is equivalent to *dividends declared* because those dividends are paid in the same reporting period in which they're declared.)

If the entity has majority interests in subsidiary companies, changes in these three amounts also change the parent entity's equity.

	HARVEY NORMAN HOLDINGS LIMITED STATEMENT OF CHANGES IN EQUITY FOR THE YEAR ENDED 30 JUNE 2015	CONSOLIDATED June 2015 $'000	CONSOLIDATED June 2014 $'000
3a	**Total equity at 1 July of HVN and non-controlling interests**	2,491,106	2,363,855
3b	**Other comprehensive income**		
3c	Reserves, revaluation of land and buildings HVN	11,060	16,639
	Non-controlling interests, revaluation of land and buildings	–	2,706
3d	Reserves, reverse expired or realised cash flow hedge reserves HVN	12	47
3e	Reserves, currency translation differences HVN	(5,317)	27,647
3f	Non-controlling interests, currency translation differences	1,757	882
3h	Reserves, fair value of interest rate swaps HVN	3,255	2,680
3i	Reserves, fair value of forward foreign exchange contracts HVN	26	(13)
3k	Reserves, fair value of available-for-sale financial assets HVN	1,302	829
	Other comprehensive income including that attributable to non-controlling interests (2i in figure 11.4)	12,095	51,417
	Profit for the year HVN (from PorL, figure 11.2)	268,095	211,695
	Ditto attributable to non-controlling interest (from PorL, figure 11.2)	819	543
	Profit for the year HVN plus non-controlling interests (2a in figure 11.4)	268,914	212,238
	Total comprehensive income for the year HVN plus non-controlling interests(2k in figure 11.4)	281,009	263,655
	Reserves, employee equity benefits reserve, net cost of share based payments HVN	217	420
	Reserves, aquisition reserve, acquisition of non-controlling interest	–	(7,313)
3l	Shares issued pursuant to Renouncement Rights Offer	120,718	–
	Non-controlling interests, aquisition of non-controlling interest	–	(16,513)
	Non-controlling interests, dividends and distributions to members	(2,526)	(1,455)
3m	Dividends paid to HVN shareholders	(333,664)	(111,543)
	Total equity at 30 June of HVN and non-controlling interests	2,556,860	2,491,106

Figure 11.6 A summary of HVN's statement of changes in equity for 2014–15. >

> [3a] The $2,491,106,000 of total equity is the amount as at 30 June 2014.

[3b] to [3k] These amounts are of other comprehensive income for HVN during 2014–2015, and have been introduced in the figure 11.4 statement of comprehensive income.

[3c] The $11,060 is net of income tax and is the difference $13,115 – $2,055 from [2f] and [2h] in figure 11.4. This increase in reserves arises from the upward revaluation of the carrying amounts of tangible assets as described in subsection 9.2.2.

[3e] and [3f] Currency translation differences arise from translating the financial statements of foreign operations. The difference $5,317 – $1,757 = $3,560 is repeated as [2b] in figure 11.4.

[3h] An interest-rate swap is one in which the interest on a loan or loan facility is changed from a fixed rate to a floating rate or vice versa.

[3k] Results from revaluations as at the reporting date of the carrying amounts of available-for-sale financial assets.

[3l] HVN offered shares to shareholders at a discount during 2014–15. The acceptances increased HVN's capital invested by $120,718,000.

[3m] The dividends declared between 30 June 2014 and 30 June 2015 (here called *dividends paid*) totalled $333.664,000, and comprised:

- an 8c ($84,986,000) per share final dividend for 2013–14 paid on 1 December 2014,
- a special dividend of 14c ($148,724,000) per share paid on 30 December 2014,
- an interim 2014–15 dividend of 9c ($99,954,000) paid on 4 May 2015.

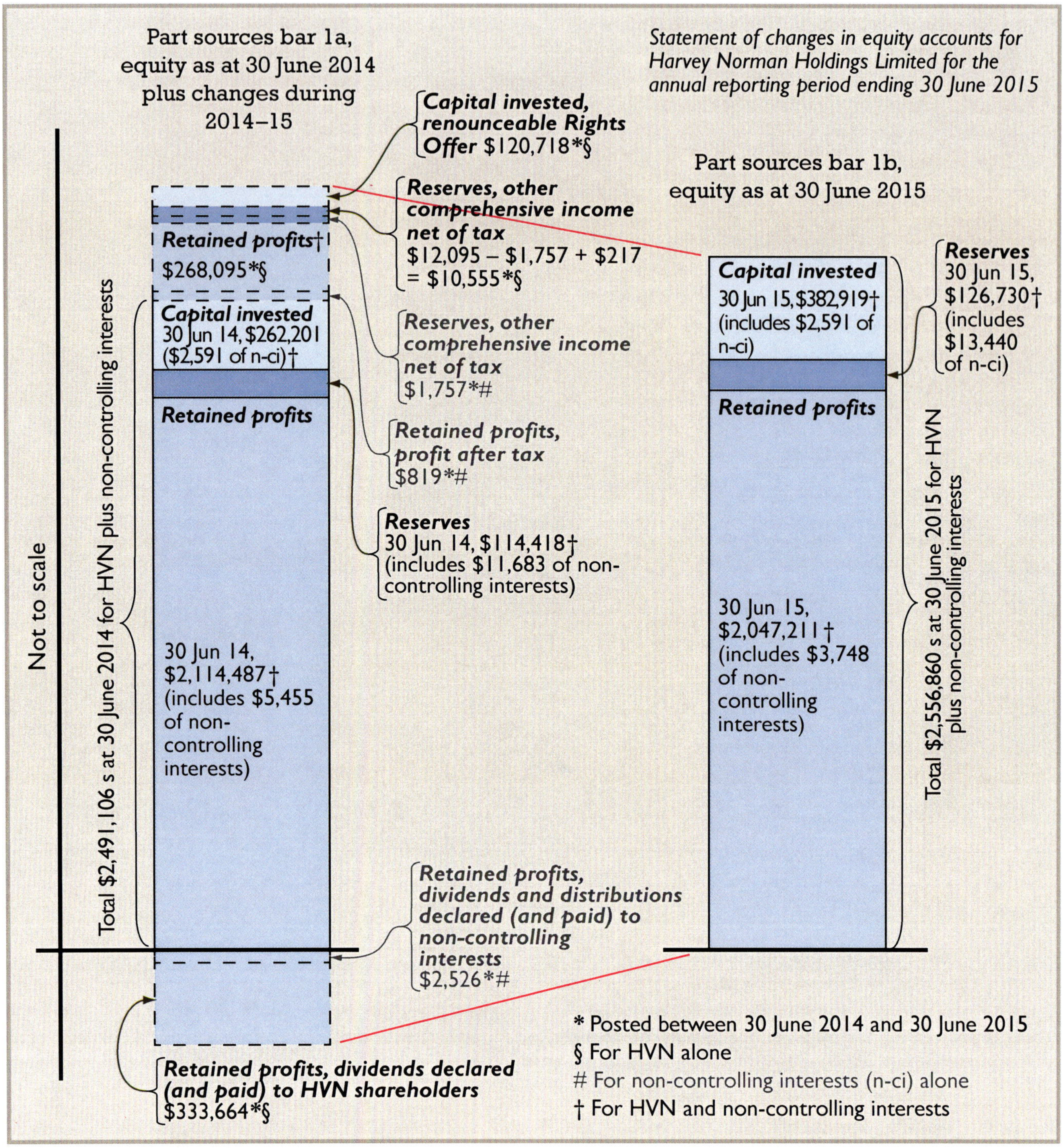

Figure 11.7 Harvey Norman's statement of changes in equity for 2014-15 represented graphically.

The six amounts of equity attributable to non-controlling interests shown within the brackets are given in Notes to the Financial Statements number 26 in HVN's 2015 annual report.

Part sources bar 1a Shows the balances of the three equity control accounts as at 30 June 2014, plus the totals posted to those accounts during the 2014-15 annual reporting period. Capital invested during 2014-15 increased by $120,718,000. Reserves increased by $12,312,000. There were two increases in retained profits ($268,095,000 and $819,000) and two decreases ($2,526,000 and $333,664,000).

Part sources bar 1b Shows the balances of the three equity control accounts as at 30 June 2015.

11.4 BALANCE SHEET

A balance sheet (statement of financial position) reports the financial position of the organisation as at midnight on the reporting date. It is a restatement of the post-closing trial balance pictured on the right-hand side of figure 11.1.

The form of balance sheet used in figure 11.1 has two parts: the top part lists and totals the amounts which constitute the net assets, the bottom part lists and totals the amounts which constitute the equity. The items of equity shows how the net assets have been financed. The totals of the net assets and equity should be equal. Some nations prescribe a format of balance sheet in which the top part states the assets, and the bottom part the liabilities plus the equity.

Figure 11.8 shows HVN's balance sheet as at 30 June 2015; figures 11.9 and 11.10 show balance charts prepared from it.

Figure 11.8 Harvey Norman's balance sheet as at 30 June 2015. It shows account balances as at both 30 June 2014 and 30 June 2015. The notes column shown in the original has been omitted here.

The amounts of assets and liabilities (but not of capital invested, reserves and retained profits) include 100% of the liabilities and 100% of the carrying amounts of the assets of the two companies majority owned by HVN.

The differences between the equity account balances at 30 June 2014 and 30 June 2015 shown at the bottom of the balance sheet are explained in the statement of changes in equity shown in figures 11.6 and 11.7.

HARVEY NORMAN HOLDINGS LIMITED BALANCE SHEET FOR THE YEAR ENDED 30 JUNE 2015	CONSOLIDATED June 2015 $'000	 June 2014 $'000
Current Assets		
Cash and cash equivalents	185,840	144,957
Trade and other receivables	1,142, 551	1,119,393
Other financial assets	26,148	21,596
Inventories	298,381	297,670
Other assets	23,072	23,010
Intangible assets	476	541
Total current assets	1,676, 468	1,607,167
Non-Current Assets		
Trade and other receivables	71,815	64,526
Investments accounted for using equity method	21,425	24,912
Other financial assets	16,570	16,176
Property, plant and equipment	552,603	569,057
Investment properties	1,935,936	1,903,504
Intangible assets	83,727	77,898
Total non-current assets	2,682,076	2,656,073
Total Assets	4,358,544	4,206,131
Current Liabilities		
Trade and other payables	813,474	740,681
Interest-bearing loans and borrowings	408,438	469,872
Income tax payable	34,807	24,142
Other liabilities	2,870	2,043
Provisions	23,490	25,494
Total current liabilities	1,283,079	1,262,232
Non-Current Liabilities		
Interest-bearing loans and borrowings	290,000	238,094
Provisions	12,249	10,293
Deferred income tax liabilities	198,728	188,980
Other liabilities	17,628	15,426
Total non-current liabilities	518,605	452,793
Total Liabilities	1,801,684	1,715,025
NET ASSETS	2,556,860	2,491,106
Equity		
Contributed equity	380,328	259,610
Reserves	113,290	102,735
Retained profits	2,043,463	2,109,032
Parent entity interests	2,537,081	2,471,377
Non-controlling interests	19,779	19,729
TOTAL EQUITY	2,556,860	2,491,106

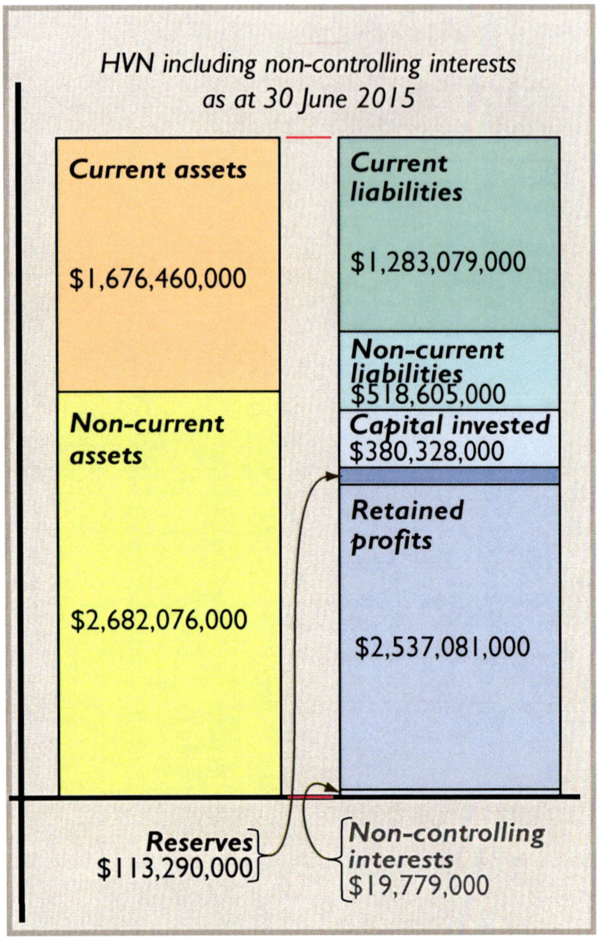

Figure 11.9 A balance chart showing the main control accounts in the balance sheet for HVN and non-controlling interests as at 30 June 2015. A more detailed representation is shown in figure 11.10

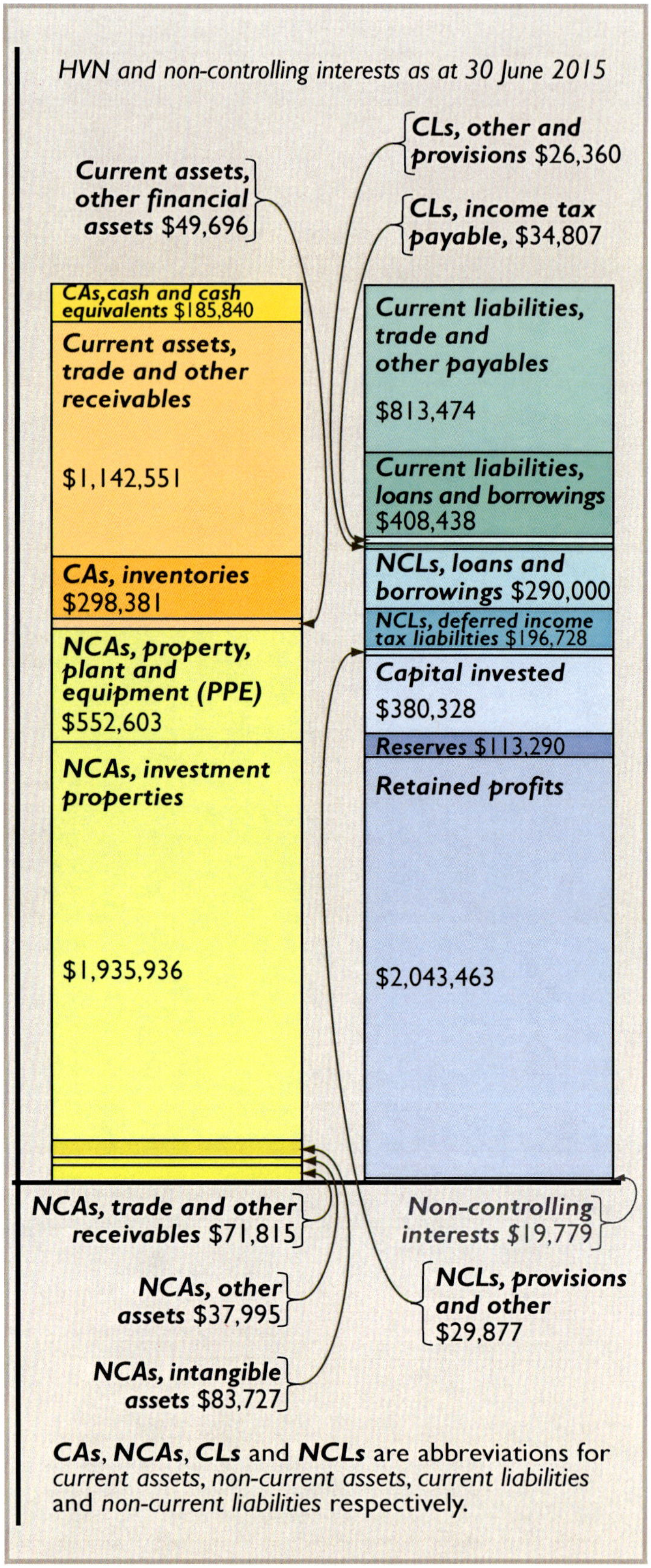

Figure 11.10 A more detailed representation than figure 11.9 of the balance sheet for HVN and non-controlling interests as at 30 June 2015. >

> The relative heights of the NCA (non-current assets), investment properties control account in the assets bar shows that HVN has about 45% of its assets in the form of investment properties. The sources bar shows that about 45% of HVN's funding is from retained profits.

11.5 STATEMENT OF CASH FLOWS

A statement of cash flows (figures 11.11, 11.12 and 11.13) is a statement of the entity's cash and cash-equivalent inflows and outflows during a period. (Another term for *inflow* is *receipt*; another term for *outflow* is *payment*.)

A cash flow statement is important because it:

- shows where receipts have come from and payments have gone to
- shows whether an entity's cash holding has increased or decreased during the period. A significant negative or fall in cash flow is often a sign of liquidity problems now or ahead
- gives a guide as to whether the entity will be able to meet its commitments. These can include: repaying loans as they fall due, paying dividends or drawings, paying taxes payable, and conforming to conditions imposed by banks or other lenders.

Cash flow statements are produced using cash, not accruals, accounting. Payments and receipts are recorded gross; therefore value added tax components aren't deducted. The end-of-period adjustments explained in chapters 8 and 9 shouldn't affect any cash ledger account balances unless the adjustments have corrected any cash account errors.

Cash includes cash-on-hand, undeposited funds, petty cash, cash-at-banks, and cash equivalents which should be convertible into cash within three months with minimal risk of losing value. Cash equivalents are held for paying future commitments, not for investment.

Accounting standards may require that an entity's cash flows be separated into three classifications:

1. **Operating activities** are the principal revenue-producing activities excluding financial and investing activities. Cash flows include: income tax payments and refunds, dividends paid, drawings paid, cash payments for expenses and the purchase of current assets, cash payments to manufacture such assets, cash receipts from the disposal of such assets, and for an entity which deals or trades in securities and loans the cash flows which result.
2. **Investing activities** concern the acquisition and disposal of non-current assets including shares and debentures in other entities, and lending to other entities. Cash inflows include repayments of loans, and interest and dividends received where not included in operating activities.
3. **Financial activities** affect the capital invested and borrowings, including bank borrowings but not a typical overdraft. In the cash repayment of a loan the interest component would be included in operating activities, the repayment of the principal in financial activities.

11.5.1 Reporting operating activities cash flows

In figure 11.11, the cash receipts from and cash payments for each main operating activity are listed.

The accounting standards may also require that cash flows from operating activities be reconciled to net profit in a note to the cash flow statement (note 28(b) in Harvey Norman's figure 11.11 cash flow statement is shown in figure 11.12). This indirect method first reports the period's profit after tax (the $268,914,000 in figure 11.2), and then reports the adjustments which when added and subtracted bring the total to the net cash flows from operating activities ($340,448,000 in figure 11.11). These adjustments are the changes in operating activity account balances during the period. They include for example:

- the depreciation during the period
- the increase (or decrease) in accounts receivable
- changes in inventories.

Statement of Cash Flows for the Year Ended 30 June 2015

	NOTE	Consolidated June 2015 $000	June 2014 $000
Cash Flows from Operating Activities		Inflows/(Outflows)	
Net receipts from franchisees		830,844	871,251
Receipts from customers		1,707,259	1,590,489
Payments to suppliers and employees		(2,056,114)	(1,994,315)
Distributions received from joint ventures		13,905	15,512
GST paid		(43,258)	(39,087)
Interest received		8,657	8,874
Interest and other costs of finance paid		(33,059)	(36,583)
Income taxes paid		(89,284)	(78,626)
Dividends received		1,498	1,420
Net Cash Flows From Operating Activities	28(b)	340,448	338,935
Cash Flows used in Investing Activities			
Payments for purchases of property, plant and equipment and intangible assets		(55,012)	(64,970)
Payments for purchase of investment properties		(15,828)	(54,665)
Proceeds from sale of property, plant and equipment and properties held for resale		7,152	10,459
Payments for purchase of units in unit trusts		(395)	(106)
Payments for purchase of equity accounted investments		(4)	(2,608)
Proceeds from sale of listed securities		1,477	134
Payments or purchase of listed securities		(4,048)	-
Loans granted to other entities		(15,145)	(1,361)
Net Cash Flows Used In Investing Activities		(81,803)	(113,117)
Cash Flows used in Financing Activities			
Proceeds from Renounceable Rights Offer		120,718	-
Payments for purchase of shares in controlled entities		-	(22,618)
Repayments of Syndicated Facility and Syndicated Working Capital Facility		(52,000)	(122,855)
Dividends paid		(333,664)	(111,543)
Loans repaid from related parties		37,153	19,925
Proceeds from other borrowings		7,196	1,878
Net Cash Flows Used In Financing Activities		(220,597)	(235,213)
Net Increase / (Decrease) in Cash and Cash Equivalents		38,048	(9,395)
Cash and Cash Equivalents at Beginning of the Year		115,172	124,567
Cash and Cash Equivalents at End of the Year	28(a)	153,220	115,172

Figure 11.11 A scan of Harvey Norman's statement of cash flows for 2014–15. It shows the details of the three types of cash flows. Note 28(b) explains how the net cash flows from operating activities for 2014–15 are related to the same period's profit after tax; note 28(a) explains how the cash and cash equivalents are held at 30 June 2015. Both notes are shown in figure 11.12.

NOTES TO THE FINANCIAL STATEMENTS (CONTINUED)

	CONSOLIDATED June 2015 $000	June 2014 $000
28. Cash and Cash Equivalents		
(a) *Reconciliation to Cash Flow Statement:*		
Cash and cash equivalents comprise the following at end of the year:		
Cash at bank and on hand	169,694	119,092
Short term money market deposits	16,146	25,865
	185,840	144,957
Bank overdraft (Note 17)	(32,620)	(29,785)
Cash and cash equivalents at end of the year	153,220	115,172
(b) *Reconciliation of profit after income tax to net operating cash flows:*		
Profit after tax	268,914	212,238
Adjustments for:		
Net foreign exchange gains	(220)	(588)
Bad and doubtful debts	2,785	129
Provision for inventory obsolescence	1,258	(192)
Share of net profit from joint venture entities	(8,657)	(17,501)
Depreciation of property, plant and equipment	64,399	68,398
Amortisation	13,047	9,235
Impairment of fixed assets and IT projects	-	217
Impairment of investment in joint venture	274	-
Revaluation of investment properties and properties held under joint ventures	(7,604)	9,529
Property revaluation adjustment for overseas controlled entity	(1,123)	2,123
Deferred lease expenses	244	214
Provision for onerous leases	667	135
Discount of interest-free long term receivables	-	32
Accretion of interest-free long term receivables	-	(59)
Executive remuneration expenses	4,246	2,926
Transfers to provisions:		
- Employee entitlements	2,662	2,059
Loss / (gain) on disposal and revaluation of:		
- Property, plant and equipment, and listed securities	2,271	(1,331)
Changes in assets and liabilities net of effects from purchase and sale of controlled entities:		
(Increase)/decrease in assets:		
Receivables	(81,322)	(58,618)
Inventory	(1,970)	(28,697)
Other current assets	(62)	4,645
Increase/(decrease) in liabilities:		
Payables and other current liabilities	69,973	133,716
Income tax payable	10,666	325
Net cash from operating activities	340,448	338,935

Figure 11.12 A scan of Harvey Norman's notes to the financial statements 28(a) and 28(b).

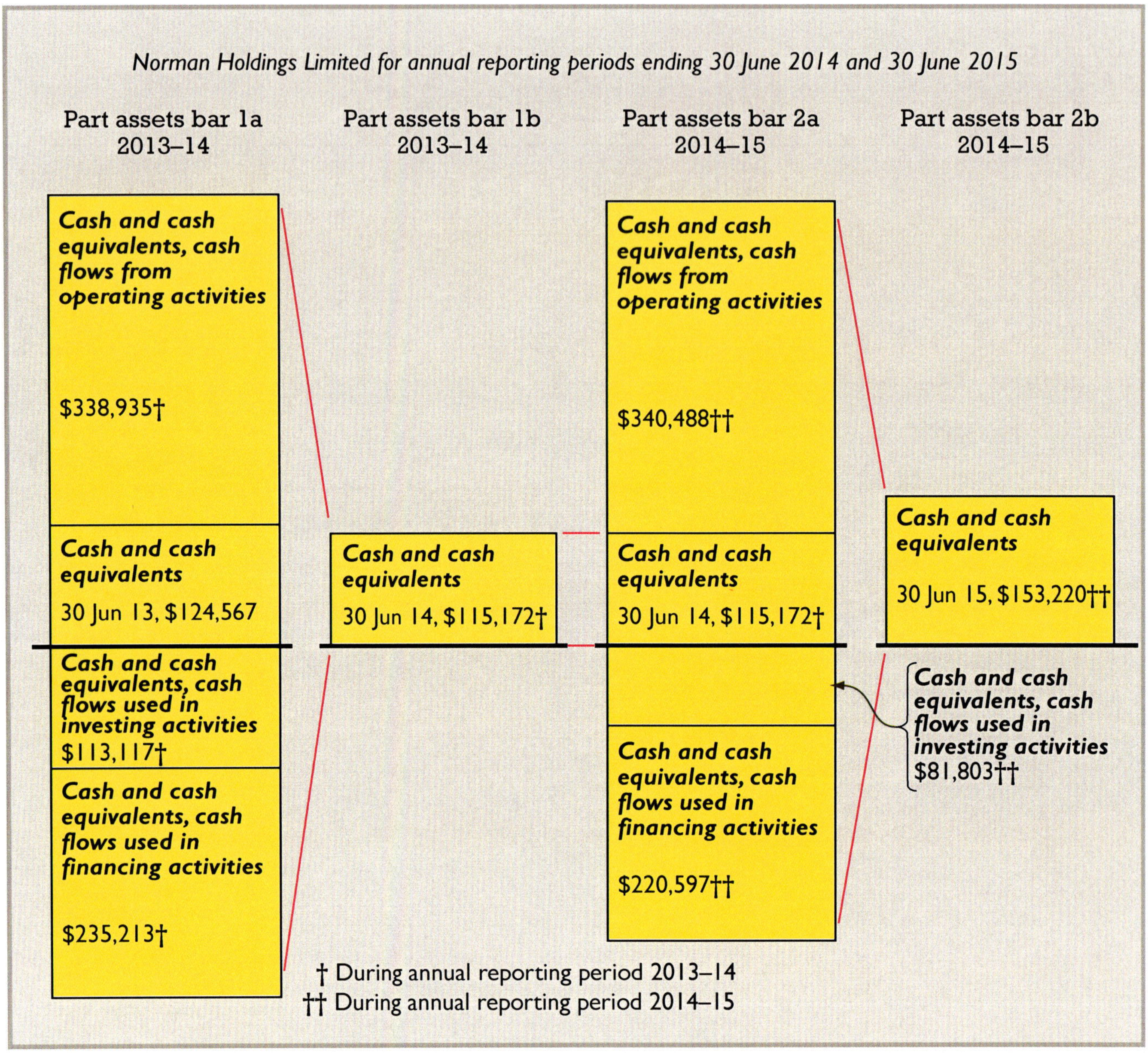

Figure 11.13 A graphical comparison of Harvey Norman's 2013–14 and 2014–15 cash flows. The amounts in this chart are shown in text in figure 11.11.

The cash flow used in financing activities in 2014-15 includes dividend payments totalling $333,664.

11.6 OTHER PARTS OF FINANCIAL STATEMENTS

The fifth item in the set of financial statements listed on page 78 was *notes*. In them accounting standards usually require the disclosure of any contingent assets or liabilities, where:

- A *contingent asset* is a 'possible asset whose existence will be confirmed only by the occurrence or non-occurrence of one or more uncertain future events not wholly within the company's control'.
- A *contingent liability* is similarly a 'possible liability whose existence is yet to be confirmed'.

The accounting standards usually then require that both contingent assets and contingent liabilities be continually assessed, be disclosed by being discussed in notes to the company's financial statements, but not be posted to accounts which are then reported in the company's balance sheet and profit or loss financial statements.

If the company assesses that the realisation of a contingent liability has become probable, and if the amount and/or timing can be reliably estimated, that liability should be recognised as a *provision*, a 'liability of uncertain timing or amount' in the balance sheet.

Companies may also be required to include in their annual reports:

- **a directors' declaration** that:
  - the financial statements comply with the accounting standards
  - give a true and fair view
  - there are reasonable grounds to believe that the company can pay its debts, and
  - the financial statements have been prepared in accordance with the relevant laws
- **a directors' report** to the company's shareholders on the company's activities during the subject annual reporting period and on the company's future prospects. Directors are appointed by shareholders to carry out the day-to-day business of a company. Their salaries and fees are therefore a normal payroll expense
- **an auditor's report** Auditors are particularly qualified accounting professionals who are independent of and external to the entities they report on. Auditors report primarily on the adequacy of disclosure in annual reports, and on the adequacy and accuracy of an entity's financial statements. An auditor who materially disagrees with the content of an entity's annual report should issue a qualified auditor's report.

11.7 BALANCE CHARTS AND FINANCIAL STATEMENTS

This chapter has shown that financial statements are easier to understand when displayed as graphical accounts charts. Stakeholders are then be better able to decide how well the entity has performed. And where a company is publicly listed, members of the public can then judge whether to invest, or increase or decrease their current shareholdings. However the information in financial statements is historical and, depending on the interval since the reporting date, may not be a reliable guide to the entity's current financial position despite the requirement for continuous disclosure.

Balance charts can also be used to analyse and compare investment opportunities. This is explained in the next chapter.

Chapter 12

FINANCIAL ANALYSIS

Would an annual profit of $200,000 before tax for the reporting period 2015–16 be laudable? Jane would have been thrilled had Drone achieved that, but had a major bank only achieved that profit, its shareholders would have been horrified. However by calculating for Drone and for the poorly performing bank the ratio of profit divided by some measure of the entity's size, the performances of the two businesses could be meaningfully compared.

Financial analysis is the use of financial statements, and other available data to monitor and evaluate the financial position of an organisation, and its performance in areas including:

- profitability
- management efficiency
- productivity
- liquidity, the ability of the entity to pay its debts as they fall due
- financing, how appropriately the entity funds its activities
- for entities listed on a securities exchange, stockmarket performance.

The main tool used in financial analysis is ratio analysis, but before concentrating on that, a look at how managers can use the data in the accounts.

12.1 ANALYSING THE ACCOUNTS

For those within an entity who are permitted access, the individual ledger and control accounts are an invaluable source of information. The data is available in three forms:

1. **Ledger account balances.** They provide a snapshot of the amounts associated with the entity's centres of interest at the specified balance date. Account balances often consulted include:
   - those of individual debtors and creditors
   - those of the entity's bank accounts
   - taxes payable.
2. **The record through time of an account's debits and credits.** This can provide both date-specific and trend information. Examples of the latter include whether a customer is a prompt payer, and whether the rate of sales to a customer has increased or decreased through time.
3. **Control account balances.** As explained on pages 14 and 15, the balance of a control account is derived by totalling the balances of the two or more accounts which directly feed into it. Control account balances can, like ledger accounts, provide both date-specific and trend information. For example, the control account balance of the total of all the accounts-payable account balances at regular intervals may show a trend or recurring seasonal variations.

Today accounting software can display the above data or any of a host of different reports as at any date or for any period at the click of a mouse. But to gain full benefit from the powerful facilities of accounting software the accounts have to be fully up-to-date.

12.2 PROFIT AND SIZE

The major criterion of entity performance is profit, but, as illustrated in the first paragraph of this chapter, an entity's profit is far more meaningful when it's related to that entity's size. There are several definitions of profit and of entity size.

12.2.1 Definitions of profit

Analysts commonly use measures of profit other than profit before tax (*accounting profit for the period before subtracting the income tax payable for the period*). One is EBIT (*earnings before interest and tax*), that is the profit before tax with the period's interest expense added back and before subtracting any distributions to owners. In assessing the profitability of an entity's activities, interest and tax are not subtracted from EBIT because:

- The interest expense during a period depends not on the efficiency and profitability of the entity's operations but largely on what proportion of the entity's sources of funds are borrowed and therefore attract interest.
- Income tax payable is affected by deferred tax assets carried forward from previous years, by any available tax offsets, and by for example whether the entity uses an overseas tax haven or similar.

Another measure of profit is EBITDIA which is EBIT with the period's non-current assets' depreciation, impairment, and amortisation expenses added back, again because their amounts have little to do with the performance of the business's operations.

For Harvey Norman for 2014–15 the three measures of profit are stated on page 6 of the 2015 annual report and are:

- Accounting profit before income tax payable on that profit is subtracted (net profit) = \$378m
- EBIT = \$411m
- EBITDIA = \$489m.

12.2.2 Definitions of business size

There are several amounts which could be used as a measure of an entity's size: total annual income, total assets, net assets (total assets less total liabilities which equals equity), and capital employed.

An entity can be conceptually split into two parts:

1. **Operations.** For example, a manufacturer's operations are its manufacturing. Operating then includes managing those current liabilities such as trade creditors and taxes (other than income tax payable) which are inherently part of operations of the business.
2. **Funding.** The part of an entity which only provides the funding, receives and reinvests amounts of retained profit in the operations, manages any distributions to owners, and pays any income tax. The composition of the sources of an entity's funds is called its *funding structure.*

If any account balance in a balance chart is shifted diagonally, the two bars' net heights change, but remain equal, and the balance sheet equation isn't violated. Diagonally shifting the five operational current liability account balances and the cash account balance in figure 12.1 diagonally results in figure 12.2. Its left- and right-hand bars are called respectively *capital employed* and *funding structure.* (This particular definition of capital employed is taken from *Accounts Demystified* by Anthony Rice.) And *capital employed* is the denominator (the amount below the line in a fraction) of the preferred starting ratio in ratio analysis.

12.3 RATIO ANALYSIS

Ratio analysis has been developed to enable an entity's financial health to be assessed, and the reasons for that health or otherwise to be investigated.

Vertical analysis is the fundamental tool of ratio analysis. It typically starts from a single profitability ratio for the whole entity. The most meaningful ratio is ROCE (return on capital employed), also called ROIC (return on invested capital). Starting from ROCE, the entity's operations and funding structure can be analysed separately as outlined in figures 12.3 and 12.4 respectively. Vertical analysis thus enables you to bore down through a branching, multi-level structure of ratios to investigate performance in those areas which appear appropriate.

There's no point in calculating ratios unless their values mean something. There are two ways to provide meaning:

- by calculating the same ratio for a series of dates (often the ends of annual reporting periods), or for each of a series of consecutive periods of equal length. The reasons for any trends are then investigated—a process called *horizontal analysis* (figure 12.6)
- by comparing the values of particular ratios for the subject entity with those for similar entities, or with those typical for similar entities. These ratios are often called *KPIs* (Key Performance Indicators), and their values for specified situations are called *benchmarks.*

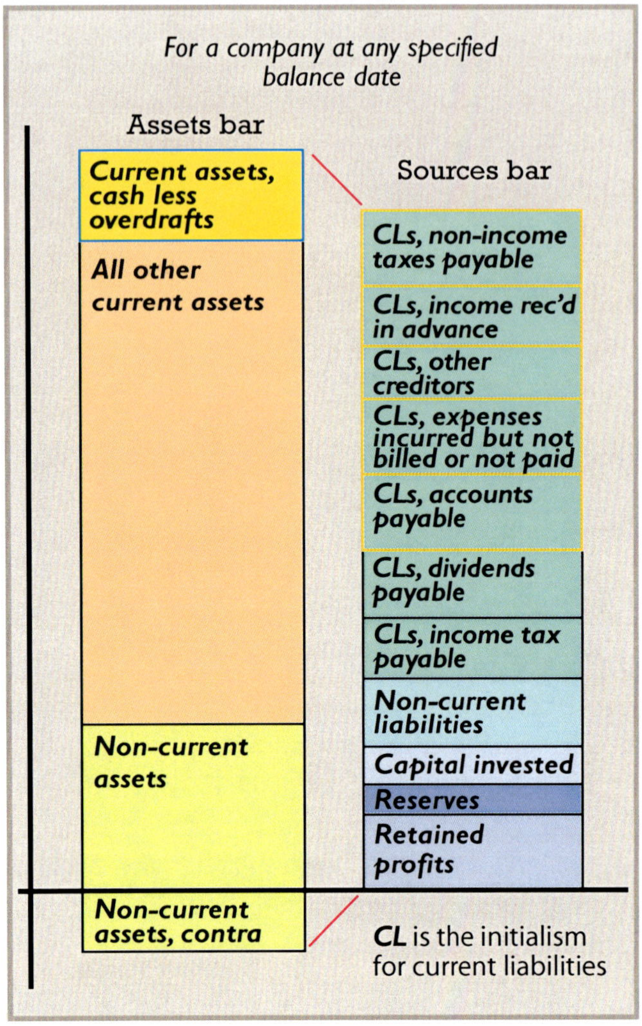

Figure 12.1 A balance chart showing the accounts which need to be moved diagonally to separate a company's operational accounts from its funding-structure accounts as shown in figure 12.2.

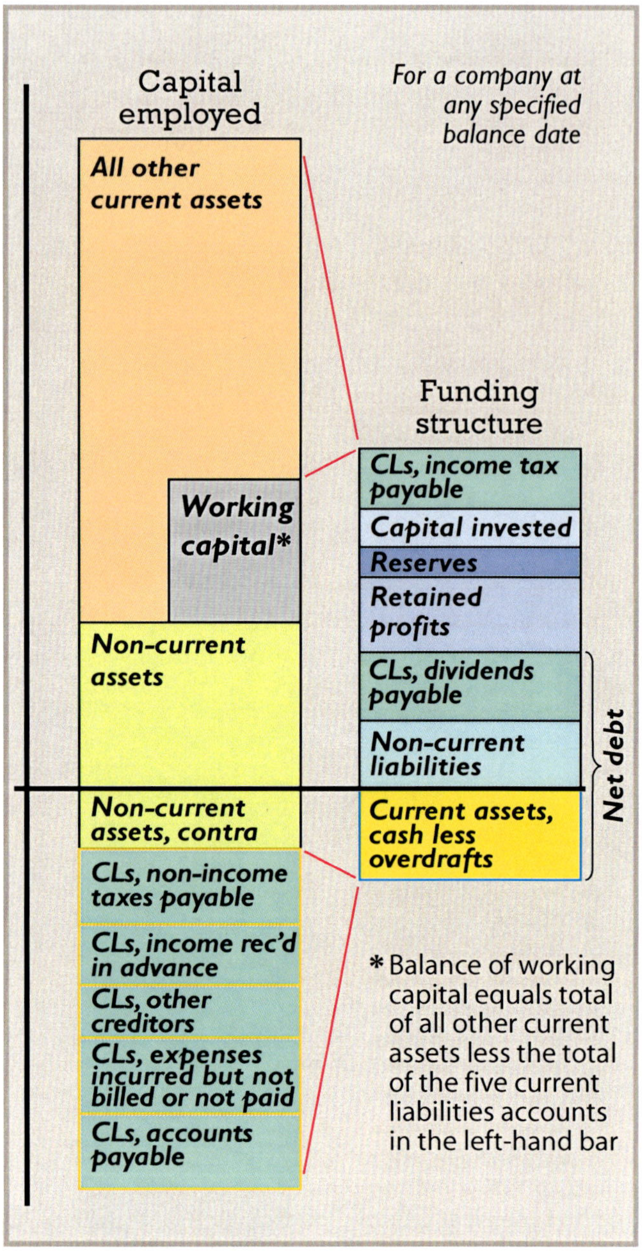

Figure 12.2 Definitions of capital employed, funding structure, and working capital. A more common but cruder definition of *working capital* is 'current assets minus current liabilities'.

The cash less any overdrafts account (outlined in blue) will be shifted diagonally because if the company didn't have this amount of cash, it wouldn't need to be provided by the funding structure.

Shifting the five current liabilities accounts with yellow outlines diagonally excludes them from the funds structure. They're then managed as part of the business's operations. However the following balances are retained in the funding structure:

- income tax payable because its amount varies according to what proportion of the funds structure attracts loan interest or similar which is a deduction, and therefore decreases income tax payable
- dividends payable because if not distributed these would be free funding for the company.

Working capital is the business's net amount of current assets, and gives an indication of the business's liquidity and freedom to act. Too high an amount of working capital suggests that the company's inventories and work-in-progress are being under utilised; too low and potential sales may be lost because customers can't be serviced as quickly as they expect.

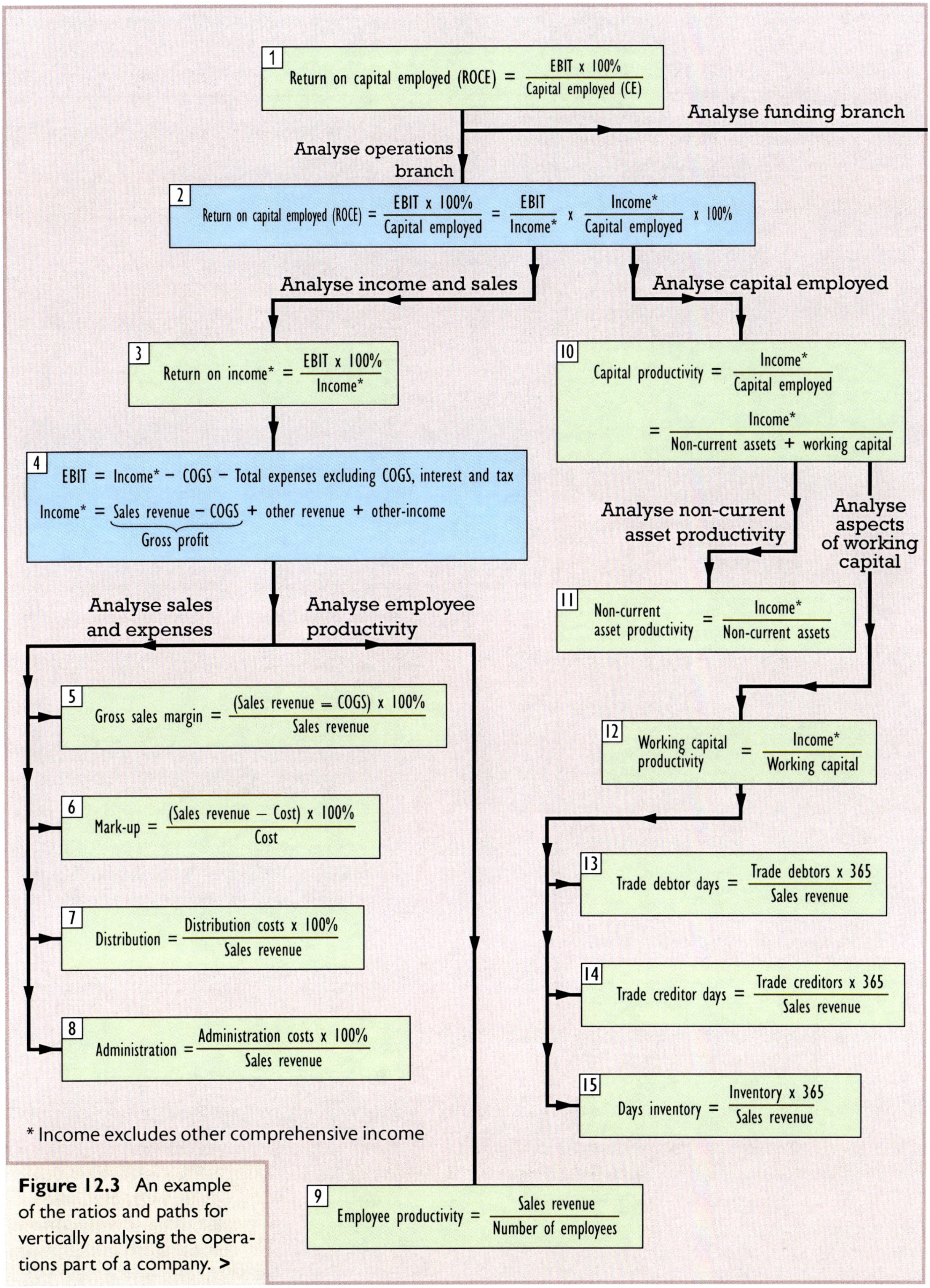

* Income excludes other comprehensive income

Figure 12.3 An example of the ratios and paths for vertically analysing the operations part of a company. >

> [1] ROCE is a measure of how effectively the business is using its funds. A common but less accurate measure of ROCE is total assets less current liabilities.

[2] The formula for ROCE expanded to introduce the business's income for the reporting period.

[3] Return on income. A high number doesn't necessarily indicate a high ROCE.

[4] Detailed definitions of EBIT and income.

[5] Gross sales margin is a measure of the profitability in purchasing and producing goods before other business expenses are taken into account.

[6] Mark-up is the 'arithmetic mean percentage which the business adds to its products' costs to get the selling price'.

[7] Distribution costs as a percentage of sales.

[8] Administration costs as a percentage of sales.

[9] Employee productivity. If management is implementing efficiencies and introducing new technologies soundly, this amount should be increasing faster than inflation.

[10] Capital productivity is a measure of how efficiently the business's capital employed is being used. Although the higher the better, the value doesn't inform whether the sales have been profitable.

[11] Non-current asset productivity is the sales per dollar of non-current assets.

[12] Working capital productivity measures the sales per dollar of working capital.

[13] Trade debtor days is a measure of how efficiently the business collects the monies owing by its customers. If greater than the payment period specified on the business's invoices, corrective action is required.

[14] Trade creditor days. The longer the better as thus the business's suppliers provide free funding. However too long and suppliers become more difficult to deal with and may increase the prices they charge the business. >

> [15] Days inventory measures the time it takes to sell inventory from the time raw materials (or for a retailer finished goods) are purchased. A business needs to strike a balance between the costs of holding stock including the increased probability of having to devalue that stock and being unable to service customers quickly if stock is too low.

> **Figure 12.4 caption continued**

[16] The constituents of a business's funding structure.

[17] Debt to total funding is a measure of the business's reliance on debt to operate.

[18] The current ratio is a measure of liquidity. The ratio's norm varies with business type; for example, a manufacturer's is typically greater than a greengrocer's. A sound current ratio isn't an absolute guarantee of liquidity because payments may have to be made before accounts receivable are due.

[19] The quick ratio is a more stringent test of liquidity than the current ratio because the former assumes that inventories can't be quickly converted into cash, and prepayments can't be reversed.

[20] A high value of interest cover indicates that profit would have to fall greatly before the business would be unable to service its debts.

[21] Gearing. The higher the gearing (the proportion of funding by debt) the greater the change in return to owners resulting from a change in profit. Thus if gearing is high, an increase in interest rates can greatly reduce the return to owners, perhaps sufficiently to turn it negative.

[22] Return on equity. If this return is below that obtainable from alternative investments, investors will consider investing elsewhere.

[23] Dividend cover is a measure of how likely the company is to be able to maintain the same dividend in the future.

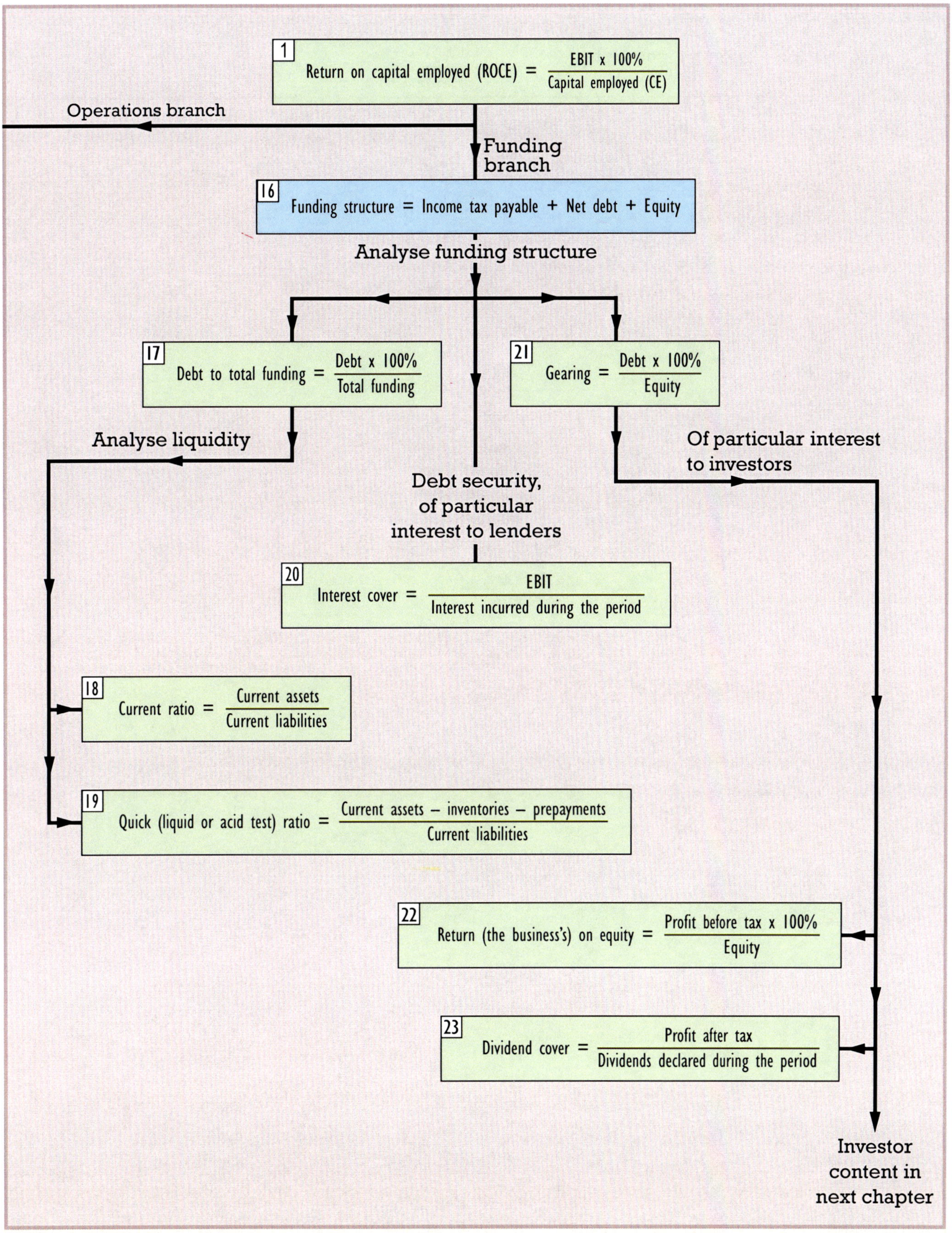

Figure 12.4 An example of the ratios and paths for vertically analysing the funding structure part of a company. (This caption continues on the preceding page.) <

12.3.1 Benchmarks

There are four potential sources for benchmarks:

1. commercial sources
   - industry associations. Some can supply benchmarks for their industry. This is usually a separately chargeable service to association members
   - commercial consultants—although the data has to be purchased, it can be tailored to ensure relevance.
2. non- or less-commercial sources
   - from textbooks, articles and other sources which provide detailed discussions of financial analysis (also called *ratio* or *DuPont* analysis)
   - from institutions including banks, university business schools, and taxing authorities (figure 12.5).
3. ratios calculated from an entity's own accounts. This is the most common source of benchmarks.
4. ratios calculated from the financial data of those entities which are relevant and which can be accessed.

Benchmarks should be used with caution. For example, benchmarks obtained by analysing the easily accessible annual reports of public companies will typically have limited relevance to small entities.

Key benchmark ratio	**Annual turnover range**		
	$65,000 – $200,000	$200,000 – $500,000	More than $500,000
Income tax return			
Cost of sales/turnover	26% – 41%	29% – 41%	33% – 45%
Average cost of sales	35%	35%	39%
Total expenses/turnover	68% – 82%	75% – 86%	83% – 91%
Average total expensesl	75%	81%	87%
Activity statement			
Non-capital purchases/ total sales	53% – 69%	53% – 65%	53% – 63%

Figure 12.5 An example of free benchmarks, here published by the Australian Tax Office and therefore of limited relevance to businesses in other countries. This table is just one of the many the Australian Tax Office publishes for a wide range of different small businesses. This table is for the printing industry, and is located at <www.ato.gov.au/Business/Small-business-benchmarks/In-detail/Benchmarks-A-Z/L-Q/Printing/>.

12.3.2 Using ratio analysis

The three financial analysis tools of vertical analysis, horizontal analysis and benchmarking are powerful investigative tools in assessing the financial position, recent performance and prospects of an entity.

As figure 12.6 shows the results of such analyses can be more readily appreciated if displayed graphically. Graphical display can also be adapted to facilitate comparisons between several entities as shown in figures 12.7 and 12.8. Similar graphical percentage comparisons can be prepared for other financial statements.

When using ratio analysis certain factors need to be born in mind:

- Variables other than benchmarks and KPIs can be relevant, for example the prevailing rates of interest for borrowing
- It's important to strike a balance between short-term and long term factors.
- The applicability of ratio analysis to what are sometimes called micro businesses is limited. More direct analysis may be preferable; for example, a fall in sales of a hairdressing establishment could be due to a staff member whose behaviour irritates customers.
- About thirty ratios are in common use. However an analyst should also consider developing bespoke variables and ratios which have greater relevance to the particular situation.
- Be alert for explicit or, more often, unrevealed differences in the detailed definitions of the variables used in ratios
- Be consistent when calculating ratios. Account balances typically vary through a period, in some cases seasonally. Consider whether to use end-of-period balances or average balances (typically half the sum of the balance at the end of the subject period plus the balance at the end of the previous period).
- If you're not an employee or an owner, it may be difficult or impossible to access the financial data needed to properly perform a detailed analysis.
- The financial-statement account balances may be unreliable because of innocent subjective judgements, tweaking to improve the results, or intentional distortions.

This chapter has introduced financial analysis. Financial ratios are also used in business valuation, explained in the next chapter.

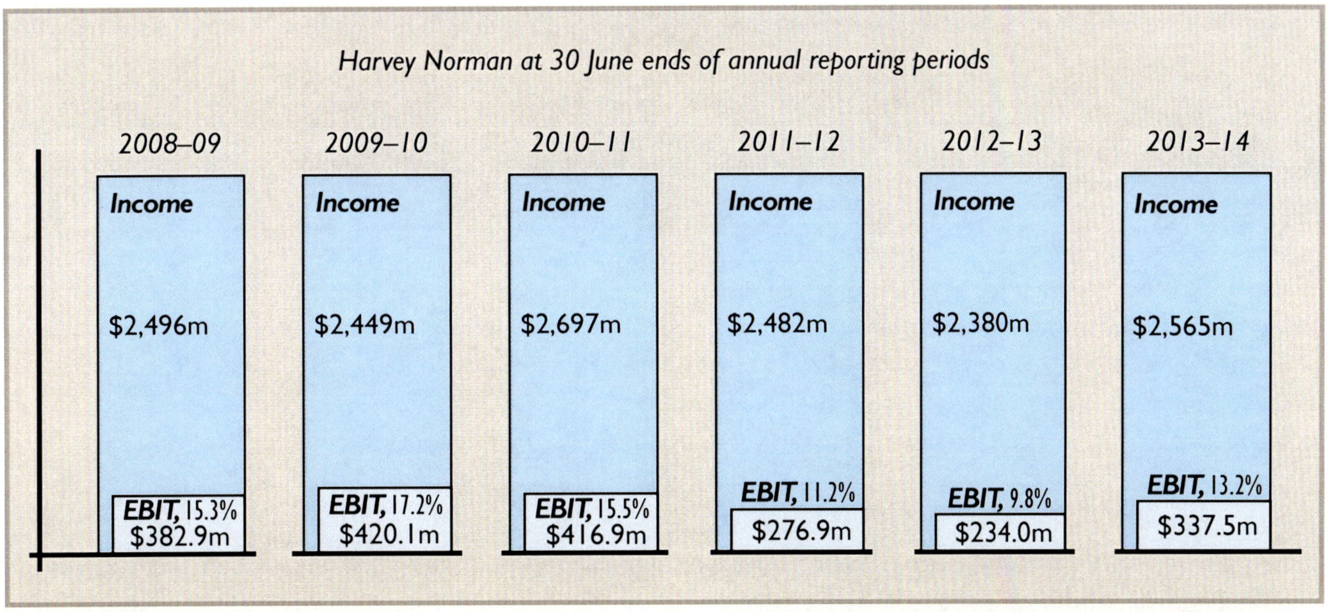

Figure 12.6 An example of horizontal trend analysis, here ratio 3 in figure 12.3, return on income. By making the physical heights of each year's income the same, the values of the ratio EBIT÷Income through the annual reporting periods are shown by the heights of the paler rectangle and can be readily compared.

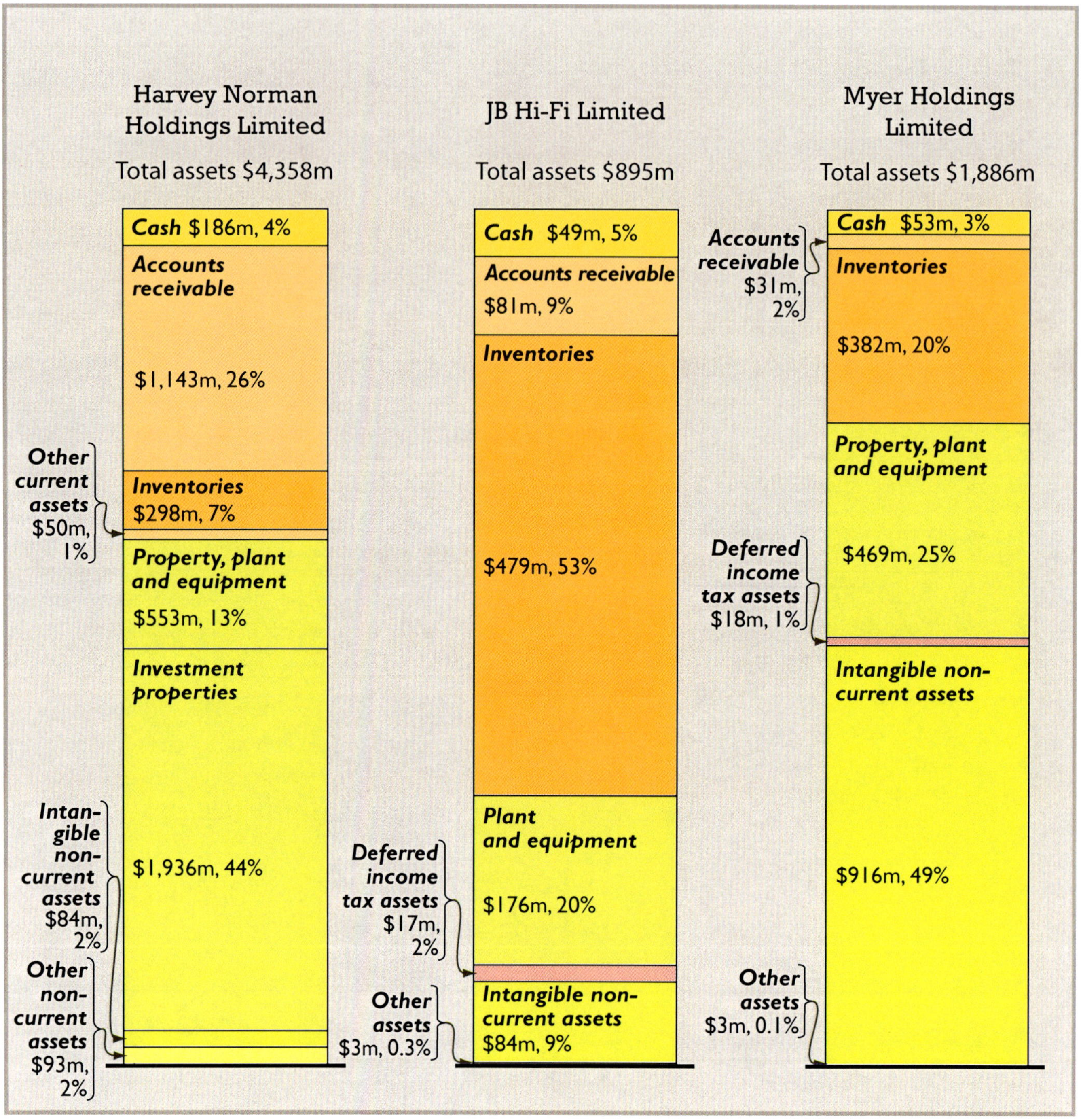

Figure 12.7 A balance chart of the balance sheet assets bars for Australian public companies Harvey Norman Holdings Limited, JB Hi-Fi Limited and Myer Holdings Limited as at 30 June 2015 prepared from their 2015 annual reports.

The three companies have different amounts of total assets, but by displaying them at a common size (the same total height) you can readily see that the proportions of the balances of their major asset categories differ considerably although all three companies are major retail chains:

- 44% of HVN's asset's are investment properties reflecting that an important part of HVN's business is leasing HVN stores to franchisees.
- JB Hi-Fi is nearer to a conventional retailer and has 53% of its assets in inventories.
- Myer is unusual with 49% of its assets intangible, and consisting mainly of goodwill and trademarks.

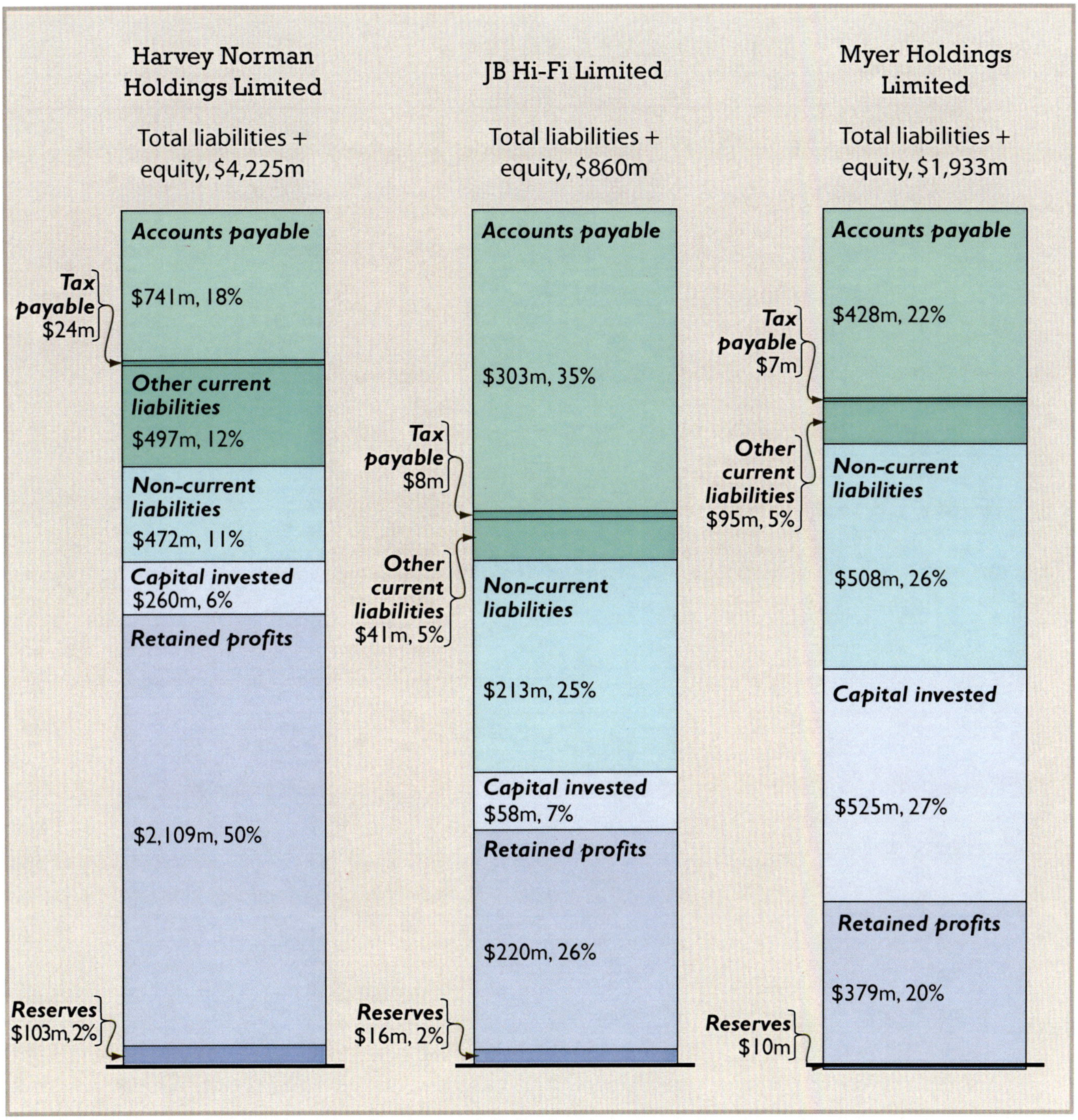

Figure 12.8 A balance chart for the balance sheet sources bars for Harvey Norman Holdings Limited, JB Hi-Fi Limited and Myer Holdings Limited as at 30 June 2015 prepared from their 2015 annual reports.

The three public companies have different amounts of total liabilities plus equity, but by displaying these totals at a common height you can readily see how the fundings of the three companies differ:

- 47% of HVN's funds are retained profits and attract no interest nor dividends.
- JB Hi-Fi's proportion of funds from accounts payable is about double that of HVN and Myer, and reflects JB Hi-Fi's larger inventories.
- Myer's proportion of funding from capital invested is about four times higher than that for HVN and JB Hi-Fi, and reflects the high share price achieved when Myer was re-listed on stock exchanges in 2009. This has also contributed to Myer's very high proportion of intangible assets.

Chapter 13

VALUING BUSINESSES

In this chapter for-profit entities are called *businesses*. This chapter introduces some of the factors which can determine:

- how much a business might be valued at, or
- whether a business's quoted valuation is higher or lower than some other relevant valuation.

A company traded on stock exchanges already has a readily-accessible valuation: its share price.

13.1 WHY VALUE A BUSINESS?

Those interested in valuing businesses include:

- owners wishing to sell their interests in a business
- potential buyers of all or part of a business
- those wishing to investigate how the value of a business can be increased
- those required to decide the price at which to issue shares in a company to increase its capital invested, or whether and at what price to underwrite such an issue
- those wishing to rank or compare businesses
- those needing to calculate appropriate amounts of compensation for damage caused to businesses.

13.2 NEED FOR ACCOUNTING INFORMATION

A sound assessment of the value of a business requires up-to-date and adequate financial statements. When valuing a business as a going concern, a forecast of future cash flows with supporting information is also needed. These and other financial reports and information should be vetted in a process often called *due diligence*. This process includes assessing:

- whether any assets are over- or under-valued
- the accuracy of the sources-bar account balances, particularly of the income and expenses accounts
- the reliability of forecasts.

Once sufficient and reliable financial information is available, the value of a business can be assessed. Such assessments will be both objective and subjective.

13.3 CRITERIA AFFECTING CHOICE OF VALUATION METHODS

The choice of method, or usually the combination of methods, most appropriate for a valuation are affected by:

- The reason for the valuation.
  a. a business which is expected to continue operating can be valued in many different ways as explained later
  b. if about to be wound up (closed), a business's value will usually be related to the value of its net assets (total assets minus total liabilities).
- The tangibility of the assets. Many businesses have significant tangible assets which can be valued with some confidence. At the other end of the spectrum, businesses can be without significant tangible assets—the valuations of such businesses are then typically related to expected future profits. Some businesses have relatively-high book values of intangible assets—these book values tend to be severely written down in asset-based valuations.
- The age of the business. Many young businesses have low or negative net assets, and/or are making losses even though their values based on expected future profits can be high.
- The likely volatility of cash flows and profits. For example, mature, asset-rich businesses operating in relatively stable markets with high bars to entry by competitors can be valued with more confidence than start-up businesses intending to exploit unproven new technologies.

13.4 VALUATION METHODS

There are many valuation methods. This section will introduce just five:

1. discounted cash flow (DCF) methods
2. asset valuation methods
3. entry cost
4. methods is which the valuation is some multiple of a particular amount
5. industry rules of thumb.

13.4.1 Discounted cash flow methods

The discounted cash flow methods (of which there are several) only apply to businesses with stable, predictable cash flows. This is because these methods assume that the present value of the future cash flows which it's estimated that the business will generate could be made available to investors and therefore represent a value of the business. To introduce these methods, I'll re-explain *cash flow* and explain *present value.*

Cash flow

As explained in chapter 11, an entity's cash flow for a period is the total cash inflow for the period minus the total cash outflow for the period. An entity's cash flow for an annual reporting period is reported in that period's cash flow statement. Harvey Norman's cash flow statement for 2014–15 is explained on pages 91 to 94. Cash flow is a measure of liquidity, not of profitability, although strong positive cash flows tend to be associated with good profits.

Present value

If you expect to earn 10% per annum compound on your investments, the present value of having \$110 twelve months from now is \$100. Similarly the present value to you of \$121 twenty-four months from now is \$100. And the present value of a forecast cash flow for an annual reporting period which will end t twelve-month periods from now is

$$\frac{\text{forecast cash flow for the annual reporting period}}{(1 + r)^t}$$

where *r* is the rate of return required by the potential buyer (the *hurdle rate*) expressed as a fraction, and *t* is the number of years from now to the end of the reporting period for which the cash flow was forecast. The fraction $1/(1 + r)_t$ is called the *discount factor*—discount factors for single and multiple years can be readily found in present value discount tables. For example, if you expect to earn 10% on your investments, and are confident that a business's annual cash flows will remain constant for the next five years, the present value of those cash flows is (0.909 + 0.826 + 0.751 + 0.683 + 0.621 = 3.79) x amount of annual cash flow.

13.4.2 Asset valuation methods

The assumption that the value of a business is strongly related to the amount of its net assets ignores that business's present and future profitability. It's therefore particularly applicable to a buyer who just wants to buy the business's assets. The starting point for asset valuation methods is the book value of the business's net assets (total assets – total liabilities). However, the current book values of assets may be significantly different to their current fair values because:

- there have been recent unrecorded changes in fair value; for example, property prices may have risen (or declined), some debts are uncollectable, or inventories may have fallen in value
- the accounting standards used don't permit upward revaluations. For example, it was explained on page 62 that the accounting standards could allow a business to value its non-current assets by the cost model or the revaluation model. The former doesn't permit upwards revaluations, and therefore any non-current assets which are likely to appreciate, such as land, may be undervalued under the cost model.

The current fair values of a business's assets and the amounts of its liabilities assume that that business is a going concern. Even so, the values of identifiable intangible assets are difficult to value, and net tangible assets (net assets – intangible assets) is usually more reliable than net assets. Also, the asset values realisable in a liquidation or a forced sale may be very different to their going concern fair values.

13.4.3 Entry cost valuation

An alternative to buying an existing business is to start a similar business from scratch. The cost of the latter is illustrated in figure 15.1 and would help establish a maximum buying price for the existing business. The costs of starting a business include:

- raising the required finance
- purchasing and acquiring the appropriate assets
- obtaining the necessary approvals and rights
- developing the necessary goods and/or services to sell
- recruiting and training staff
- establishing a market presence and a customer base.

Investigating starting a new business also provides the opportunity to look for potential savings or improvements; for example, by employing different technologies. These might then be applied to either the existing or a new business.

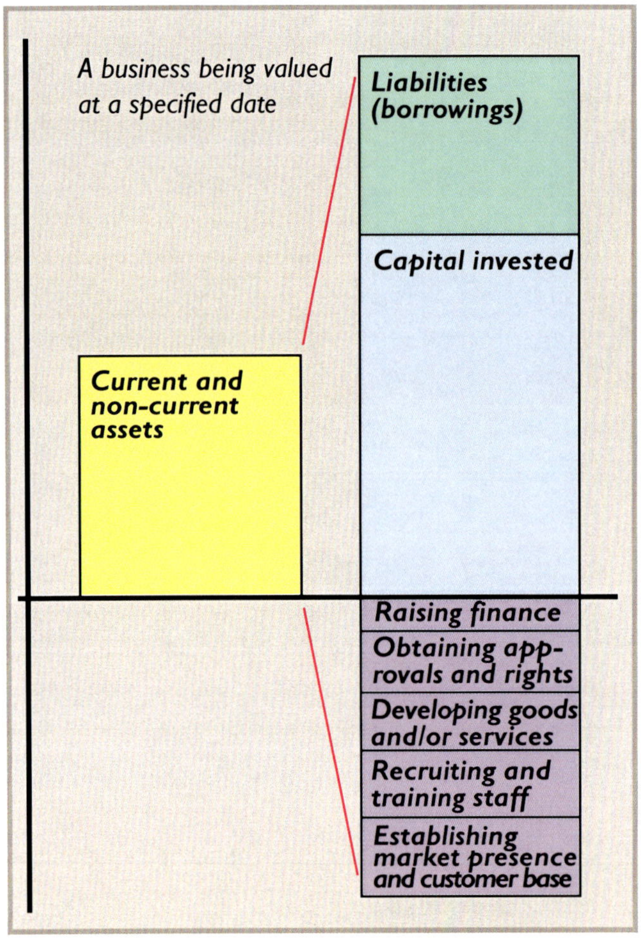

Figure 13.1 Entry cost valuation. Once the totals of the expenses and assets needed to start a business equivalent to the subject business have been determined, their sum equals the total of borrowings and capital invested required to start that equivalent business, and is thus a measure of the value of the subject business.

13.4.4 Price multiple valuation methods

There are several price (meaning 'valuation') multiples which can be used to calculate a valuation. They include:

- price/earnings ratios including price/EBIT and price/EBITDIA
- price/sales
- price/net assets book value.

In the price/earnings ratios earnings is the profit for the annual period after tax, excluding any exceptional items which have temporarily distorted the profit. Other measures of earnings which may be used are EBIT and EBITDIA which are explained on pages 96 and 97.

Price/earnings ratio

The price/earnings ratio (P/E) is the number of years the business would take to earn its market value or price if the business's annual earnings remained the same during those years as those published in the most recent annual report. This particular ratio is called the trailing P/E ratio. The value of the ratio by which the business's earnings are multiplied to produce a price indicates the investors' or valuer's forecast of the business's future profitability and/or changes in share price. And although the four quarters' most recent earnings are those usually used, other options include: double the earnings of last two quarters, double the forecast earnings for the next two quarters, or the forecast earnings for the next four quarters.

At any particular date there is an approximate typical P/E ratio for a public company with good earnings prospects in a particular industry. That P/E ratio varies over time due to many factors, and will usually be smaller for other businesses working in the same industry. The more the P/E ratio used in a valuation

ASX 300 Leaders — **To close of business Wednesday, March 23, 2016**

Company Name	ASX Code	Last Sale	Move +/-	Quote Buy	Quote Sell	Volume 100s	Day's High	Day's Low	52-Week High	52-Week Low	Dividend ¢ per Share	Dividend Times cov'd	Net tang assets	Div yield %	Earn share ¢	P/E ratio	Week % move
1	2	3	4	5	6	7	8	9	10	11	12	13	14	15	16	17	18
GUD Hldgs	GUD	6.92	-	6.91	6.94	2867	6.99	6.89	10.18	6.07	42.00 f	.56	.23	6.07	23.60	29.3	+.29
GWA Grp..................	GWA	2.27	-4	2.27	2.28	4673	2.30	2.23	2.75	1.765	7.00 f	2.00	.02	3.08	14.02	16.2	-.44
Hansen Tech..............	HSN	3.60	-3	3.60	3.61	2264	3.63	3.57	3.98	2.00	6.00 p	2.00	.11	1.67	12.00	30.0	-.55
Harvey Norman	**HVN**	**4.69**	**-**	**4.67**	**4.69**	**23791**	**4.71**	**4.65**	**4.99**	**3.65**	**24.00 f**	**1.17**	**2.48**	**5.12**	**28.02**	**16.7**	**+.43**
Healthscope..............	HSO	2.62	-1	2.61	2.62	77285	2.65	2.60	3.09	2.12	7.20	1.45	.22	2.75	10.43	25.1	+1.55
Henderson Grp cdi.......	HGG	4.86	-4	4.86	4.87	12705	4.88	4.81	6.56	4.34	21.48	1.39	.65	4.42	29.82	16.3	-.82
HFA Hldgs	HFA	2.41	-5	2.40	2.41	1593	2.43	2.34	3.22	1.865	14.66	1.29	.29	6.08	18.97	12.7	-1.23

Figure 13.2 An extract from *The Australian Financial Review* of 24–28 March 2016 showing the quotation on the ASX (Sydney Stock Exchange) for Harvey Norman Holdings Limited for 23 March 2016. The black column numbers superimposed on the white squares correspond to the item numbers in the list of explanations below.

[1] Company's name.

[2] Official ASX abbreviation for the company.

[3] Most recent (closing) price paid for shares in the company. This price may be that paid by or to a stockbroker.

[4] How the closing price paid on 23 March (see column 5) compared with the closing price on the trading day before.

[5] Highest price bid on 23 March for shares in the company.

[6] Lowest price at which the shares were offered for sale on 23 March.

[7] Number of shares traded during 23 March in 100s.

[8] Highest price paid for the company's shares during 23 March.

[9] Lowest price paid for the company's shares during 23 March.

[10] Highest daily closing share price for the company during the 52 weeks ending 23 March.

[11] Lowest daily closing share price for the company during the 52 weeks ending 23 March.

[12] Dividend in cents per share. 'f' indicates that the most recent dividend declared was fully franked. 'p' indicates that the most recent dividend declared was partly franked (see pages 75 and 76).

[13] Times covered (dividend cover), earnings÷dividend.

[14] NTA (net tangible assets/share), net tangible assets÷number of ordinary shares.

[15] Dividend yield, the dividend per ordinary share declared during the preceding 52 weeks x 100% divided by the price of last sale in column [3].

[16] EPS, earnings per share, operating profit less tax, less dividends to minority and preference shareholders ÷ average number of ordinary shares.

[17] P/E, price/earnings ratio, the last sale price from column [3] divided by the EPS from column [16].

[18] Movement in the share price expressed as a percentage over the week.

The above explanations are based on information from <*www.afr.com/whats_in_a_table/*>, and they and the extract are reproduced with permission of the ASX Limited.

exceeds the approximate typical P/E ratio for a similar businesses with good earnings prospects, the more the valuer believes the earnings and/or share price of the subject business will rise. Similarly the further below the approximate typical P/E ratio the P/E ratio used in a valuation lies, the more earnings and/or the share price are expected to fall.

Figure 13.2 shows quotations for public company shares on the Sydney Stock Exchange. The format of those quotations is similar to those used elsewhere. The immense variation in the P/E ratios of different businesses is illustrated in figure 13.2 where those for just the seven companies shown lie between 30.0 and 12.7. Extreme values of P/E ratio are associated with businesses whose earnings have little relevance to their valuations.

13.4.5 Industry rules of thumb

For types of businesses which are commonly bought and sold there may be established valuation rules of thumb, for example an amount per customer or per subscriber or per branch, or a multiple of annual revenue. However such rules-of-thumb should not be accepted without question, and should be used in conjunction with other valuation methods.

13.5 FACTORS WHICH CAN AFFECT VALUATIONS

Valuations of the same business using different methods can be far apart as figure 13.3 demonstrates. Although valuations can be determined as described in the preceding section, those valuations all rely on assumptions. The choice of those assumptions, or the decision to amend a valuation can be influenced by:

- factors particular to the business
- factors external to the business
- subjective factors.

Factors particular to the business

Factors particular to a business which should be considered when making a valuation include:

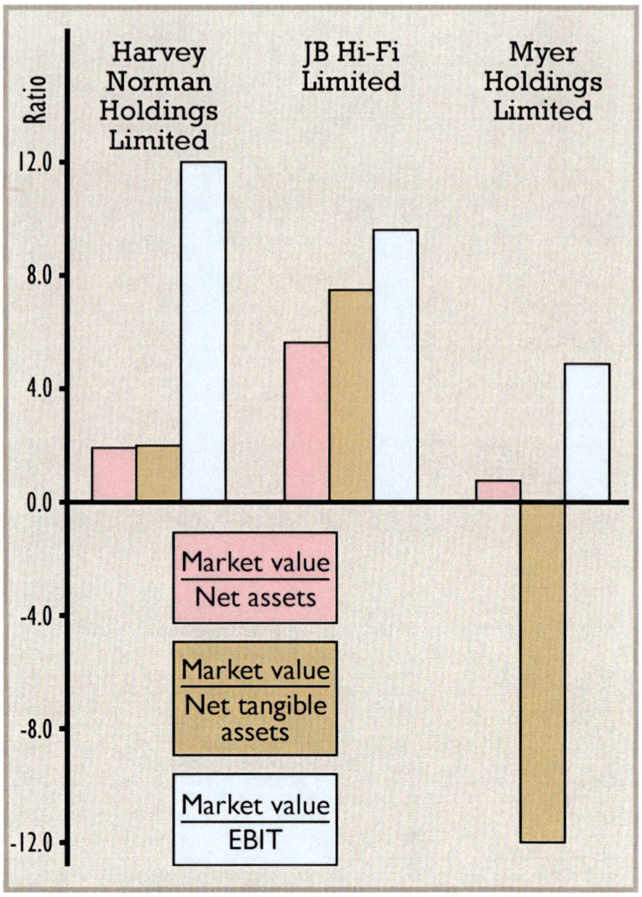

Figure 13.3 The unreliability of any one criterion as a measure of a business's value. The values of three ratios for three apparently similar companies as at 30 June 2015 for Harvey Norman and JB Hi-Fi, and as at 27 July 2015 for Myer Holdings. Net tangible assets is net assets minus intangible assets.

This chart suggests that while earnings is the most reliable valuation criterion for long-established companies, forecast future earnings is more reliable than historical earnings. However, valuations are affected by many other factors both objective and subjective.

For Harvey Norman: net assets, $2,557m; net tangible assets, $2,473m; market value, 1,095m shares @ $4.50 = $4,927m; EBIT $411m.

For JB Hi-Fi: net assets, $343m; net tangible assets, $259m; market value, 99m shares @ $19.51 = $1,931m; EBIT $200.9m.

For Myer Holdings: net assets, $863m; net tangible assets, ($53m); market value, 586m shares @ $1.11 = $650m; EBIT $133.5m.

- the strengths of relationships with important suppliers, subcontractors and customers
- the importance of contracts, rights, patents, distribution agreements and similar held by the business
- the expertise of particular owners or other staff. How vulnerable is the business to their leaving, joining a competitor or setting up a competing business?
- particularly with small businesses, earnings can be distorted by owners' payments strategies; for example, a company's retained profit will be inflated if the salaries of working owners have been unreasonably low.
- costs such as those of closing the business's premises, fulfilling product warranties, and making redundancy payments to its employees are relevant for a valuation which assumes that the business will close.

Factors external to the business

Factors outside a business's control typically influence its valuation. Such factors include: prevailing interest rates, the availability of credit, the current and expected international, domestic and local economic climates, the outlook for the particular sector of the economy in which the business operates, and the contemporary market emotion.

Subjective factors

Valuations are subjective; for example, different buyers may be willing to accept different rates of return or may value a business's assets differently. A buyer who would seek to optimise the subject business's future performance, or combine it with businesses the buyer already owns, or buy it to create some sort of monopoly might be prepared to pay more than a buyer who wants to break-up and sell the business's assets. And a buyer who is emotionally desperate to own that particular business rather than a similar one may be willing to pay a premium.

A transfer of ownership requires the seller and the buyer to agree on a price. The greater the need for the seller to sell, and particularly if this is known by potential buyers, the lower the sale price is likely to be. Where there are competing potential buyers or the seller is reluctant, the buyer may have to pay a premium.

13.6 MARKET VALUE

A tiny proportion of Australian businesses have their ordinary shares quoted on stock exchanges. Figure 13.2 shows an extract from the Sydney Stock Exchange share quotations for 23 March 2016, and also explains its meanings. The challenge for a potential buyer or seller of quoted shares is to decide whether those shares are overvalued or undervalued.

For those companies whose shares are quoted on stock exchanges, their market value or market capitalization is:

$$\begin{bmatrix}\text{Number of shares}\\ \text{purchased by investors}\end{bmatrix} \text{x} \begin{bmatrix}\text{Quoted price}\\ \text{per share}\end{bmatrix}$$

For example, on 23 March 2016 Harvey Norman's share price was \$4.69, the number of ordinary shares issued was 1,095,116,804 and the market value of the company was \$5,136m. However, on 30 June 2015 Harvey Norman's net asset book value was \$2.557m, its share price was \$4.50, and its market value therefore \$4,927m. The increasing difference between the market and book values during the period 30 June 2015 to 23 March 2016 reflects the higher earnings in 2014–15 (figure 12.6 on page 103) and investors' confidence in the company's future prospects.

A company's shares may not be fully paid. For example, if shares were issued by a company at \$4.00, with \$2.00 payable immediately and \$2.00 payable a year later, the quoted price per share during that year would be lower than if the company's shares were fully paid because shareholders would shortly be called upon to pay the \$2.00 owing.

The number of ordinary shares can in some companies increase, particularly if the share price increases, for example by stock options being exercised. If the number of shares are thus increased without a commensurate rise in earnings, the share price would fall. Hence in such a situation the potential for significant dilution tends to depress the share price.

Chapter 14

BUDGETING

To explain budgeting this chapter discusses:

- what a budget is,
- the structure of a master budget,
- the rationale behind budgeting,
- preparing budgets,
- implementing budgets.

14.1 WHAT A BUDGET IS

A budget is a plan of action for an entity for a specified period, usually of one to three years, agreed by the entity's management. A budget should include both financial and non-financial targets, and the supporting assumptions and data on which that budget is based. The comprehensive budget prepared for an entity is called a master budget.

14.2 STRUCTURE OF A MASTER BUDGET

An entity's master budget is a set of interdependent function budgets and budgeted financial statements (the financial statements which would report the changes in and the financial position of the entity were the function budgets all achieved). The function budgets consist of budgets for functions such as the management of cash, of raw materials, of overheads, and of revenues. An entity's function budgets and budgeted financial statements are usually grouped under the headings:

- **operating budgets** Operating budgets are concerned with the functions which contribute to income and to expenditures related to earning income. These function budgets are summarised in a budgeted profit or loss statement
- **financial budgets** The financial budget's function budgets show the funding targets needed for the entity to achieve its budgeted operating targets plus any additional changes in funding which will be needed for the entity to achieve the control account balances in its budgeted balance sheet. For example, a company might decide to issue additional shares to obtain enough cash to take advantage of new investment opportunities which are expected to arise. The budgeted balance sheet is produced by adding the budgeted changes in its constituent control account balances during the budget period to the balance sheet account balances as at the beginning of the budget period.

A master budget's constituent budgets are designed to realise the subject entity's objectives, make clear how those objectives will be achieved, and show how the entity will match its capabilities to the opportunities and challenges expected in its market. The entity must therefore ensure that it has the appropriate organisational structure, personnel, and financial and other resources taking into consideration risk and contingency plans.

14.3 WHY BUDGET?

The purpose of budgeting is to improve an entity's performance, particularly during the budget period. Budgeting requires that the entity's management provide a defined plan so that:

- managers switch focus from dealing with day-to-day problems to planning ahead. Having a budget with targets helps an entity's manager forestall many day-to-day problems and provides a means to judge progress
- people within the entity can better communicate and collaborate to achieve the agreed and defined goals
- the actual performance of each function can be monitored relative to its budget targets
- the manager of each function will be motivated by being held accountable for that manager's function budget and its achievement.

- the entity can efficiently obtain the resources required by the budget by the required dates and for the durations specified. Having budgets also enables potential resource excesses and shortages to be foreseen and appropriate action taken.

14.4 PREPARING A BUDGET

If not done already, before preparing an entity's master budget the management functions within the entity which will have their own budgets must be identified.

An entity's chart of accounts may also need modifying so that each management function has its own control accounts. The number of such functions will reflect the size and complexity of the entity. Each function should have a manager who is involved in preparing that function's budget, making efficiency improvement plans, and monitoring and reacting to that function's performance in comparison to that function's budget targets during the budget period. Those targets should be demanding but realistic, and require efficiency improvements.

Most entities prepare a master budget for the next 12-months period. An alternative is to have, say, a three-year budget which is updated every year.

Budgets are now usually prepared using spreadsheet-based software. This facilitates:

- preparing and combining schedules. A *schedule* is a 'component of a budget which shows the changes in the subject function through the budget period, not just the targets which the function should have achieved as at the end of the period'
- revising master budget component budgets as new information and feedback is received
- preparing separate budgets for a small number of different likely scenarios
- trialling different budget assumptions.

Stage 1

The first stage in preparing a master budget is to clarify the assumptions on which the master budget's component budgets will be based. In this process inputs are typically sought from both internal and external sources, and include historic, present and forecast values and trends for:

- the entity's sales and those of competitors
- the entity's production and those of competitors
- amounts and timings of price changes
- market growth or shrinkage
- interest and inflation rates
- the entity's required return on investment
- the costs and availabilities of relevant resources
- technological developments recent and anticipated
- changes in the political climate and events
- seasonal factors.

Once clarified and stated these assumptions are used to agree the target revenues during the budget period in numbers of the various types of units sold and their unit selling prices and/or in the quantity of services and their selling prices. In agreeing these revenue targets, the entity's objectives, capabilities, and any relevant restrictions should be taken into account.

Stage 2

The second stage is to prepare the individual function budgets, and then group them under the operating and financial budget headings. The entity's senior and function managers need to consult during this process so that the resulting function budgets are compatible with the entity achieving the sales targets agreed and stated in the revenue budget. Any bars to achieving the sales targets revealed by the managers of other functions should be evaluated and the affected budgets modified if necessary.

Consensus budgeting is desirable. However there can be situations when an entity's senior management is justified in dictating harsher targets than those determined by consensus.

Because of the interdependent and myriad factors which typically affect budgets and because budgeting decisions and information neither flow exclusively from the top down nor the bottom up, the conventional explanations of master budget preparation using flow charts are unsatisfying. This chapter instead promotes a holistic explanation using balance charts.

Figures 14.1 to 14.5 illustrate how a manufacturer might prepare a master budget. The figures are presented in reverse order to make the process easier to understand.

- Figure 14.1 shows target sales during the budget period and the changes in the manufacturer's production-related control account balances which are necessary to achieve those target sales and some other production-related targets.
- Figure 14.2 shows the target changes in non-production function related control account balances. After balancing, this balance chart becomes the manufacturer's budgeted balance sheet as at the end of the budget period.
- Figure 14.3 shows the budgeted profit or loss statement for the budget period. Its stated profit (or loss) will result if the targets are exactly achieved.
- Figure 14.4 shows how target changes to control account balances during the budget period are aggregated by function prior to combining them into function budgets.
- Figure 14.5 illustrates how a function's schedules are combined to produce a single function budget. A single budget is much easier to use as a management tool than a collection of related schedules or component budgets. However the schedules or component budgets provide the back-up information needed to fully understand the function budget and, if required, revise it.

Although figures 14.1 to 14.5 relate to a manufacturing company, the budgeting process they illustrate is applicable to service and retail entities, and to those entities active in more than one of these areas.

14.5 IMPLEMENTING A BUDGET

The manager of each entity function should be accountable for that function's performance against its budget. Similarly, the CEO (chief executive officer) of the entity should be responsible for the performance of the entity as a whole, and each senior manager should be responsible for the performance of the functions under his or her control.

The record keeping needed for budgeting needs to be integrated with the entity's chart of accounts. For efficient budget implementation the entity needs to have systems which monitor performances and compare them with the relevant targets in the current master budget. Any resulting variances in performance from budget targets or budget assumptions can arise suddenly or become apparent as trends. The appropriate managers should then investigate the variances and decide what actions to take bearing in mind that corrective actions can affect other functions. Hence the need for continuing consultation between function managers. If variances suggest that budget targets will not be met or will be exceeded, managers should consider whether the related budgets remain valid and whether the master budget should be flexed (updated to reflect variances and/or changes to assumptions). A budget which isn't changed is a static budget.

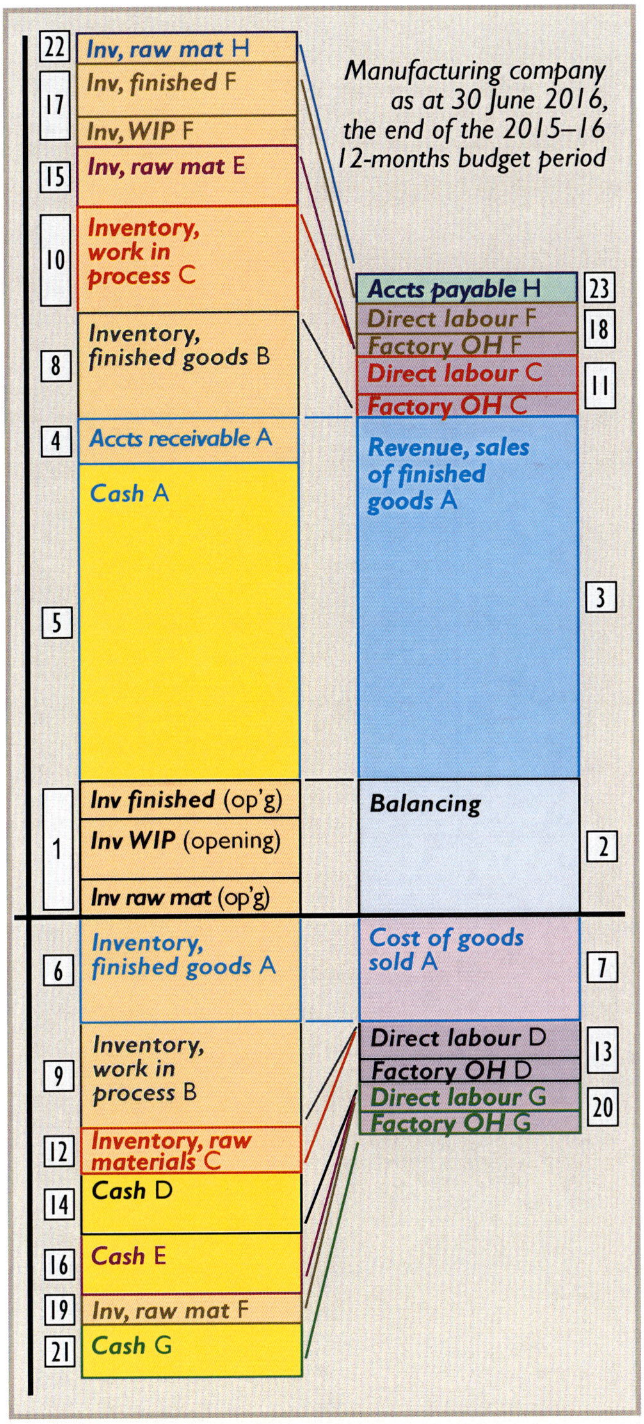

Figure 14.1 A balance chart showing a manufacturing company's target sales of finished goods and target increases in inventory during the budget period. The chart also shows the cash and debt-financed expenditures on raw materials, direct labour and factory overhead required to achieve the targets. These expenditures are derived from the targets.

The box heights are accurately drawn to the y axis's monetary scale. Each box represents an > opening control account balance or a budgeted change to a control account balance during the budget period. The subject entity should therefore have a control account for each budget function in its chart of accounts.

Abbreviations used in this chart are: *inv* for 'inventory', *finished* for 'finished goods for trading', *WIP* for 'work in process', *accts* for 'accounts', *OH* for 'overhead', *raw mat* for 'raw materials', and *opg* for 'opening'.

To aid comprehension, related account balances and target changes to account balances have box outlines and account names of the same colour and the same reference letter.

[1] The manufacturer's opening inventory at the beginning of the budget period consisted of amounts of: raw materials and purchased components which are intended to manufactured into finished goods; partially manufactured items called *work in process*; and unsold finished goods. Indirect materials such as solvents, cleaning materials, lubricants, small tools, etc. are recorded as expenses as they are purchased and aren't therefore included in inventory. Also, the expenses accounts are closed at the end of each reporting period.

[2] The account balance to balance [1].

[3] The agreed target revenue for the budget period.

[4] and [5] The target assumption is that by the end of the budget period, most of the revenue in [3] will have been received in cash.

[6] To achieve the target revenue finished goods of the shown cost must have been sold.

[7] The reduction to assets recorded in [6] must be balanced by an equal cost-of-goods-sold expense.

[8] and [9] The finished goods sold during the budget period were completed work in process.

[10], [11] and [12] The cost of the work in process recorded in [9] consists of the constituent raw materials, direct labour, and factory overhead costs. Factory overhead includes: factory council rates, factory rent, maintenance, insurance, supervisory and other indirect labour, employee benefit costs for direct and indirect labour, and indirect materials >

> (used in the factory but not incorporated into the finished manufactured goods). Factory overhead also includes the depreciation of factory-related non-current assets, but as this expense doesn't involve any expenditure (but does reduce income tax payable), it's not included here.

[13] and [14] The direct labour and factory overhead expenses recorded in [11] would be paid for in cash during the budget period.

[15] and [16] The manufacturer's management agreed that at the end of the budget period the manufacturer should have somewhat higher inventories than at the start of the period to facilitate the higher sales envisaged for 2016–17. Subtracting the usage of materials in [12] from the opening raw materials in [1] shows that raw materials would run out before the end of the budget period. [15] shows the additional raw materials needed to avoid this and provide sufficient opening raw materials for 2016–17. The cash payment for these raw materials is recorded in [16].

[17], [18] and [19] The target increases in finished goods and work in process by the end of the budget period recorded in [17] would require expenditures on direct labour and factory overhead [18] and raw materials [19].

[20] and [21] The direct labour and factory overhead recorded in [18] would be paid for in cash.

[22] and [23] The raw materials component of [17] recorded in [19] would be purchased on credit, and the related cash wouldn't be paid out by the end of the budget period.

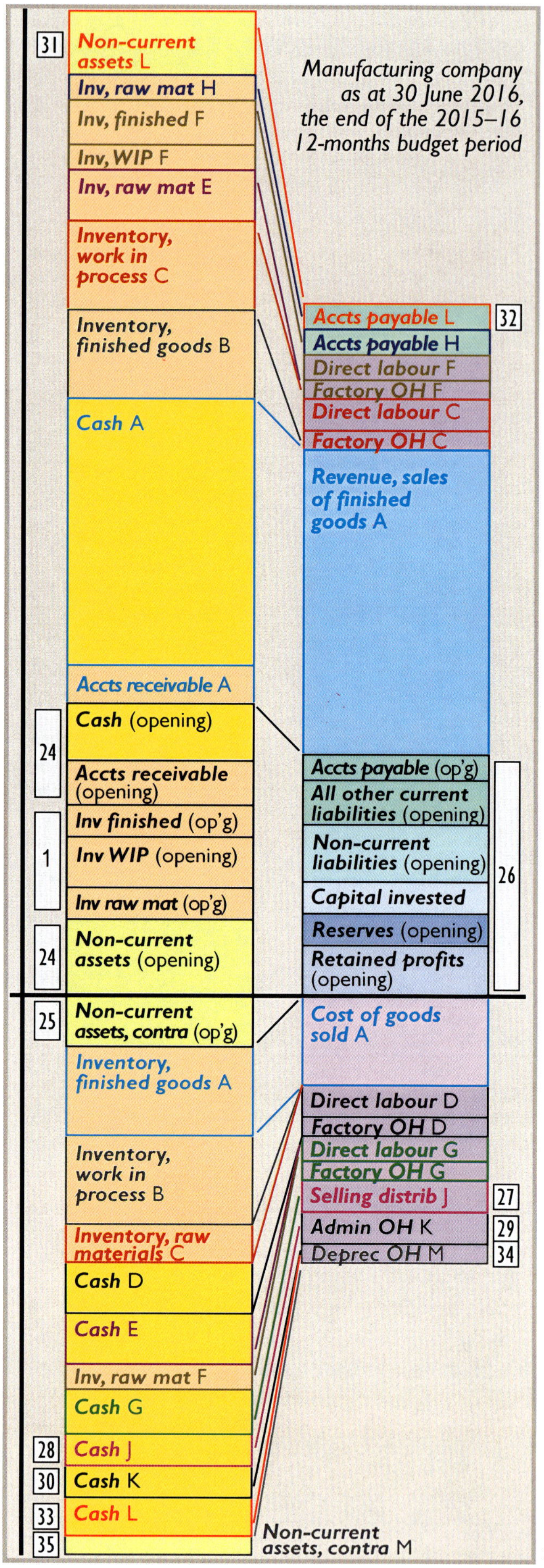

>

> **Figure 14.2** The balance chart as at the end of the manufacturing company's 2015–16 budget year, also called a *budgeted balance sheet*. The box heights are accurately drawn to the y-axis's monetary scale.

To achieve the target sales and increases in inventory shown in figure 14.1 will involve expenditures on selling and distribution, and administration overheads. Additional non-current assets (for example, production machinery, and computer hardware and software) will need to be acquired. And existing and newly-acquired non-current assets will depreciate. These target changes are highlighted in this figure.

The central grouping of boxes [1], [24], [25] and [26] with black outlines and account names represents the company's financial position at the start of the 12-months budget period. The chart's other boxes represent the target changes agreed to by company's managers for the budget year. So as not to add more boxes, this balance chart assumes that no changes are envisaged to the balances of other current liabilities, non-current liabilities, capital invested or reserves accounts, and that the company won't pay or declare any dividends during the budget period.

Only the target changes to account balances not shown in figure 14.1 are explained below:

[27] and [28] The targeted selling and distribution expenses which will be paid for in cash.

[29] and [30] The targeted administrative overhead which will be paid for in cash.

[31], [32] and [33] The targeted expenditure on additional non-current assets will only be partially paid for in cash by the end of the budget period.

[34] and [35] Because it doesn't involve any expenditure, the depreciation of non-current assets expense for the budget period is shown separately rather than being included in administrative and factory overheads.

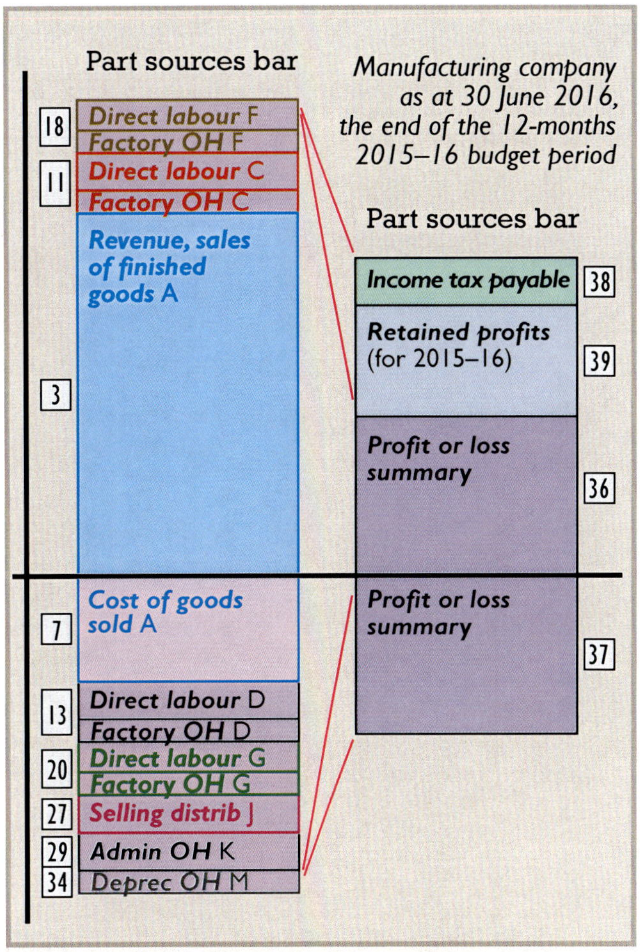

Figure 14.3 The example manufacturer's budgeted profit or loss statement for the budget period prepared from the changes to account balances shown in figures 14.1 and 14.2. If the resulting budgeted profit were insufficient, some or all of the target changes to control account balances would have to be revised.

[36] The balance of the profit or loss summary account resulting from closing the profit-related temporary accounts in the left-hand bar.

[37], [38] and [39] Separating the budgeted balance of the profit or loss account into the retained profit for the budget period and the income tax payable. The resulting amount of income tax payable [38] is added to the opening balance of the other current liabilities account [26] in figure 14.2 to give the balance of other current liabilities as at the end of the budget period. The amount of income tax payable doesn't here take into account deductions such as those resulting from falls in the unit values of inventories and any impairment losses of non-current assets.

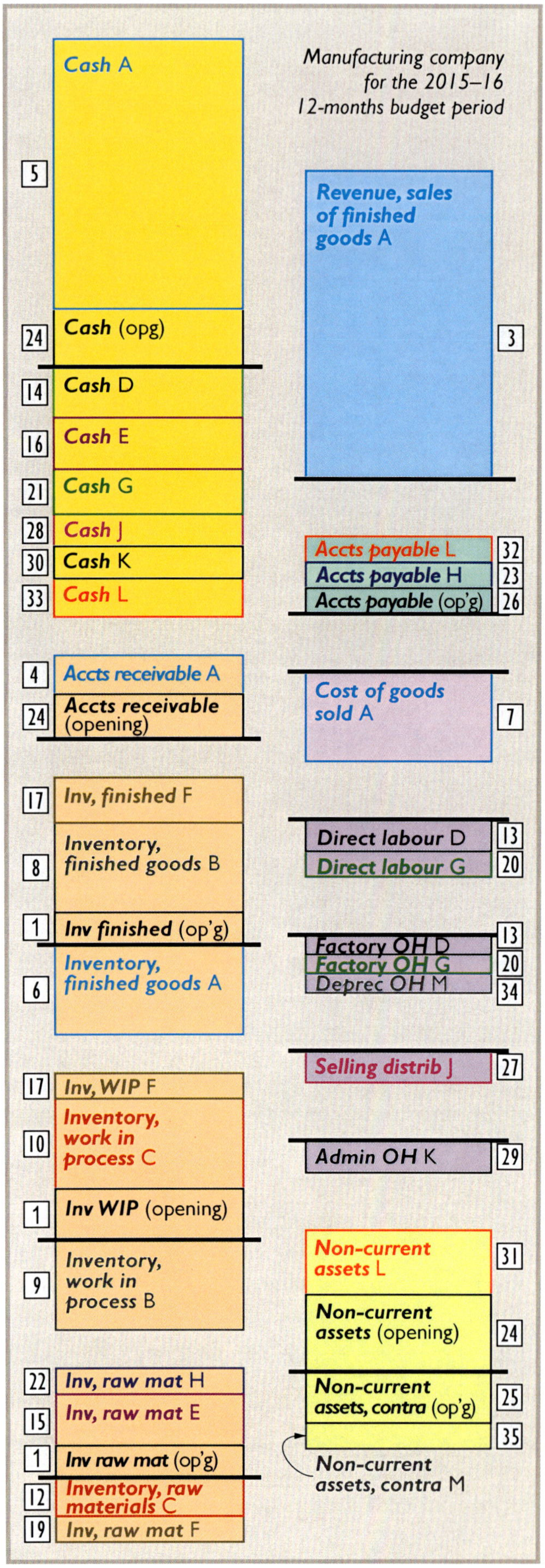

Figure 14.4 Combining account balances and target changes to account balances related to the same function (control account) to produce function budgets. The boxes are abstracted from figures 14.1 and 14.2, and the position of the x axis for each function is shown. Boxes 11 and 18 for factory overhead and direct labour aren't included here because boxes 13 and 20 fully define the targets for these expenses.

This balance chart shows thirteen budgets. These budgets are in turn be grouped into an operating and a financial budget as below:

- Operating budget
    - Revenue (sales) budget
    - Selling and distribution budget
    - Administration budget
    - Production budget
        - Direct labour budget
        - Finished goods budget
        - Work in process budget
        - Raw materials budget
        - Factory overhead budget
    - Budgeted profit or loss statement

- Financial budget
    - Capital expenditure budget (expenditures on facilities and equipment)
    - Cash budget
    - Budgeted balance sheet
        - Accounts receivable budget
        - Accounts payable budget

Because of the interdependency of budgets, preparing them is demanding. Entities therefore need to decide how detailed and complete their budgeting is going to be. If any significant expected or required changes to any control accounts are ignored, the resulting master budget will be to some extent compromised. For example, the cash budget here excludes any dividend payments during the budget period. If however a dividend payment were made during the budget period, then the cash budget shown here understates the company's budgeted cash outflows and hides the real likelihood that the company will run out of cash.

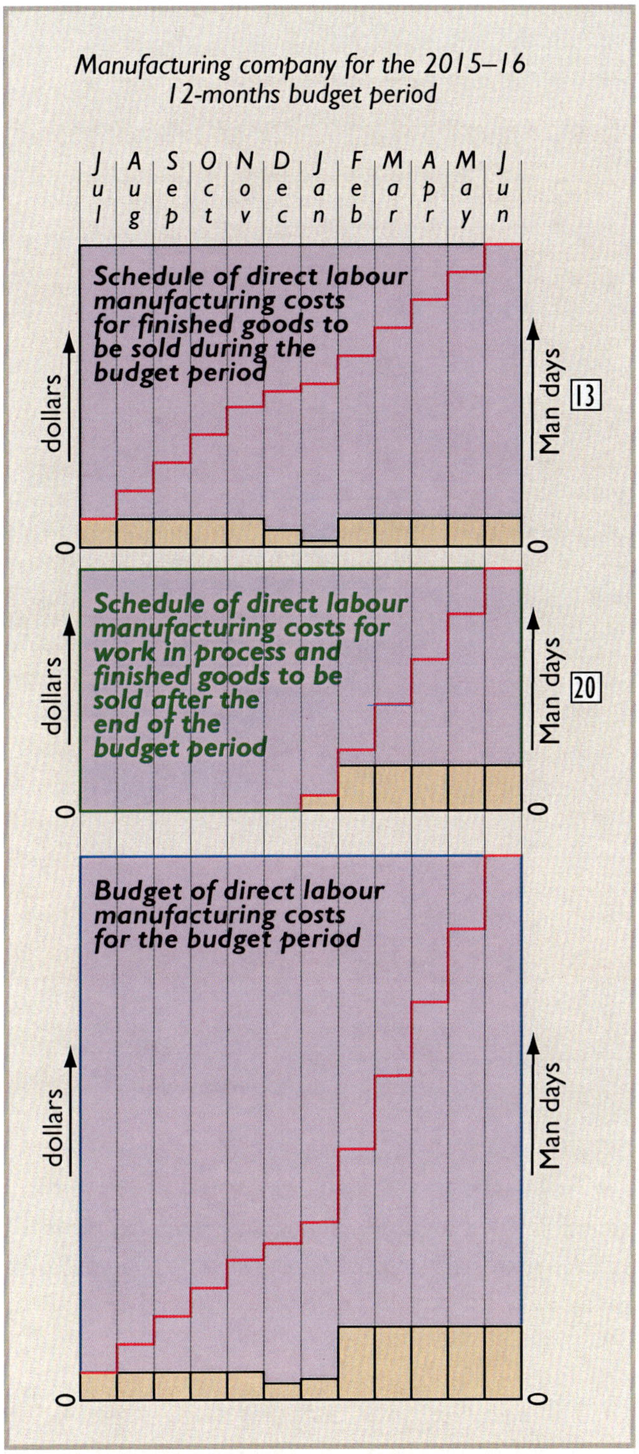

Figure 14.5 Showing how a function budget, here for the expense of direct labour, is prepared. The target direct labour costs [13] and [20] shown first in figure 14.1 have had their figure 14.1 heights multiplied by eight and their figure 14.1 widths doubled.

The budgeted direct labour costs in [13] and [20] and their combination into the direct labour budget are shown as schedules. In them > the brown boxes represent the budgeted monthly direct labour costs, and the magenta stepped lines represent the accumulated total of direct labour costs through the budget period. The number of workers which need to be directly employed in this company's manufacturing is proportional to and can therefore be readily calculated from these labour costs.

Breaking down annual budget targets into schedules with multiple shorter time periods enables better monitoring. Such usually quarterly or monthly targets should take into account seasonal factors.

Chapter 15

CONCLUSION

As explained in chapter 4, Pacioli's book *Summa de Arithmetica* was first published in 1494, and contained a treatise which was the first printed explanation of double-entry bookkeeping. That treatise (figure 15.1) did not contain any illustrations which helped the reader better understand bookkeeping. Since that treatise's publication there been little progress towards explaining accounting graphically, until my invention of balance charts.

Graphical explanations are more easily understood because patterns and relationships are more readily perceived. The understandings a reader thus achieves are also retained for longer. These advantages encourage learning from graphical sources.

Accounting has a wonderfully elegant two-bar structure. Balance charts explain by exploiting and stressing that structure. They're easy to understand, and also make the concept of double entry easier to understand. Therefore:

- It's generally easier to understand explanations which use appropriate balance charts than their purely textual (which includes columns of amounts) equivalents.
- It's easy to convert and relate balance charts to text and vice versa.
- Balance charts are versatile. This book features several variants, each designed to aid the explanation of a particular accounting topic.

Having read this book, you're well-placed to judge whether these claims are true. If they are, shouldn't balance charts be introduced into accounting education?

This international edition of *Know Accounting Graphically* is intended to help anyone who wishes to understand bookkeeping and/or accounting in a country where consumption tax is levied. However being for such a wide readership, it cannot provide the specific detail particular to a single country's accounting standards and tax law. If anyone is interested in producing an edition of this book which is country specific, please contact me because I hold the copyright.

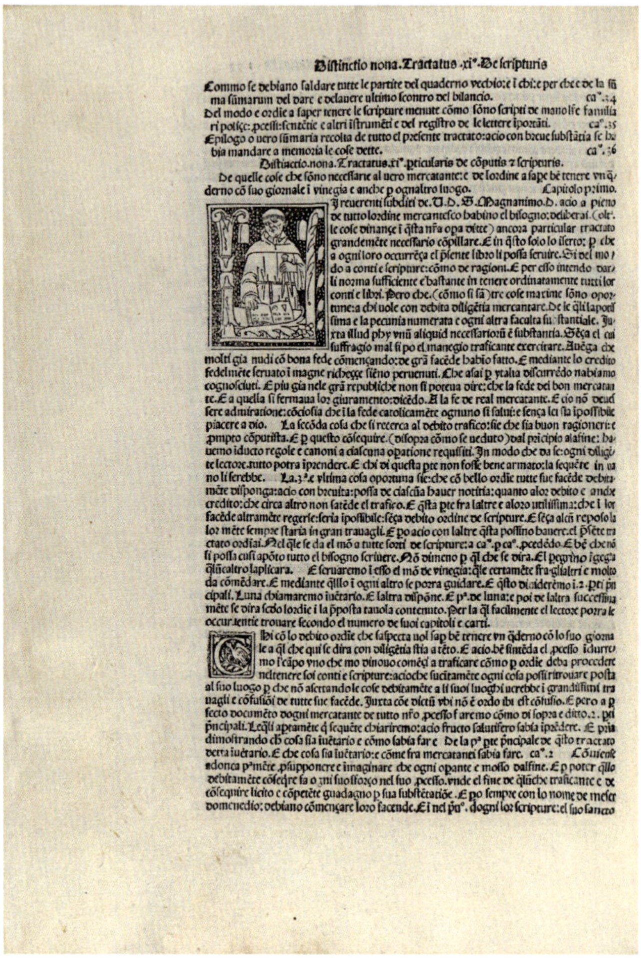
Distinctio nona. Tractatus .xi°. De scripturis

Figure 15.1 The first page of the 27-page, 24,000-word treatise on double-entry bookkeeping from Pacioli's 1523 edition of *Summa de Arithmetica*. The treatise is usually called "Particularis de Computis et Scripturis" (Particulars of Reckonings and Writings), the treatise's title in the 1494 edition.

Illustration courtesy of Edinburgh University Library.

I'd be grateful for your inputs on how the book could be improved. You can contact me via mike@knowaccountinggraphically.com.

Last, if you have found this book to your liking, please spread the word. The refusal of accounting educators until now (May 2017) to recommend this book and my lack of contacts in accounting, education and business means that only through personal recommendation will the use of balance charts spread.

Appendix

BALANCE CHARTS

This book explains with balance charts. This appendix introduces balance charts, and is mainly intended for those who already know accounting and whose interest is the charts rather than the basics of accounting.

The arithmetical basis of accounting is the accounting or balance sheet equation:

Assets = Liabilities + Equity

For, say, a company, this equation's three control account balances can be separated into the balances of the fourteen accounts represented in the figure A1 balance chart. The balances of these accounts can then be separated to produce the balances of all the control and ledger accounts the company would need in its chart of accounts.

Figure A1 and all other balance charts have three common features:

- a vertical y axis with a suitable monetary scale (here in dollars) which runs from zero both upwards and downwards
- a horizontal x axis drawn at y = 0 which doesn't have a scale. Therefore the width of a balance chart box has no significance
- two vertical bars of boxes projecting upwards and downwards from the x axis. The height of each box is proportional to the dollar amount it represents.

In figure A1 the left-hand bar's boxes represent the balances of the assets accounts shown; the right-hand bar's boxes represent the balances of the liabilities and equity accounts—it's these balances which provide the sources of the monies which enable the entity to control its assets. In balance charts a box can represent a posting to a ledger account and/or an account balance.

As figure A1 also illustrates, because the balances of its accounts are aggregated from the balances of all the company's ledger (posting) accounts, the balance sheet equation can be restated as:

[Net height (in dollars) of all assets bar ledger account balances] = [Net height (in dollars) of all sources bar ledger account balances]

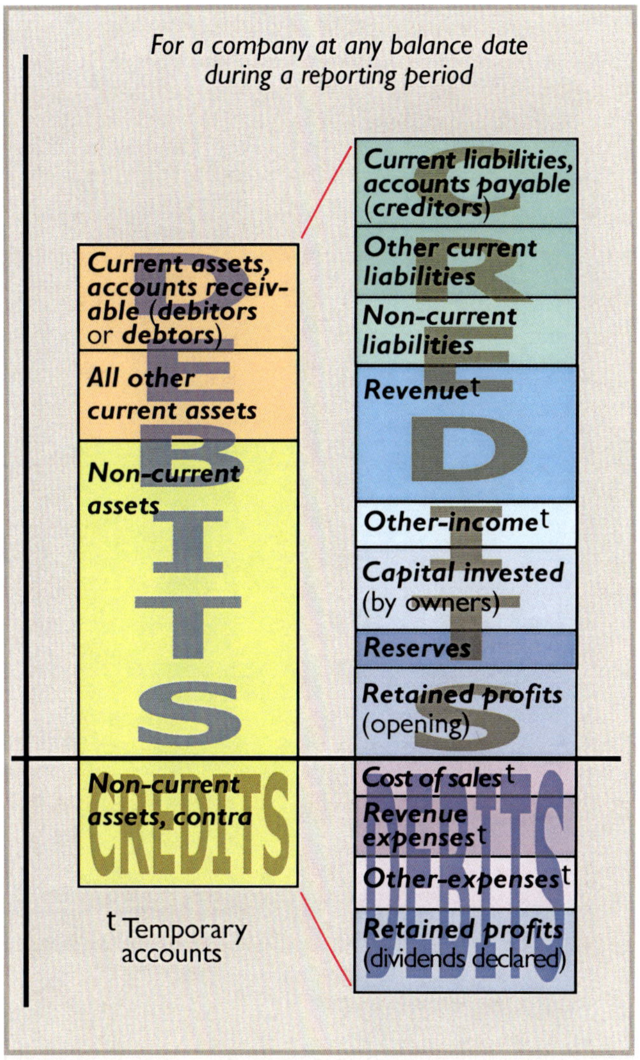

Figure A1 A balance chart which represents the balance sheet equation, and the financial position of a company at a balance date. This chart is identical to figure 5.1.

Each box represent an account balance. The name of the account is printed in bold italic type at the top of a box. The dollar amounts of the individual account balances will be different for each company and vary through time for an active company subject to the imperative of the balance sheet equation shown left.

Here and throughout this book, balance chart boxes have coloured fills: yellowish for assets accounts, greenish for liabilities accounts, and bluish for equity accounts. This feature is unnecessary if you're sketching a balance chart.

In this equation the net height of a bar equals its total height in monetary units (here dollars) above the x axis minus its total depth in dollars below the x axis. The equality between the two net bar heights is signified and confirmed in this book's balance charts by magenta lines which join the internal corners of the two bars.

When an entity is involved in a single transaction, the entity's financial position both immediately before and immediately after that transaction must conform to the balance sheet equation imperative. Therefore the postings for one or for any number of transactions must also conform to the balance sheet equation imperative. Therefore any balance chart irrespective of whether its boxes represent account balances and/or one or more postings must conform to two equations:

$$\begin{bmatrix}\text{Net height (in} \\ \text{dollars) of assets} \\ \text{bar above x axis}\end{bmatrix} = \begin{bmatrix}\text{Net height (in} \\ \text{dollars) of sources} \\ \text{bar above x axis}\end{bmatrix}$$

(Equation 5.f on page 27)

and

$$\begin{bmatrix}\text{Total (in dollars)} \\ \text{of debit account} \\ \text{balances and} \\ \text{postings}\end{bmatrix} = \begin{bmatrix}\text{Total (in dollars)} \\ \text{of credit account} \\ \text{balances and} \\ \text{postings}\end{bmatrix}$$

Figure A2 conforms to both these imperatives, and shows the main features of the most common forms of balance chart.

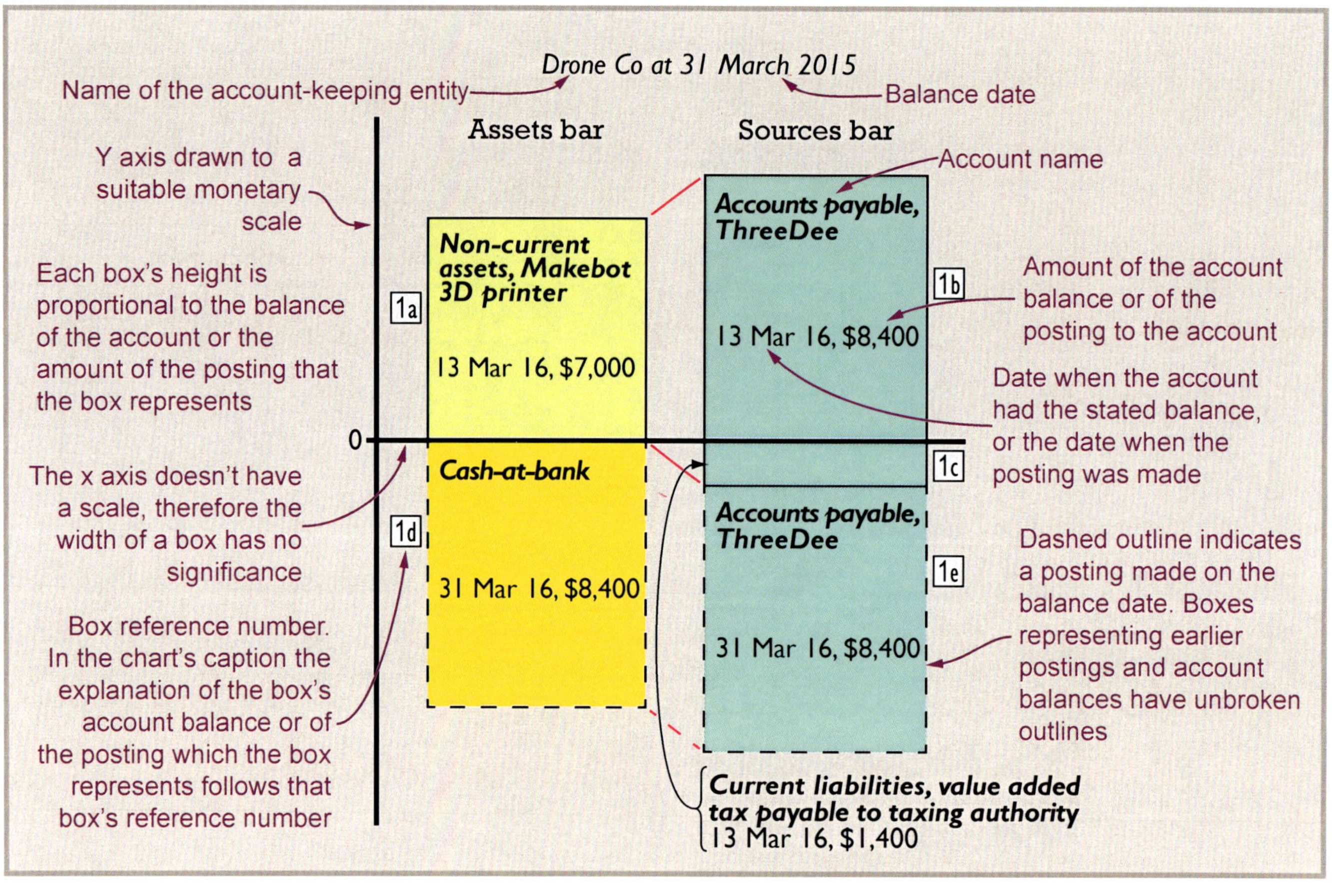

Figure A2 An balance chart based on this book's figure 6.5 on page 33. This chart represents the purchase by Drone Co of a 3D printer from supplier ThreeDee on 13 March 2016, and Drone's payment on 31 March of the related bill.

Boxes always represent positive amounts. The location of the box representing an additive posting to, and/or the positive balance of, an account will be in the same bar and on the same side of the x axis as the box representing the category of accounts to which the subject account belongs in figure A1. When an account balance and/or a posting to an account is negative, the box will be in the same bar but on the opposite side of the x axis.

INDEX

A bolded page number signifies a definition of the entry.

Other The Melaleuca Press publications by Mike Darlow include:

Books

The Fudamentals of Woodturning
Woodturning Methods
Woodturning Techniques
Woodturning Design
Turned Chessmen

DVDs

The Practice of Woodturning
The Taming of the Skew
Sharpening Woodturning Tools

Details provided at <www.mikedarlow.com>